BLUE

ALSO BY ERIC NISENSON

ASCENSION: JOHN COLTRANE AND HIS QUEST

ROUND ABOUT MIDNIGHT

BLUE

THE MURDER OF JAZZ

ERIC NISENSON

DA CAPO PRESS

Library of Congress Cataloging in Publication Data on file
ISBN 0-306-80925-7

First Da Capo Press Edition 2000

Reprinted by arrangement with St. Martin's Press

Published by Da Capo Press
A Member of the Perseus Books Group
http://www.dacapopress.com

1 2 3 4 5 6 7 8 9 10——03 02 01 00 99

For my brother Peter,

who first introduced me

to the world of jazz

Contents

ACKNOWLEDGMENTS

FIRST OF ALL, I want to thank my editor, Jim Fitzgerald, for giving me the chance to write this book. Thanks, Jim, for your support, your integrity, and, of course, your patience.

Special thanks to Alice Schell for reading through most of my manuscript and giving me superb suggestions. And thanks to Bill Kenz, who helped me with so much of the research. I am also greatly indebted to Bill Kirchener for his words of wisdom and insight. And thanks to Gene Lees, for showing me that it is possible to write about jazz with passion and depth.

Special thanks to George Russell, who as friend and genius musician has shown me the rewards of daring and how a great artist can continually renew himself—and how necessary those traits are for the creation of the greatest jazz.

There are many others to whom I am indebted and whom I cannot omit: Maureen Barnes, for emotional and spiritual support, my wonderful doctor, John Falencki (and thanks to Helena too!), who has helped give me the strength to overcome certain difficult obstacles; James Hale, my Canadian friend who, thanks to the Internet, has been a constant source of support and enthusiasm. Thank you Cya Coleman for being a constant booster of my spirits. And, of course, thanks to my old pal Sean Ducker, for no real reason at all.

Then there is my father, who all my life has shown me how exciting a life of creativity can be. Thank you, Dad, for always believing in me.

And although he has been gone for more than half a decade, Miles Davis must also be acknowledged. He changed my life more than once and was my greatest teacher when it came to understanding just how profound a life dedicated to the creation of art and, in particular, the making of jazz could be. Wherever you are Miles, this book is, of course, for you too.

INTRODUCTION

MY LAST BOOK, *Ascension: John Coltrane and His Quest*, was about the musician generally considered to have been the last great jazz innovator and his search for the ultimate essence of music and the mind of God. In the last chapter of that book, "After the Trane," I discussed what happened to jazz after Coltrane's death in 1967, and in particular my misgivings about the current jazz scene and the fact that this once continually innovative music has now become so reactionary and staid. After *Ascension* was published, I was astonished at how many jazz critics, fans, and musicians felt as I did about the current state of jazz, many of whom went so far as to write letters, send e-mail, or even call me on the phone to express their concurrence with my concerns. Most of them avidly encouraged me to expand on these ideas (as did my publisher). *Blue: The Murder of Jazz* is the result of my thoughts on these matters, and of the thoughts of the writers, musicians, and fans with whom I have discussed many of these ideas after the publication of *Ascension*.

The cry that "jazz is dead" has been so ubiquitous throughout jazz history that it has almost become a tradition in itself. So let me state the obvious. *Blue: The Murder of Jazz* is not an obituary for jazz, because jazz is quite clearly not dead. As a matter of fact, according to a number of jazz critics and fans, we are experiencing a "jazz renaissance," a great golden age for this music, which is reaching unprecedented aesthetic and commercial heights.

On the other hand, there are those who have grave and dark feelings about the state of jazz and its apparent current course. According to a number of jazz fans and critics, jazz is actually in its death throes. This great music, they say sadly, that was born with the inception of this century is also going to die at its end.

How can there be such totally dissimilar views of this current period of jazz? How can intelligent men and women observing the same phenomenon come to such divergent conclusions? That alone has caused me to think through many of the ideas in this book. The truth, I believe, is that there have always been completely divergent views on the very nature of jazz, dating back to very early in its history.

There has lately occurred the greatest amount of rancor in jazz since the advent of free jazz, rancor maybe even as great as during the birth of bop in the 1940s. I feel at least as strongly as anybody else about the current course of jazz. However, I am not trying so much to win a debate here as I am attempting to understand what has happened to jazz in the last ten or fifteen years. For those who vehemently disagree with me, don't simply write me off as a crank; there is a surprisingly large—and growing—contingent in the jazz world who feels the way I do, and many who feel even stronger. The feelings among critics range from unease and growing disillusionment with the current jazz generation to the belief that the latest developments in jazz are an indication of the music's impending doom. These critics range in vehemence from such currently important voices as Francis Davis and Gary Giddins, the veteran critic and former editor of *Down Beat*, to Gene Lees, who is convinced that jazz, like vaudeville, is probably going to breathe its final breath in New York City. The musicians who are unhappy with the current jazz mainstream include reedmen Wayne Shorter, Gary Bartz, and David Murray; trumpeters Lester Bowie and veteran Clark Terry; and composer/arranger George Russell. The renowned pianist Keith Jarrett has been most eloquent on the subject: in an article in *Musician* magazine called "The Virtual Jazz Age," he wrote: "Now we're told its a new jazz age by the same blind media industries who, along with a bunch of opportunistic critics, lackeys, panderers, cronies, and hangers-on, bought the Young Lions in the first place. It's easy to handle them because they are ultra-conservative, not risk-takers, and easy to track. But jazz is about risking everything to your personal muse and accepting the consequences." In other words jazz, which was once one of the most consistently progressive and visionary cultural wellsprings in American life is increasingly becoming a suffocatingly arid and reactionary desert.[1]

It is very painful to write such a sentence. I have loved jazz since I was fifteen years old, and in many ways it saved my life. At the time I discovered jazz, I was a miserable student at a rah-rah football high school in Westchester suburbia. I felt deeply alienated from almost everything and everyone around me, floating in my own sea of longing and fantasy. Because of being borderline cerebral palsied, I was lousy at athletics (although my handicap was not obvious (and therefore I received no sympathy), and sports at Rye High School were ultimately how one was judged (and, sad to say, it didn't help much that I was Jewish). So I was, of course, regularly teased and derided and humiliated, and my grades came to reflect my deep sadness. I was an outcast and, except for a few other fellow outcasts, I was profoundly lonely. I was far too shy to ask a girl out and risk probable rejection. So I never went to proms or hung out with the gang at the malt shop and, except for a few friends (some of whom would pretend not to know me when in school), had little social life. My problem was worse than just very low self-esteem. I was lost.

Further alienating me was the fact that I could not stand the pop music of the period, the early 1960s, that was so much a part of the teen scene of that time. Those were probably the worst years in the history of rock and roll: post-Elvis (rather, post–Elvis's army years) and pre-Beatles, a time when Fabian and Frankie Avalon and Paul Anka made music apparently aimed at the brain-dead in failing efforts to become "the new Elvis." Having grown up in a home where classical music was almost a religion, I could not ignore the vapid nature of the pop music of the time. Naturally, my feelings about this music put further space between myself and most of my peers.

One person I looked to for direction was my older brother, Peter. He seemed to me to be brilliant at everything he did (he still is—he is now a leading astrophysicist who works for Harvard and NASA). The first jazz I ever heard (or at least was conscious of) was a Dukes of Dixieland album that he bought. It was a treat to hear music other than classical played on our hi-fi system—my parents loved classical music, and my brother played cello, and played it well enough to participate in student symphony orchestras and to be accepted as a student by a cellist with the New York Philharmonic. (I had attempted several instruments, but with my poor coordination I had little chance of mastering them.) Needless to say, there was little pop music heard in our house. So when my brother, who up until this point had been snobbish toward any kind of music other than classical, bought a Dukes of Dixieland album on the recommendation of a friend, I was glad for this fresh musical breeze in our house. But I hated the music itself: loud, brash, blaring (these albums were on a label that specialized in showing off your hi-fi system). I decided that if this is what jazz was about, it was a music from which I would stay far away.

But my brother's taste in jazz broadened. First he bought Lambert, Hendricks, and Ross singing Basie. The point of that album was that Jon Hendricks put lyrics to classic Basie pieces, including the solos, and then, through overdubbing the vocal trio, produced a big sound that to some degree paralleled the big band sound of the original performances. Needless to say, I had no idea who Basie was or why the melody line seemed to meander at points (at those times when they were singing what had been an improvised solo). I kind of liked Lambert, Hendricks, and Ross, and I liked even better the Brubeck record my brother subsequently bought. This, he explained, unlike the Dukes of Dixieland, was "progressive jazz." I was immediately intrigued. I quickly caught on to the idea that most of the performance of the Brubeck quartet was made up on the spot. This seemed absolutely magical to me. I wondered: How were they able to do this?

The next jazz album I heard was Miles Davis's *Round About Midnight*, but I only heard this once or twice because it was owned by my brother's friend, who loaned it to him. My brother did mention that somebody named John Coltrane was becoming a very important jazz musician. (I was unaware that Coltrane was the saxophonist on *Round About Midnight*). Since it was close to Peter's birthday, I decided to give him a John Coltrane or Miles Davis album as a gift. At the record store I found the perfect album, one with both musicians playing on it. It was called *Kind of Blue*. My life would never be the same.

My brother left *Kind of Blue* behind when he went off to college, and I started to listen to it every day; often more than once a day. Bill Evans's brilliant liner notes—brief but implying many fascinating ideas, almost like haiku—in which he compared jazz improvising to a Zen style of painting especially intrigued me, since I had already developed an interest in Zen Buddhism. I found the connection between Zen and jazz exalting and revelatory—in both of them, the experience of living in the moment, in the here and now, was the source of all wisdom and transcendence. The music itself was astonishing; each solo seemed more beautiful than the last. It was like a perfect primer for understanding jazz improvisation. The musicians seemed to be expressing feelings and truths that could never have been conveyed through words. And the indigo mood of the music was perfect for my frame of mind at the time. This was music, I decided, that could be my salvation, that could show me how to live.

Jazz became my obsession, the core of my life. I felt as if jazz were a lifeline that had saved me from drowning. I read everything I could about it, spending all my money on albums whose liner notes I would read with the same amount of intense scrutiny as an archaeologist examining the Rosetta stone. I subscribed to *Down Beat*, and with my subscription I received a free copy of *The Essential Charlie Parker* on Verve. At this point, I barely knew who Bird was, except for the fact that he was a legend and sort of a mystical figure who had apparently been virtually worshiped—why else would the graffiti *Bird Lives* have become so ubiquitous?

It took me a while to really appreciate Parker's music, longer than for Miles or even Coltrane; his playing was so dense. But once I got the message I came to understand why the great alto saxophonist was regarded as virtually a holy figure: His feverishly ecstatic improvisations reflected a different way of looking at the world, one perhaps of a person close to madness but also that of someone whose every sense was filled with the wild swirl of life. I knew absolutely that his playing pointed to a different way of living, and toward a world waiting for me that had all kinds of possibilities undreamed of there in suburbia.

One of the most obvious aspects of jazz that deeply affected me was that its greatest musicians and innovators were for the most part black. I was brought up in a household in which my parents strived to shield me from the racism so endemic to our society. When I was still very young my mother told me that "the ugliest word in the language was *nigger*" (not *kike*—and we were Jews!) and that I was never to speak it. Even now, when I use that word in a context like the preceding sentence, I still feel uncomfortable. Nor did they let my brother and I watch shows like *Beulah* or *Amos and Andy*, which they—rightly—believed presented a demeaning portrait of black life (once again, however, there was no objection to our watching *The Goldbergs*, a show about a stereotypical Jewish family).

But even my parents were a little surprised by my devotion to this African-American music. (I discovered, incidentally, that, much to my delight, the sound of, say, Coltrane played loudly drove them at least as nuts as my friends' parents were driven by rock and roll records). And my few friends could not understand my love for this music at all. Most of them were casually racist, and they assumed that every other white person had the same attitude toward blacks. This alienated me even further. I knew as a fact, that a great number of black people were indisputable geniuses, responsible for most of this music that was so close to my heart. Very quickly I learned about the position of a white person who happens to love jazz deeply. And I try to write about jazz as conscious as I can be of that special position, or at least I hope that I do.

When I was still a kid, knowing and loving jazz was a way of rebelling against the bourgeois suburban lifestyle for which I had developed an acute contempt. I viewed the musicians themselves as rebels—which to a degree is true, but not in the way that I thought then—and the more antisocial the musician, the more I admired him. Bird was my god, of course. And I was fascinated by Mingus's apocalyptic rage and larger-than-life temperament, Miles's turning his back to his audience, the often bizarre eccentricity of Lester Young and Thelonious Monk, and Bill Evans's junked-out asceticism. Like many others, particularly the Beats (whom I read and also admired around this time), jazz musicians were almost supernatural creatures. I especially romanticized those musicians who were self-destructive, particularly those who died young.

Of course, Charlie Parker was at the head of that list: Imagine—when he died at the age of thirty-four, his body was so used up that the attending doctor assumed he was well into his fifties. I got hold of a book called *Bird: The Legend of Charlie Parker* that purported to be something of an oral biography of Bird and which mesmerized me; it was really a collection of every outrageous tale of Parker's excessive behavior—much of it obviously apocryphal—that the author could find.

Then of course there was the brilliant bop trumpet player Fats Navarro. Navarro was a junkie who died at the age of twenty-six (Miles Davis told me, incidentally, that Navarro was his all-time favorite trumpet player). Bud Powell did not die young, but he spent much of his life in and out of psychiatric institutions, and there are many famous stories about his erratic behavior ("I taught him how to act crazy," claimed Charlie Parker—that was my Bird!).

All this kind of lore was probably as important to me as the music itself. The image of these sensitive musicians, driven insane by the insensitivity of bourgeois American society and racism, sacrificed on the cross of their art, was a compelling one, which in itself was an indictment of the suburban life from which I was so alienated. Of course, once I really came to know jazz musicians as friends I realized how much pure myth was involved in this stereotyping. Unfortunately, these ideas about jazz musicians are still popular. Just witness movies like *Bird*, *Round Midnight*, and *Lady Sings the Blues*, or books like *But Beautiful*. Portraying these great artists as pathetic victims has little to do with the real lives of most jazz musicians.

The miraculous thing about jazz is that after I outgrew this phase of romantic fantasizing, it continued to fascinate and reward me. But as I grew older, jazz remained important to my life for somewhat different reasons. With maturity, the music took on increasing profundity and value for me, something I could not say about many of my other youthful pursuits. For instance, some of the books that I had read and loved as a teenager, like the novels of Thomas Wolfe, Sinclair Lewis, or Herman Hesse, lost their meaningfulness when I got older. The works of other writers I had read at this time—Faulkner, Hemingway, Fitzgerald, and Ellison—took on new layers of depth as I experienced more of life. Jazz was like these novels; even though I lost my romantic images of the jazz musician and the jazz world itself, the music became increasingly meaningful and inspirational. I still got goose bumps when I listened to *Kind of Blue*, but as I got older, it seemed to gain emotional and spiritual resonance and become even more a central part of my life. And I discovered the same thing to be true of of the best albums that I first discovered in my early years with jazz.

Jazz, in its offhand way, was a constant source of wisdom and revelation for me. Certainly one of its key lessons was the ineluctable nature of change. In this early period of my involvement with jazz, the greatest teacher of this principle was John Coltrane. Watching him, at first with great dismay, become increasingly influenced by the free jazz movement, I wondered, Why would he change his music so drastically? As he wandered farther and farther outside, I was forced to realize that Coltrane simply had to continue moving on, even if it meant making music that was considerably less perfect than his earlier work. And perhaps the idea of "perfection" was irrelevant to somebody committed to the concept of improvisation, and with it change, and all that it entails.

In the 1960s, like so many of my generation, I became involved in the counterculture. Now legions of young people seemed to have come around to my way of thinking, rebelling against the limitations of mainstream American life. I recognized that the counterculture was to a degree an offspring of the jazz world. Music was at the center of both cultures, the thing that united those in the alternate cultures, and was a source both of wisdom and direction. Of course, in the 1960s the counterculture music was rock. Thanks to the Beatles, whom I loved (for one reason, their ability to change and grow), I was able to break free from the bonds of "jazz snobbery" and be open to the new rock. For a while I thought that maybe jazz was too idiosyncratic and introspective to unite a cultural revolution. And rock seemed to be changing from a cheap thrill into a music of far more depth and complexity. Rockers even began improvising, often for long stretches, attempting the spontaneity of jazz. Unfortunately, much of this improvisation did nothing but demonstrate how hard it is to improvise on the level I had grown used to from jazz. But rock could only go so far before it was no longer the music of lowest common denominator, which had always been the glory of this good-time music. In the 1970s, the punks would remind the world that not only was rock *supposed* to be a cheap thrill, but that its basically simple quality was something to be reveled in.

As the 1960s turned into the 1970s, my hopes for the counterculture, and rock and roll, began to fade. But jazz and the great jazz musicians were still able to astonish me. They were finding ways of taking what was most valuable from both rock and the free jazz of the 1960s, fusing it with the music's great legacy, and pushing on. Once again, jazz illuminated a path forward in the rapidly changing world around me. And in the forefront, once again, was the genius who had first got me hooked on jazz, Miles Davis.

Jazz was so central to my life that I felt almost proprietary toward it. There were so few people I knew, really, who were as obsessed with this music as I; one critic compared the experience of being a jazz lover meeting other dyed-in-the-wool fans to that of an alien from Venus running into another Venusian. To me the great jazz musicians, wearing their hearts on their sleeves every time they played, were almost like actual friends for whom I felt the same kind of love and loyalty as I did for any of my other close friends.

I believe this special feeling toward jazz and its musicians is very common. Jazz seems to speak to us so directly that we feel our understanding and views about it are personal matters. Jazz fans—real jazz fans, the ones who know, say, who Jimmy Blanton or Dave Tough or Tina Brooks are—are so few and far between that we tend to be solipsistic, believing that only we and a small elite truly know what jazz is all about.

So when there is some kind of controversy in the jazz world, it often results in debate that seems ludicrously ferocious to non-jazz fans. After all, to us these arguments are personal because the music has such an intense grip on our inner lives. Such disagreements have often caused anger, as if the partisans of each side of the issue were really attacking the decency of the other's wife or mother. After all, it is only jazz, isn't it? Well, depending on your point of view, yes and no.

Jazz is now going through a period of controversy that has been as fierce and uproarious as the advent of bop and the birth of modern jazz in the 1940s. And like that period, at stake is not just musical style but, on a deeper level, widely divergent views of jazz's meaning and place in our lives. Such matters as race, "high" versus "pop" culture, and the differences between Western and non-Western sensibilities lurk just under the surface. Deeper still, I believe, is the perception of what jazz tells us about our lives, and in particular what is happening to this country, here in the last decade of "the American century."

As we shall see, I believe that some of the most vital aspects of jazz are being throttled by a group of musicians and critics that has come to dominate the jazz mainstream. All of these people profess the greatest love for jazz and what they call the jazz "tradition." I believe them; their love for this music is certainly no less than my own or than the love of those who agree with me. But they are smothering the heart and soul of jazz with their love. It should be clear by now that it is very difficult for me to remain objective about these matters—as you can gather, this music has a personal meaning and importance to me, and if it is being smothered then so am I, in a way.

I have to admit that when I first started working on this book I had great trepidation. I began to wonder if I had overstated the case. But the more I read, both about the current scene and also about certain elements of jazz history, the more I realized that this book was absolutely necessary. In order to explain what was wrong with the current mainstream of jazz, I had to explore what had made jazz and the jazz revolution—for that is what the emergence and development of jazz was—so important to our lives and so triumphant as a positive force in American life, both social and musical.

All of us on both sides of this current controversy, needless to say, truly love jazz and have found great meaning in it for our lives. But somehow the jazz vision, at least that of the mainstream, has become myopic. An entire generation of jazz musicians seems to have lost sight of what has made jazz unique in the history of Western culture, and what elements have kept jazz so vital and relevant over the years. To at least some degree, they have trivialized jazz and forgotten or overlooked what made it, in the words of one musician, "as serious as your life."

Does jazz have a future? Will it survive into the next century? These are key issues now. And at the heart of this controversy is the question, What is jazz anyway and why do those of us who love it feel that it is so damned important? Is it just an enjoyable form of music and not much more than that? These are questions I have been asking myself ever since I first became fascinated with this music. Perhaps I should thank those with whom I take issue about the current state of jazz for inadvertently forcing me to reach at least tentative conclusions about these vital matters.

Ever since I first got hooked by *Kind of Blue*, I sensed that jazz had a unique power that I had not found in other forms of music or other art forms, for that matter. My attempts to understand the strange and powerful emotions I felt listening to jazz had a profound effect on the course of my life. And I am certain I was not the only one to feel this way. Perhaps the best way to convey the effect that jazz has had on my life is to say that I, like many white jazz fans, often felt quite a bit like that ultimate icon of American culture, Huckleberry Finn, floating on the currents of the great American river with the black slave Jim, both of us finally, ecstatically, free, lighting out for new territories. The direction and meanings of our fateful jazz journey—and how that journey has been thwarted in the last decade or so—is what this book is ultimately about.

1.

The Case for Murder

IN A RECENT edition of the *New York Times Magazine*, there was a whole section devoted to jazz, a rare event for this usually ignored music (at least by the mainstream press). On the cover was the trumpeter Wynton Marsalis, and in the section itself were lengthy laudatory articles about Marsalis and the bassist Christian McBride and a photo display of a group of young up-and-coming jazz musicians with the title "The Next Miles Davis Is on This Page."[1] To anyone unfamiliar with the current contretemps in jazz, these pieces might not seem like the grist for anger and fierce argument. After all, an article extolling the brilliance of Marsalis as a player and composer and another one doing the same for McBride hardly seem the stuff of controversy. But jazz has become so polarized at this point that the *Times* section is viewed by many solely in terms of cultural politics. For it is Marsalis and his mentors and acolytes who have been at the heart of the current uproar in jazz.

The thrust of the entire section is that this current era is a "golden age" for jazz. The author of the Marsalis piece, novelist and occasional jazz writer Frank Conroy, points to the plethora of young jazz musicians who have emerged in the last ten years or so. And Conroy believes that successful programs like that of Jazz at Lincoln Center are encouraging the composition of large-scale works. These long works, Conroy believes, will finally make jazz a truly important form of art. According to Conroy, jazz has at last begun to earn the respect of the cultural elite, thanks to these new long-form pieces (most of those that have been performed at Lincoln Center have been composed by Marsalis).

As we shall see, there are many others who feel the way Conroy does. And then there are those who feel quite the opposite. Because once one leaves New York, the true sorry state of jazz is obvious. Outside of Manhattan, there are very few clubs that feature name jazz musicians anymore. It is true that festivals are well attended—but they are once-a-year events that attract jazz fans from all over the world.

And jazz radio? It is virtually dead. One of the last commercial jazz stations, KJAZ in San Francisco, recently (as I write in mid-1996) gave up its struggle and went out of business. The only way to hear jazz—true jazz—on the radio, even in New York, is on college stations. It is true that stations that play what is called "lite jazz" have become increasingly popular. But that in itself is a signal of what is happening to jazz. For lite jazz—such as the music of Kenny G., Grover Washington, Jr., and Bob James—is so diluted and soft-edged that it is closer in depth of feeling to elevator music than to "heavy" jazz. I am old enough to remember WRVR, a wonderful New York all-jazz station that played the best of the music. It is long gone. And it was not the only station in New York that regularly broadcast jazz. They are all gone.

Record sales? It is ironic that in the same section in the *New York Times Magazine* that extols the glories of today's "golden era" there is a listing of the top ten jazz albums: The first two were Tony Bennett albums, which were followed by a Harry Connick, Jr., funk album. Other albums were from such "lite jazz" acts as Spyro Gyra. A Joshua Redman album was the only straight-ahead jazz CD on the list.

Before the advent of this golden era, jazz albums consisted of about 5 percent of all albums sold. Now in the midst of this glorious "golden age," jazz records account for about 3 percent. Even albums by this era's biggest star, Wynton Marsalis, the most famous jazz musician of his generation, have not been faring very well. A used-record-store owner who specializes in jazz was once so inundated with returned Marsalis albums that he refused to buy up any more.

Marsalis—considered by many as being the equal of Miles Davis or John Coltrane in his influence on the jazz scene—has had trouble, for that matter, even filling a small jazz club. During a recent performance at Manhattan's Village Vanguard, *New York Times* critic Peter Watrous was astonished that Marsalis was able to fill only half of the place.

Tenor saxophonist Joshua Redman, a current favorite, has been doing better than Marsalis. Redman is a talented saxophonist, although, like most of his generation of jazz musicians, he lacks originality and that adventurous spirit we associate with the best jazz musicians (his father is Dewey Redman, also a tenor saxophonist, who is a far more idiosyncratic and innovative player). Perhaps Redman is aware of his limitations as a jazz player; maybe to make up for them he has apparently begun to pander to his audience. A critic of one of his recent performances noted that he got the crowd into an uproar by holding notes and by honking and wailing. The critic seemed to believe that both this sort of playing and the reaction of the audience were unprecedented. He should have gone back and listened to Jazz at the Philharmonic records from the 1940s and 1950s, when this style of pandering to the crowd was commonplace and the crowd reacted with predictable loud, unruly enthusiasm. Redman's antics prove once again that bad taste is timeless in its appeal.

However, the clearest indication that jazz is fading as an art form is the increasing diminution of genuine creative vitality. Indeed, there seems to be a wholesale avoidance of the kind of fresh inventiveness and risk-taking that had always kept jazz a vital and continually stimulating art form. At times there seems to be a conscious attempt to prevent jazz from being as fiercely creative and innovative is it has been in the past. This violence to the driving motor of jazz is what I, and a number of other longtime lovers of this music, consider to be nothing less than the murder of this one-time feverishly fecund and innovative art form.

Conroy's, and others', insistence that this is a golden age is really based on two phenomena. One is the Lincoln Center jazz program, called Jazz at Lincoln Center (JALC), which admittedly is a critical and popular success. The other is this large crop of young jazz musicians who have emerged in recent years—new, fresh, talented musicians seem to appear almost on a monthly basis. One has to wonder how Miles Davis would have reacted to that two-page-wide photo layout of about thirty of these musicians (most latter-day boppers with little new to add to the music) in the *New York Times Magazine*. He was angrily outspoken in his denunciation of the current "back to bop" movement. Upon hearing young musicians playing hard bop or post-bop, he would rhetorically ask, "Didn't we do it good the first time?"

Both of these phenomena are directly related to Wynton Marsalis and his mentors; they are the producers and artistic directors of the Lincoln Center program and many, if not most, of this current generation of jazz musicians are admitted acolytes of Marsalis. There is no avoiding him if one wants to come to terms seriously with the current state of jazz.

Wynton Marsalis is usually described as "the leading musician of his generation." Partly this is due to his indisputable ability as a trumpet player, but much of it is also due to his ideas about jazz, ideas he has tirelessly proclaimed since he was a novice jazzman in the 1980s. His influence on an entire generation of jazz musicians is as widespread as that of Charlie Parker or John Coltrane, but it is very different in kind. While Parker and Coltrane and the other great jazz innovators, such as Louis Armstrong, Lester Young, Duke Ellington, and Ornette Coleman, pointed to new directions for musicians to explore, Marsalis has done just the contrary. His concern has been with the "jazz tradition" and playing music based on his great knowledge of jazz of the past, particularly post-bop of the 1950s and early 1960s.

Marsalis believes that the free jazz of the sixties and the fusion of the seventies removed jazz too far from that "tradition." He continually insists on bringing jazz back to swing and blues, which to him are the essence of jazz, although he has never really defined those terms; this I will try to do later on in this book. Lately, he has also exhibited the influence of Duke Ellington in his composing and arranging, creating large-scale works for jazz orchestra that have received, at best, a mixed reception. And in order to expand his style, Marsalis has once again moved backwards rather than forward, unmistakably attempting to graft elements of Louis Armstrong's style to his own. Those young musicians who follow in his footsteps have been labeled neoclassicists by critic Gary Giddins. The term comes from the description of some critics of 1950s hard bop as being a "classic" jazz style. These young imitators of that style in the 1980s and 1990s are therefore neoclassicists. But as we shall see, there is a more accurate term for them based in jazz history.

In addition to being one of the producers of the Lincoln Center program, Marsalis has written some lengthy Ellington-esque "suites" for the program, which has a working band of some of the best jazz musicians in New York. There is a strong didactic nature to virtually everything Marsalis does; his love of and commitment to this supposed jazz tradition is not unlike a fundamentalist's view of the Gospels, and Jazz at Lincoln Center constantly reflects his beliefs.

Marsalis's main mentors in terms of his jazz "philosophy" are the writers and social critics Stanley Crouch and Albert Murray. Crouch began his involvement in jazz as a free jazz drummer whose style was based on that of avant-gardists Sunny Murray and Milford Graves. He also wrote poetry; one of his more notable poems was a eulogy for Albert Ayler, who became famous for playing the sort of white noise on his saxophone that Crouch—and Marsalis—now spurn as not really being part of the jazz tradition. In the 1970s he began to write jazz criticism, especially boosting players in the free jazz community. But over the years, Crouch's musical outlook began to change drastically, and that change reflected his slide to the right politically. He gave up playing the drums altogether, joined the staff of the *Village Voice*, and increasingly began to write about mainstream, hard-bop musicians and less about free players. His nonjazz writing often involved harsh criticism of black militants and separatists like Amiri Baraka (Leroi Jones) who had been closely associated with the free jazz movement. Eventually Crouch moved so far from his past positions that former close colleagues, like the saxophonist David Murray (who had been especially close to Crouch until he was apparently replaced by Wynton Marsalis), would openly wonder what had caused such a sea change in their former associate and booster.

It was Crouch and especially Murray who developed what could be called a theory of jazz and its so-called tradition. Basically the theory is this: Jazz has developed over the years certain techniques and aspects of music-making that constitute an important part of its tradition, a tradition that arises directly out of African-American life and the "blues philosophy" that Murray and Crouch perceive in that life. Playing within this tradition gives a musician a kind of legitimacy, placing him within a community that supports and understands his music, while playing outside this tradition is simply amorphous music-making. Music played outside the tradition was music in a vacuum, unconnected to people's lives, particularly black people's lives, which is basically what jazz is, and always had been, about—at least according to this theory.

What are these techniques? Possibly the most concrete and succinct statement of what this tradition is all about is in Tom Piazza's *Guide to Classic Recorded Jazz*. Piazza is a vociferous supporter of both Marsalis and Crouch and the neoclassicist movement. He states in his book: ". . . Stanley Crouch has made a short but useful list of the essential musical elements that jazz musicians deal with: the blues, the romantic ballad, Afro-Hispanic rhythms, and the attitude toward the passage of time (at slow, medium, and fast tempos) that is called swing. To these I would add that jazz always demonstrates a call-and-response sensibility derived originally from the African-American church and which is present in the music's most basic structures."[2]

This is, I suppose, as close as one can get to a succinct statement of the principles or elements of the jazz tradition according to the neoclassicists. But it is not very well thought out, and worse, it severely limits the imaginative parameters of this art form. Having a list that includes the blues, ballads, "Afro-Hispanic" rhythms, and the concept of swing is very confusing to say the least; the first three items in the list are musical forms that are, according to Crouch/Piazza, used by jazz musicians, but the fourth, the element of swing, is not a musical form at all but refers to the supposed rhythmic attack of *all* "true" jazz performances. Another major problem is that most jazz performances are neither blues nor ballads nor Latin numbers (and do Latin numbers really swing, in the strict definition of swing employed by Crouch and Marsalis?); they are usually pop songs or original tunes often with a harmonic base borrowed from a pop tune. And, as we shall see, the concept of swing is at best an amorphous one. I have no idea what Piazza means when he says he hears "call and response" in most jazz performances. Does he mean that all soloing and accompaniment is essentially call and response? It does *sound* good to mention a quality associated with the black church, since several elements of the black church were quite influential on the development of jazz and the early musical consciousness of a slew of important jazz musicians. But stating that call and response can—and therefore must—be heard in every "authentic" jazz performance is a great exaggeration, and again it limits rather than frees the musician: in order to create "authentic" jazz, according to Piazza, a musician has to make sure his music includes that quality that can be called call and response. There are numerous examples where call and response has been used by jazz musicians, and it can be an effective musical device—Horace Silver's "Sister Sadie" comes to mind—but declaring that it is an essential quality for the performance of jazz is quite an overstatement, to say the least.

The whole problem with this concept of the jazz "tradition" is that the truth is, the only real tradition in jazz has been no tradition at all, or rather, the tradition of individual expression and constant change and growth. Those who disagree with this neoclassicist concept of the jazz tradition believe that not only is there no real jazz tradition (except the continual breaking down of the perimeters of that supposed tradition), but that jazz itself is almost impossible to define in any narrow, dogmatic fashion. Piazza writes, "Many of the people who use the word most vociferously insist on a usage for it that is so broad as to be, in my mind, meaningless." Well, maybe the word *jazz* has finally lost its meaning, because there is no definition that really embraces the music—or at least the music that is generally perceived as jazz—in all its complex variety.

For instance, does the blues have to be part of a jazz performance? Of course not. There are even some undeniably great jazz performers, such as Art Tatum, Teddy Wilson, Earl Hines, and Coleman Hawkins, who, although they could play within the blues form, nevertheless had little affinity for the blues. Jazz musicians are diverse in the music that has influenced their style, and reducing it all to blues is greatly simplistic. For example, Hawkins listened almost exclusively to opera, and certainly its influence can be heard in his dramatic, bravura style much more than that of the blues. As we shall see, this insistence on the primacy of "blues expression" in jazz is part of a particular agenda rather than a clearly thought out principle.

The more we study jazz, the greater its possibilities and the fewer its limitations. André Hodeir has pointed out that jazz does not even have to involve improvisation.[3] He gives as an example, a tune played by the Basie band that does not include any solos; it is still indisputably jazz. However, I do believe that both the *feeling* of improvisation, which is essential for the creation of jazz, and the musical philosophy that lies behind improvisation are essential factors that make jazz both unique and relevant to our time.

And where does the concept of swing fit into the basic definition of jazz? Well, that depends on your definition of swing. The neos are always insisting on the primacy of swing in a jazz performance—"It don't mean a thing if it ain't got that swing"; to them, music without swing simply is not jazz. But what is swing? I usually take swing to mean music played in the straight-ahead 4/4 meter that conveys a sense of linear movement forward. Most jazz performances do swing in this fashion, but what about other meters, such as 3/4 or 6/8 or 5/4? Are pieces played in these meters not jazz? This would mean that Coltrane's version of "My Favorite Things," Miles Davis's "All Blues," Sonny Rollins's "Valse Hot," and Paul Desmond's "Take Five" are not jazz, an absurd premise. And what about jazz played with funk or Latin rhythms? Such performances do not swing in the traditional manner—which would mean that everything from Herbie Hancock's "Watermelon Man" to all bossa nova pieces are not jazz, which is ridiculous. Everyone from Coleman Hawkins to Archie Shepp has recorded bossa novas—what an absurdity to suggest these are not jazz.

Beyond these examples, there are certain musicians who play jazz and do not swing in the manner demanded by the neos. For example, Cecil Taylor does not swing, at least not in the narrow definition of swing upheld by Crouch and Marsalis. Anthony Braxton's solo performances also don't swing. And it should not be forgotten that many critics insisted that Coltrane did not swing in the late 1950s, mainly because his style at the time was based on glissandos played over the beat. Interestingly enough,

Crouch insists that Coltrane's bandmate in Miles Davis's magnificent late 1950s sextet, Bill Evans, could not swing because (like Trane) he had an unusual but personal and legitimate rhythmic approach. And even if, according to somebody's code, these brilliant and tremendously influential musicians did not swing, so what? Their rhythmic approach was the right one for their particular conception.

How do we know that the above examples are jazz? Because they *feel* like jazz; they are players of improvised music created with a sensibility obviously derived from that unique jazz conception—that is as close as I can come to answering such a question.

It is at least partly because of the insistence of many of the leading musicians in the jazz mainstream today—that is, the leading musicians of this new young generation of jazz musicians—to define both swing and jazz itself in a narrow, parochial fashion that is causing so much of the formerly vibrant creativity of jazz to diminish so greatly.

I think that there would be better understanding of the music of Wynton Marsalis's young acolytes who have been dominating the jazz mainstream if they were given a better descriptive rubric. I believe "revivalist" perfectly fits the bill. As I noted earlier, the first jazz record I ever heard was by the Dukes of Dixieland. They were among the original revivalists. In the 1950s and 1960s, they, too, played jazz in a style that had dominated the music forty years earlier. There were several other bands that followed in their wake; the Firehouse Five was almost as popular. The difference between those earlier groups and this group of neoclassicists is that nobody considered the earlier musicians to be part of an important movement in jazz history, and none of those who played in these bands were taken very seriously.

The young musicians of the day, at least the bulk of them, paid little or no attention to such revivalists. They were too involved in investigating the new areas for musical exploration opened up by the bop revolution of the 1940s. Occasionally important jazz musicians did make nods toward earlier jazz styles and players, like when Coltrane recorded "Blues to Bechet" or Charles Mingus played half-humorous pieces like "My Jelly Roll Soul" based on his fondness for Jelly Roll Morton's music. But both of these pieces were put in a modern context, and of course nobody would ever brand the music of Coltrane and Mingus as being revivalist (or neoclassicist, for that matter).

This current generation seems so transfixed by jazz's magnificent past that they are as paralyzed as deer standing on a highway staring into the headlights. They seem unable to move ahead, unwilling to create music made out of the grist of their own time and place. And unfortunately, there are a number of critics who proclaim their music as being important and equal to any music created in the history of jazz. Record companies have been signing up the "neos" with the hope that the flak these young musicians have attracted will translate into big CD dollars.

Actually, the record companies are more at fault than probably any other single party for this sick situation. Most of them have gotten on the neo bandwagon, signing young players to large contracts despite the fact that most of these youngsters have not found an individual voice or discovered an innovative way to express their own lives in music based in the here and now.

Wynton Marsalis was made a victim of his own success. Given unprecedented public relations marketing, the record companies created the illusion that a talented young player was actually one of the all-time jazz greats. Much of his immediate fame was due to the fact that he had a separate career as a classical trumpet player. To the cultural elite, this meant that Marsalis was a "real" musician who could play "real" music and of course also that jazz stuff. Marsalis was immediately acceptable in the higher strata of America's cultural construct.

And his attitude toward jazz was not dissimilar to his attitude toward playing Bach or Handel: He studied the "tradition," learned all about it, and played within the sanctity of the music's past without challenging listeners through musical exploration and innovation. No one had to worry about Marsalis jarring his audience with the shock of the new as, say, Mingus had with *The Black Saint and the Sinner Lady* or George Russell had with *Living Time* or Coltrane had with *Meditations* or Miles with *Bitches Brew*. The enclaves of Lincoln Center were safe for the ladies and gentlemen who had built that cultural museum.

If Wynton Marsalis's own career is any indication, there is little hope that his generation will develop into genuine innovators, and by that I mean musicians who will reinvent jazz in reflection of their own lives in their own time. For years he and his supporters have entreated his critics to be patient; he was quite young and his important innovative work would come with time. But now, as I write, Marsalis is thirty-four years old. That is the same age Charlie Parker was when he died. Parker had done his most innovative work while in his twenties, like most great jazz innovators. Louis Armstrong, Lester Young, Ornette Coleman, Coleman Hawkins, Earl Hines, and Dizzy Gillespie all did their most innovative work in their twenties or early thirties. By the time they were thirty-four, Miles Davis had recorded *Kind of Blue* and *Porgy and Bess,* and Coltrane had developed most of the elements of his style and, at age thirty-four, would form his classic quartet and record *My Favorite Things*. If anything, Marsalis has become even more of a revivalist the older he has become, reaching back to Duke Ellington for his long-form compositions and suites and to Louis Armstrong as a direct influence on his trumpet style.

I do not want to attack Marsalis as a musician; that would be silly. And his ambition is admirable. I especially admire his work with kids—going to schools, especially inner-city schools, and demonstrating for them and teaching them about this magnificent legacy of jazz, trying to inculcate in his young audience self-esteem, respect for values, and the idea that leading a decent, clean life is "hip." And one more thing: I think his knowledge of all jazz history and his insistence that those of his generation study the entire gamut of jazz's history, not just the immediate past, is important in itself and has helped develop interest in the entirety of jazz's musical riches. Most young musicians have usually ignored the earlier music and only focused on the players of the recent past. Encouraging musicians—and jazz fans, too—to listen to and know the entire jazz legacy is in itself something that Marsalis should be applauded for.

What disturbs me about Marsalis is that he seems to believe he has the right to dictate to the jazz world a very strict set of principles that define jazz and its so-called tradition. In many ways, one cannot blame Wynton Marsalis. He is surrounded by those who continue to extol his supposed genius, and because he became so famous while so young, he has, I believe, lost touch with the reality of his own talent. A while back I saw him on Charlie Rose's PBS nightly interview show. Rose began his interview by asking Marsalis what it was that made him the greatest trumpet player of all time, greater than Armstrong, Gillespie, or Miles. To his credit, Marsalis demurred, telling Rose that he did not consider himself equal to those geniuses. But Rose's ludicrous question reflects the way Marsalis is viewed by the cultural elite.

Why? Part of the reason—a very important part—is that Marsalis has a separate career as a classical-music trumpet player. As I pointed out earlier, his ability to play Bach and Haydn legitimizes him as a musician—beyond anything a musician who "just plays jazz" could even dream of—to those in the cultural establishment. This had a great deal to do with his being made the principal producer, the auteur if you will, of Jazz at Lincoln Center. Since Lincoln Center is primarily a museum for music rather than a center for the creation of a living art, Marsalis's revivalism and backward-looking musical philosophy fit right into its cultural design. When Paul Whiteman performed George Gershwin's "Rhapsody in Blue" in 1924, the critics raved that Gershwin had "made a lady out of jazz." Of course, "Rhapsody in Blue" is hardly a work of jazz at all. It has little of the most revolutionary aspects of jazz, most importantly any semblance of improvisation. But the idea of making jazz "safe" and "proper" for the sake of a supposedly "cultured" audience (read: middle- and upper-class white people) is still obviously a successful one. The only difference now is that middle- and upper-class black people are now part of this supposedly cultured audience. Treating jazz like classical music is not a new idea, but it has never been as widely accepted as it is now.

Don't confuse this new trend with the supposed "Third Stream" music that became a trend in the late 1950s. The Third Stream was an attempt to fuse elements of European classical music with elements of jazz, including improvisation and jazz rhythm. Third Stream was, if anything, an attempt at bringing a new kind of innovation to jazz, not simply treating jazz as if it were classical music. In other words, it was a step, albeit a very small step, in jazz's evolution and continuing forward progress. It was not universally applauded, however. John Coltrane had no use for it, and Miles Davis compared it to "looking at a naked woman that you don't like."

Jazz repertory is an attempt to give the great works and musicians of jazz the same kind of treatment as the great works of classical music. These are good intentions, but they are of little interest to most jazz musicians and have virtually no effect on the evolution of the music. And one has to wonder about the idea of repertory for a type of music based on spontaneity and the inspiration of the moment. Perhaps it can serve an important purpose if it is done well by really giving listeners, whether jazz fans or not, a perspective on the history of this music. The Cooper Union repertory, the American Jazz Orchestra now defunct, was repertory at its best because the producer, critic Gary Giddins, and John Lewis, who was Giddins's musical director, found imaginative ways of presenting older jazz from a contemporary viewpoint. It was repertory that could serve as an aid to young musicians wishing to push on with fresh innovation. And it gave to its audience a real understanding of the dynamics of jazz's evolution. Despite its artistic success, it failed commercially and, sadly, it did not survive.

But generally, repertory is a very slippery idea in jazz. When Gary Giddins first began exploring the idea of jazz repertory, he asked the question, If works of jazz are as great as those of classical music, why should they not be performed in repertory? But asking this question ignores the profound differences between classical music and jazz. And once again, it is an example of trying to put the square peg of jazz through the round hole of European classical music. Perhaps there is a way to present jazz in a cultural institution like Lincoln Center. But using the model that works for classical music is missing several essential elements that make jazz unique.

Perhaps the best example are the works of Duke Ellington. Ellington is generally conceded to be the greatest of all jazz composer/arrangers. If his music cannot fit into the repertory—at least most of the great body of his music—that in itself brings into question the entire concept of jazz repertory. And as we shall see in Chapter 6, the *authentic* presentation of Ellington's music is simply not possible in repertory. Not in any way that represents his music the way he intended it to be heard. And that is because Duke Ellington was a genuine *jazz* composer in the most profound sense. He understood early on the very special properties of jazz and must have realized that composing for a jazz big band was profoundly different from composing for a classical symphony orchestra.

Yes, it is important for both musicians and fans to know the wonderful legacy of jazz. But for jazz itself such things as repertory and revivalism, even if successful, have little bearing on jazz being able to survive as a creative art form. If jazz musicians—especially young jazz musicians—cannot find ways to build on that legacy and create music that reflects the reality of their own lives here and now, jazz cannot survive. This of course is the case to some degree with any art form, but with jazz it is crucial—and to understand that means comprehending why jazz is so profoundly different from music of the European tradition.

The sound of, say, the hard bop of the 1950s is the sound of people's lives. The big difference between European classical music and jazz is that European music is composed for an instrument or an ensemble; the performer's job is to play the music hopefully as close to the conception of the composer as possible. However, in jazz, improvisation—or at least the *feeling* of improvisation—is the heart of the music, and therefore the performer *is* the composer. And everything the jazz soloist plays is an expression of his personality, experience, deepest feelings and desire. The music is, in essence, being composed at the same time it is being performed. Even if the jazzman plays the same solos over and over again—which some jazzmen have done—rather than inventing them on the spot, the above holds true; after all, it is the musician's choice whether to repeat a solo, change it slightly, or improvise a completely different solo.

I suppose someone may ask why musicians of this current generation cannot simply attempt to improvise in the hard-bop idiom. The answer is the same, I believe, that would be given to somebody who wished to compose, say, Baroque music, or, for that matter, to write Elizabethan drama. Well, of course they *can* improvise—there are no laws that I am aware of preventing them from trying to do so. But I doubt if anyone would take their efforts as a serious contribution to the respective art form. We all assume that art must be created out of one's own life. And this is doubly true for an artist whose work is mainly improvised. Once one realizes that a jazz musician is a spontaneous *composer*—the bulk of the music he plays at any performance is, at least theoretically, composed on the spot—then the parallel should be obvious.

I think it is clear that the work of artists that is reflective of their own time is still of relevance over the course of time. My own belief is that those who attempt to create art based in idioms from previous eras—revivalists—produce works that may be entertaining and even may help us to understand artistic creation from the past, but ultimately they are inauthentic and have little that is profound to say to us. This is especially true in jazz because innovation is such a key part of the true jazz tradition. It is flexible and open-ended enough so as to allow often enormous change and yet still have a connection with its earliest history. In other words, jazz can survive even outright revolution and still remain true to its basic spirit.

Why is innovation so vital to jazz? It is hard to deny the genuinely rapid evolution of jazz since its beginning early in this century. Too often, however, its rapid development is ascribed to a parade of great men handing down the torch—from Morton to Armstrong to Ellington to Young to Parker to Monk to Coleman to Coltrane—but that is profoundly misleading. Change in jazz has always been a group process. Although the above individuals made great contributions, innovation in jazz has never been the result of one or two individuals' brilliant discovery. Just like the actual performing of jazz itself, innovation is the result of individuals developing ideas in a group context.

Many of the individuals who have contributed to essential jazz innovations are little noted in the jazz histories, or their true contribution to change is either ignored or underappreciated. As an example of the latter, a few years ago an astonishing album was released called *Birth of the Bebop*. It contained previously unknown recordings of Charlie Parker from the early 1940s. On some of these tracks, Bird plays tenor in a style that is quite obviously derivative of Ben Webster and in particular Chu Berry. (Incidentally, Parker named one of his children Leon—Berry's real first name—after Berry.) The usual wisdom is that Lester Young was the seminal influence on Parker. But these recordings make it clear that there were several players in addition to Young whose harmonic and rhythmic advances made modern jazz inevitable.

While I was working on my last book, *Ascension*, I talked to the late drummer Art Taylor, who frequently played and recorded with Coltrane in the 1950s, including appearing on Trane's classic *Giant Steps*. He was also the author of an essential book of interviews with jazz musicians, *Notes and Tones*. I asked him how he and the other musicians who recorded with Coltrane reacted to Trane's constant growth as a player. "It was no problem," explained Taylor, "because all of us were growing right beside him. We were all involved in innovation."

Back then, he explained, all jazz musicians were part of a tight brotherhood (which included several women, too). They worked together, hung out together, shared many of the same social values and experiences. There were some negative aspects of this brotherhood, mainly, of course, drug and alcohol abuse. These unholy practices had the effect of alienating jazz musicians as a group from mainstream society and therefore tightening their bond with one another. And it helped turn them into a society within a society where, no matter what else might have been going on, the development of this musical art form was the paramount concern. But it was mainly the music, and the knowledge of how powerful this music was, how deep was its potential as a spiritual and consciousness-raising force, that held the brotherhood together. Jazz musicians worked together to expand the possibilities of the music as well as to improve it and resolve many of the paradoxes inherent in the creation of jazz. This was never done in any formal way; jazz musicians never got together in a forum setting or some sort of a symposium to thrash out the music's problems and map its future. It was a more intuitive and casual sharing of ideas, like the way the music was performed.

For instance, jam sessions were often places where new concepts were worked over and either accepted or rejected by the jazz community. Or when a musician sat in with another's group, new ideas could be explored right on the bandstand. This is not to say that they did not discuss, verbally discuss, musical ideas. At the height of the jazz scene there were places like Jim and Andy's Bar in Manhattan, or Gil Evans's one-room apartment in the late 1940s, and a number of after-hours joints, where musicians would gather, relax, and often talk music. And in the late 1950s and 1960s, Miles Davis's home was a favorite gathering place for the many musicians who had played or were still playing with Miles.

At heart was the belief that the music they played had frontiers to be explored, and that jazz had a future that seemed as unlimited as the reaches of the stars or the depths of the oceans. It was a future that was keyed to the potential future of its home country, a country that itself still seemed to have frontiers to be explored. In other words, jazz was a powerfully progressive force in American life because it was a music based on the deepest kind of hope.

I am not insisting that all "authentic" jazz musicians must be innovators, at least not in a formal sense. Most jazz musicians are not innovators like Parker or Armstrong or Ornette Coleman, of course. But they must find a mode of expression that is singularly theirs, to "tell their own story," as Lester Young would put it, to create music that is reflective of their lives in the here and now.

ONE CANNOT DISCUSS America as a society or as a culture for very long without bringing up the concept of freedom. This country was founded by those seeking freedom, a war of liberation was fought to win its freedom as a nation, and its Constitution was written based on the needs of a truly free society. Of course, there is a double edge to the American concern for freedom since it was a country that allowed slavery for hundreds of years, and even now is not a truly free country for those in minority groups. Jazz is the most American of art forms because the concept of freedom is at its heart, albeit freedom as perceived by African Americans whose ancestors were slaves on American plantations. All the great innovations in jazz have been based in resolving the problems and paradoxes of a music that allows so much freedom to its performers.

By drawing parameters, by instituting a narrow conception of tradition, by using the word *jazz* to limit rather than extend the music's possibilities, the neoclassicists are stifling the element central to jazz, that of freedom and individual expression—within the context of a group. And without the exhilaration of freedom and the open possibilities of being able to "light out for new territories," jazz, quite simply, is being murdered.

Maybe jazz's time is simply over. After all, it was born with the century, so maybe it is not a coincidence that as the century comes to an end, so does jazz, or at least jazz as we have commonly known it. That may be so. And if it is so, it should be allowed a graceful descent into its grave. Propping up a dying art form by trying to revive a style from forty years or so in its past is futile (especially since that style—hard bop—had been so thoroughly explored in its own time in hundreds of albums), particularly when it means smothering the music's inherent freedom. As we shall see, I do not necessarily believe that jazz really is coming to its end—that is, if it is again allowed the freedom to grow in whatever direction it goes, regardless of anyone's dogmatic concept of a jazz tradition.

In a piece for the *New York Times* on the dearth of creativity in jazz today, pianist Keith Jarrett wrote that Miles Davis would rather play inferior music that was innovative and reflective of its own time than play superior music of and from an earlier era.[4] In other words, to Miles anything other than music that is played and is truly reflective of its place in time, even though it carried the risk of failure, was simply not worth playing. Indeed, without the risk of failure, there is an absence of the edge created by taking chances. It is risk-taking that results in "the sound of surprise" as well as innovation itself. Playing music that has been thoroughly explored decades in the past is like rediscovering New Jersey: It is unlikely that anything fresh will result from it. Much of Miles's "electric" music of the 1970s has to be seen ultimately as a failure—but what an audacious failure, what great risks Miles consciously took in order to connect with the soul of his time! He knew that he could continue playing "My Funny Valentine" and "So What" with a good post-bop band for the rest of his career and probably play that music better than any of his contemporaries. But to Miles there was absolutely no point in doing that; the very idea was deadening to his soul. He had to play music that was truly alive and vital, no matter how difficult it might have been to create music the equal of that in his illustrious past once again.

Wynton Marsalis's reaction to the fusion music of Miles, and such other latter-day musical adventurers as trumpeter Lester Bowie, Anthony Braxton, and the saxophonist Steve Coleman, is that they have not been jazz musicians since they went in directions that he considers "nonjazz." On the surface, this may seem only a problem of semantics, but I think it runs deeper than that.

I find it intriguing, and illuminating, that so many great jazz musicians—musicians who are a vital part of anyone's history of the music—disavowed the word *jazz* at one time or another. Louis Armstrong used to insist that he really played folk music because it was "music for folks." Ellington often expressed disdain for the word. In a famous interview, Charlie Parker insisted that the music he played, bebop, was "not a love child of jazz." Charles Mingus angrily stated that using the word *jazz* meant "the whole back-of-the-bus syndrome" and when he released what is probably his greatest record, *The Black Saint and the Sinner Lady*, he demanded it be labeled "ethnic folk dance music." And of course, Miles

Davis had little use for the word and thought of it merely as a way of keeping serious black musicians "in their place."

The main reason all these important musicians had so little use for their music being labeled as jazz had to do, to a degree, with marketing. Quite simply, jazz records really were on the back of the bus when it came to record-company promotion. Record executives firmly believed that jazz records only sold to a small minority, so they saw little reason to bother wasting marketing funds on jazz music. But I think there is a deeper reason for the attitude of these musicians. As we shall see, throughout jazz history there have always been those in the jazz scene like Wynton Marsalis and Stanley Crouch. That is, there have always been those who used the "jazz tradition" like an albatross around the necks of constantly searching, adventurous, and innovative musicians. These guardians of the "tradition" have always been stalwart in their insistence that jazz had strict limitations, and music played outside those limitations was not jazz. So the reaction of creative, iconoclastic musicians has been, naturally, "So what if I am not playing jazz?" They could not be swayed from taking their music to places forbidden by these self-appointed keepers of the "jazz tradition."

The rise of the neoclassicist generation that has come to dominate this current jazz scene gives rise to some of the most basic questions about the nature of jazz. I do not think there is any other way to argue my point of view than to look back at how and why jazz developed the way it did. But before we go down that river, I think at least one issue must be confronted immediately. It is the one issue that cannot be avoided in any discussion of American society or culture, and particularly jazz. And it has become a central element in the current bickering in jazz, whether stated outright or not. It is, of course, race and racism.

2.

Young Man's Blues: Racism and Ageism in Jazz

DURING A NATIONAL Public Radio show on the current racial controversy in jazz, New Thing tenor saxophonist Archie Shepp stated that jazz was an art form by and for black people because it developed out of the blues, which, at least according to Shepp, owes little to the European musical tradition. However, as Gerry Mulligan pointed out, jazz was really born out of the brass bands that flourished in New Orleans during the nineteenth century.

In a way, both men were right. Quite obviously the instrumentation, polyphony, and harmonic structure of early jazz groups came from the brass bands, whereas blues were mainly vocal and accompanied only by guitar or piano. But it was when black and Creole musicians in brass bands started playing black musical forms, like the blues and ragtime, that jazz came into being. Therefore racial purity is really impossible to discern even here in the birth of jazz. This idea that all black music comes from the single source of the blues seems to be another attempt at making all of black culture homogeneous. The only thing that can be said about all of African-American music is that all of it arose out of the melding of certain aspects of African music and certain aspects of the European musical tradition. Yet now, sadly, race and racism have raised their ugly heads in the current jazz scene.

One of the things I have always loved about the jazz scene has been the mutual respect among musicians, regardless of ethnicity. This is not to say there is no racism in the jazz world—an impossibility given the level of racism endemic throughout American society. But, compared to the rest of the culture, jazz has been an oasis of racial sanity and compassion. So it is downright depressing that racism—or if you prefer, racialism—has become increasingly an issue in the current jazz scene. But then again, this current movement sweeping the new generation of jazz musicians is basically reactionary (though again I stress not in any narrow political meaning of that term), and, as we shall see, racism of one sort or another has always been closely associated with such a reactionary view of jazz.

It has become increasingly difficult to discuss the issue of racism in the current neoclassicist movement; those who do discuss it are often tarred as racist themselves. It really is a new type of McCarthyism. During that unhappy period in the 1950s, criticizing Joe McCarthy or any of his fellow witch-hunters meant being accused of being a "pinko" and could even result in the loss of one's job. Obviously, Marsalis and company do not have this much power, but in that world within a world of jazz, iconoclasm of any sort has become increasingly discouraged. The jazz scene has become a place where the smart thing to do is to go along with the confused logic, self-serving historical perspective, and just plain wrongheadedness of the leaders of this movement if you want to be an important part of the scene—and that includes both musicians and jazz writers.

Race is intrinsic to the issues discussed in this book; there is no way of avoiding it. Of course, no matter what slant you might take on American culture or society, the issue of race is virtually always present, even if only indirectly. But I believe that the racial polarization that has cropped up in jazz since the advent of the neo movement is, to use a phrase of Spiro Agnew's, part of the same ball of wax as some neoclassicists' reactionary views and narrow strictures about the music itself.

It makes sense that the jazz scene should be a place of relative racial harmony since it was born from a melding of black (African) and white (European) musical techniques and sensibilities. That this should have occurred in the Jim Crow South is something of a miracle. Jazz could only have been born in the so-called melting pot of America, a place where, contrary to Rudyard Kipling, the twains of West and East (or at least non-Western) have not only met but, through jazz, have become intertwined and melded, producing something truly new under the sun. Jazz is sui generis, neither European nor African, although it was "invented" by black musicians. Even in its earliest days it was performed by both whites and blacks, and in essence it is universal like all other great arts.

However, as we shall see, the deepest part of the jazz sensibility springs from the African-American experience.

There are a number of reasons why jazz has been so free from the racism that plagues virtually every field of endeavor throughout America (and here again I must stress that it is only *relatively* free from racism). One obvious reason is that, after all, if you are a white person who wants to play jazz, you must pay obeisance to the genius of the black innovators who created and chiefly developed this music. If you clutch fondly to the fantasy of "white supremacy," the overwhelming genius of Armstrong, Ellington, Parker, Miles, Monk, Coltrane, and all the others is like a good dose of reality.

One of the unfortunate aspects of the neoclassicist movement is that it has exacerbated more racial tensions in jazz than any other time since the late 1960s. Although there are a number of white musicians in this movement, it is mostly black, and the fact that it is dominated by black musicians has given it a certain legitimacy because, with one exception, all major movements in jazz have been led by black musicians (the exception, as we shall see is cool jazz). Wynton Marsalis has been accused of practicing "Crow Jim"—the systematic exclusion of whites—mainly because of his policies at Lincoln Center. Comparatively few whites have been hired to play in the large band used at the JALC programs. Marsalis claims that he chooses musicians according to their ability, and, to be honest, I have no reason to doubt him. Of course, Marsalis is entitled to play with the musicians he feels most comfortable with. But what does bother me, and many others, both black and white, about the Lincoln Center program, is that while having focused on jazz players ranging from the greatest innovators to far lesser talents, except for one token concert (focusing on the late Gerry Mulligan), it has not saluted any white musicians. There have been no programs devoted to Bix Beiderbecke, Pee Wee Russell, Benny Goodman, Woody Herman, Stan Getz, Bill Evans, Gil Evans, Scott LaFaro, Lee Konitz, or any other notable white jazz musicians.

The answer of Marsalis and the others running JALC has been that they need to salute the most crucial jazz musicians first, all of whom happen to be black. But how can you leave out of the program, say, Bix Beiderbecke, to name just one white jazz musician? Bix, as we shall see, has been acclaimed by both white and black musicians and has long been conceded as one of the great figures in jazz by anyone with real knowledge of this music. Does Marsalis really believe that, say, Dewey Redman—who was saluted in a Lincoln Center concert—is of greater historical importance than Bix, or Goodman, or Bill Evans?

There is no question that most of the greatest jazz musicians are black, and this has been true since the beginning of the music. Yet it is simply inarguable that there have been musicians of other races (not just white) who have made great contributions to jazz. Marsalis talks constantly about jazz as a true reflection of American democracy. Yet how can he leave whites and other races out of that democracy? Is that a "true reflection" of American life? Like it or not, there really are a rather large number of white folks in this country, and, as we shall see, it is simply undeniable that there have been great white jazz musicians, and the evidence for that is overwhelming.

Perhaps such ideas might be traced to Albert Murray, whom the *Village Voice* called "the mind of Stanley Crouch," who, in turn is, according to the *Voice*, "the mind of Wynton Marsalis"—and therefore of an entire generation of jazz musicians. Murray and Crouch have been enormously influential in the neo generation and the direction (or, rather, lack of direction) the neo generation's music has taken, and that in itself is a first. In the case of every previous jazz generation, it was the musicians who pointed the way, and the critics who struggled to keep up with their advances. With this generation, however, it has been jazz critics not the musicians, who have defined the direction of jazz. The great Wayne Shorter, one of the most continually innovative jazz musicians of his generation, put it this way in an interview: "The critic is becoming the star, and the artists are the army that fights for the star." [1] Shorter is, sadly, correct—this is a perverse and unhealthy situation for any art form, and particularly for jazz, in which traditionally the musicians have marched, often defiantly, to their own idiosyncratic drum.

The influence of critics is in large part the explanation for this obsession with jazz's past. Critics, at least most of them, traditionally have had a long and deep understanding of the history of jazz, much greater than the average jazz musician who is usually aware only of the most recent developments. For instance, when John Coltrane first took up the soprano saxophone, he went back to explore the work of the first great jazz soprano saxophonist, Sidney Bechet. Bechet is one of the seminal jazz innovators, yet most of the musicians of Coltrane's generation were only vaguely aware of who he was and what his music sounded like. Of course, critics are unable to innovate and explore new musical territory. Traditionally, critics have been uncomfortable, as we shall see, with innovation, at least at first; few of them are able to separate the genuine innovators from the charlatans hiding under the guise of "avant garde." As knowledgeable as the best critics may be about the course of jazz history, inevitably when critics try to guess in what direction jazz (or any other art form) is headed, they are almost always on the wrong track. Any art form, therefore, that comes under the domination of critics, as jazz has in the last decade or so, is bound to look backward to jazz history, which is what critics know and understand best. So jazz has become like Stephen Dedalus, trapped in the nightmare of history and unable to wake up.

Some of the neos, and especially their gurus, have pushed their fascination with jazz history to the extent that they have to at times revise it, shaping it to fit their own narrow vision of the development of jazz and its so-called tradition. This is scary stuff. This is the Big Lie, a fascist invention: Tell a lie over and over again and pretty soon at least some people will come to believe it.

Albert Murray has been acclaimed as one of America's leading men of letters, and he has written perceptively about a number of topics concerning America society and culture. He has written some insightful literary criticism and is a serious novelist himself. His writings on race, such as are contained in his book *The Omni Americans*, are particularly clear-sighted and humane. He is wary of the reverse racism of some black leaders and has disdain for the Afrocentrism that has gained credence among a number of black intellectuals and writers.

So it is especially astounding to read his views on jazz and race, which are scarcely much different from those writers for whom he has little respect, such as Amiri Baraka (at least Baraka's writing about jazz in the mid- and late 1960s, when he was still known as Leroi Jones). Stanley Crouch, who has also written disparagingly about Baraka and other Afrocentrist writers, follows Murray's line closely. For some reason, when it comes to jazz, these men lose their ability simply to think logically and to face reality, and, even more sadly, to write with compassion and a true sense of humanism.

Albert Murray's book *Stomping the Blues*, on "blues music" (to him this includes jazz, which in his view is simply a somewhat more sophisticated manifestation of the blues) has been widely admired for its sociocultural insights on blues and jazz. This book is really the manifesto of the neo movement. According to Stanley Crouch, the book is "the most eloquent book ever written about African-American music." Crouch has influenced Wynton Marsalis with Murray's jazz "theories," and Marsalis in turn, of course, has been the main influence on this generation of jazz musicians. Yet overlooked by the critics who hailed this book (except for a few—Terry Teachout, Gene Lees, and Whitney Balliett) is that Murray apparently subscribes to the idea that only African Americans can play jazz (or the blues), an idea that has been repeatedly shown to be total nonsense, and for which there can be no other adjective used except *racist.* And that hand in hand with his racial views, he expresses an attitude toward the scope and vision of jazz as an art form that is provincial and narrow-minded; he views the jazz tradition in such specific terms that it becomes a straitjacket for a music that is famous for its celebration of freedom and change.

Throughout most of *Stomping the Blues,* Murray's racial views concerning jazz are implied rather than stated. To him "blues music" is by, of, and for African Americans, and only for them. Murray does not hedge, at least; he is up front—jazz can only be played idiomatically by black people, or, rather, American black people. He offers no reason why this would be so. He seems to believe that blacks are not born with some genetic propensity for playing syncopated music, that one must learn everything about jazz in order to play it correctly. So is it environmental? Then apparently, in Murray's view, all black people must be pretty much the same, completely homogeneous. They all have similar abilities, and if so, one must extrapolate, the same limitations. So according to Murray, the fact that, say, Louis Armstrong came from New Orleans and terrible poverty and Miles Davis came from a background of St. Louis and upper-middle-class privilege is irrelevant, and the only thing that is relevant, at least regarding their ability to play jazz, is the fact that they are both black; at least that is apparently Murray's view. Of course, one similarity they and virtually all African Americans share is that they have both experienced white racism, but is that the ultimate source of creativity and the way somebody is defined—by the fact and the degree of his or her victimization?

Here is what Murray, in a footnote, writes specifically about white jazz musicians: Discussing the fact that some "liberal critics" objected to the term *race records* in the early 1940s, he writes, ". . . These same writers intrude the name Bix Beiderbecke into discussions of such seminal blues-idiom trumpeters as Buddy Bolden, Bunk Johnson, Freddie Keppard, King Oliver, and Louis Armstrong." [2] Yet we know that in addition to these so-called liberal (read: white) critics who greatly admired Bix were scores of musicians, both black and white, including Lester Young, the great Ellingtonian trumpeter Rex Stewart, and even Louis Armstrong, who had great respect for Bix and recognized his importance as a true jazz innovator. Armstrong stated that Bix was working along the same lines that he was, although neither man was aware of the other—in other words, Bix was also developing the art of the improvised jazz solo. Further, Louis says about Bix (as quoted in *Hear Me Talkin' to Ya*, the classic oral history of jazz):

> And the first time I heard Bix, I said these words to myself, there's a man as serious about his music as I am. . . . Bix did not let anything at all distract his mind from that cornet and his heart was with it all the time. . . . When Bix would finish up at the Chicago Theater at night, he would haul it out to the Sunset where I was playing and stay right there until the show was over and the customers would go home.
>
> Then we would lock the doors. Now you talking about jam sessions . . . huh . . . those were the things . . . with everyone feeling each other's notes or chord, et cetera and blend with each other instead of trying to cut each other . . . nay, nay, nay. We did not even think of such a mess. . . . We tried to see how good we could make music sound, which was an inspiration within itself.[3]

Black and white musicians "feeling each other's notes" and trying to blend with each other instead of "cutting" each other is a lovely summary of the jazz sensibility coming from the man who is largely responsible for it. And what a moving description of white and black musicians playing together out of love for the music, the specter of racism for the moment forgotten. Is Amstrong "intruding" the name of Bix Beiderbecke here?

Louis Armstrong was not the only jazz titan who loved and respected the music of Beiderbecke and his colleague Frankie Trumbauer (also white). The influence of these musicians on Lester Young was profound—Young carried around two Bix records wherever he went and listened to them incessantly. Actually, all you need is ears; the deep influence of Bix and Trumbauer's songlike lyricism on Lester Young is obvious if you listen to these musicians with a sensitive ear. And of course Lester Young would become one of the most influential musicians in the history of jazz; his effect on the musicians—both black and white—who followed in his wake was almost as enormous as Armstrong's.

One more interesting comment about Bix: Rex Stewart has stated that Bix was a primary influence on his style, along with Armstrong. In turn, Stewart was one of the prime influences on Roy Eldridge who, of course, was Dizzy Gillespie's main influence. Anyone writing an honest history of jazz who refused to give a prominent place to Bix Beiderbecke would be guilty of gross negligence—and this could be based solely on the *black* musicians who vouched for or were directly influenced by him. It was through musicians—both white and black—that other jazz musicians almost always first gained notice in the jazz world.

THE TRUTH IS that most jazz musicians, despite what some may actually say, do not care about race when it comes to actually making music; they care about the *sound* created by the other musicians—everything else is irrelevant. Musicians have always loved to share ideas with each other, to learn from one another and jam together, regardless of race. This is the way jazz has grown and renewed itself. Musicians have always appreciated the actual music that was created, and have mostly ignored other, ephemeral considerations.

Murray makes the point that certain white musicians have won jazz polls over better black players, and that Benny Goodman was tagged the King of Swing over more deserving contenders for this title, like Count Basie or Duke Ellington. That may be true, but these things are not the fault of the musicians and do not denigrate their actual accomplishments. Benny Goodman may not have been the real King of Swing, although the great success of his band—thanks mainly to the brilliant arrangements of Fletcher Henderson—is generally considered to have launched the swing era. And virtually everyone in jazz conceded that he was a brilliant jazz clarinetist (Miles Davis, for example, believed that Goodman was the greatest clarinetist in the history of jazz).

Murray goes on. In this same footnote he states that the reason that "liberal critics" don't like the terms *race records* or *race music* is because "they are aiming at a redefinition of blues music that will legitimize the idiomatic authenticity of certain white musicians whose very accents prove that they are *not* native to the idiom but nonetheless enjoy reputations (and earnings) as great performers." Read it again and you will see exactly his intent: Murray is stating outright here that white musicians—all white musicians—are *not* (his italics) "native to the idiom" because of their "very accents." In other words, they simply were not born with rhythm in their bones. That is the whole point of the paragraph, that white critics ended the use of the term *race records* as a ploy to get talentless white jazz musicians accepted.

As for these so-called liberal critics, in the late 1930s and 1940s, a new generation of critics emerged in the jazz world. This generation included Leonard Feather, Barry Ulanov, and several others, such as, a little later,

Nat Hentoff. They were far more enlightened than most earlier jazz critics, both musically and socially, and did not subscribe to the racist stereotyping of the earlier critics. They were far more sophisticated and more sensitive to the feelings of black people—which is why they denounced what they believed to be such demeaning terms as *race records* and *race music.* They did not do this in order to allow white players into the jazz world, as Murray implies, but because they believed it was insulting to blacks. They also stopped calling blues or jazz "coon music" for the same reason, not because of some sinister agenda.

The fact that Murray puts this statement—of views that he certainly must realize are at least questionable, if not utterly outrageous to many readers—in a footnote rather than in the body of the book means that he does not have to explain himself. He therefore does not have to answer several disturbing questions. For example: Why is this art form, unlike all other art forms, only authentically created by one particular ethnic group? Is it sociological, or hereditary, or simply beyond understanding, perhaps mystical?

There is one other place in *Stomping the Blues* where Murray makes clear his views on jazz or as he puts it, "blues music," and race. Among the photographs included in the book is the famous "Great Day in Harlem." Art Kane, a photographer, rounded up every important jazz musician in New York and had them pose for a photograph in front of a Harlem brownstone. In the caption for the picture, Murray identifies all the black musicians as "first line"—New Orleans argot for the best musicians. He identifies some black children sitting on the sidewalk in the photo as "second line." And then he lists every single white musician (and only white musicians) and identifies them as "third line," putting their importance to the music beneath the kids on the sidewalk. Those white musicians include Gerry Mulligan, Pee Wee Russell, Marian McPartland, and Bud Freeman, all widely respected jazz musicians.

Throughout *Stomping the Blues,* Murray is more subtle in his bias. He uses only the term *blues music,* putting it in the category of African-American folk music, eschewing the term *jazz,* which is much more racially inclusive. This is why Marsalis and other neos constantly refer to "blues expression"—it is a euphemism for the African-American sensibility, which they insist is the only one out of which authentic jazz can be created.

I think the best way to determine whether or not white men and women can play jazz is to go directly to the great black musicians who have been the chief innovators and creators of this music. Certainly they cannot be accused of having an agenda of any sort except appreciation of musical talent. For example, John Coltrane named Getz as one of his four favorite all-time tenormen. Coltrane stated, "Let's face it, we'd all like to sound like that—if we could." As a matter of fact, it is difficult to find any musician, black or white, who does not admire Getz's artistry (and that includes such sticklers as Miles Davis and Charles Mingus). Bill Evans? Talk to Herbie Hancock, Ahmad Jamal, or McCoy Tyner. Or, for that matter, Mingus or George Russell, both of whom hired and admired Evans. Of course Miles Davis loved Evans's playing and said that he "sure learned a lot from Bill Evans," strong words coming from the usually taciturn Miles. Then what about Woody Herman? Both Bird and Dizzy loved Herman's band and enjoyed sitting in with it as often as they could, as did many black musicians who sat in or were actual members of the Herman band. Dizzy wrote one of his greatest tunes for Herman, "Woody 'n You."

The first bebop band to play Fifty-second Street, a quintet led by Dizzy Gillespie, had a white pianist, George Wallington. As we shall see later, bop was supposedly music that was created with the idea of showing up white jazzmen, this certainly put a huge hole in such a manifesto. Charlie Parker's favorite pianist, Al Haig, was white, and Bird played with and raved about the trumpet playing of Chet Baker. Later, he hired the trumpeter Red Rodney to replace Miles Davis in his group, although having a racially mixed band caused problems when they played the South. But Bird loved Rodney's playing and chose him over other, black trumpet players. Louis Armstrong frequently hired white musicians; Jack Teagarden was his favorite trombonist, and the two often played and recorded together. Nobody was more outspoken about America's racism than Charles Mingus, yet he often hired white players. Charlie Mariano's alto saxophone was given a prominent place in Mingus's masterpiece *The Black Saint and the Sinner Lady*, and on it he plays some of the most heart-singeing saxophone I have ever heard. Mingus even hired the pianist Toshiko Mariano, who of course is both Asian and female. Ornette Coleman's first great quartet included Charlie Haden, the brilliant bassist. Even Archie Shepp, one of the most racially militant musicians to emerge in the 1960s, once led a quartet that was half-white (Haden and the trombonist Roswell Rudd). Musicians have always known the music was paramount, not the skin color. The truth is this: Every single important white player—or I should say nonblack player—has been vouched for not by a white critic, but in virtually every case by prominent black jazzmen. That is how every jazz musician, regardless of race, first gains notice—other musicians take note long before most critics and fans are aware of the new talent on the scene. And the open-mindedness of the great musicians is extraordinary. When Weather Report, probably the best fusion band, formed in the early 1970s, none other than Duke Ellington endorsed the band. His reason? Because of his great respect for Joe Zawinul, the group's cofounder (along with Wayne Shorter) and keyboardist/composer. And Zawinul is not only white, he's Austrian!

But this is demeaning, demeaning to all concerned, to whites, to blacks, and to jazz itself, to be forced to make this sort of list of racial accountability. This debate was thought to have been decided decades ago. What has happened that race has become such an issue in jazz, of all things, here at the end of this century, when so many have died in the name of racial tolerance?

The key to the issue of race in jazz is a simple point: The reputation of all jazz musicians, black or white, begins with other musicians—and this has been true from the time of King Oliver to that of Wynton Marsalis.

Stomping the Blues is mainly an attempt to show how what Murray calls "blues music" reflects a narrowly defined African-American sensibility. He is very persuasive in his portrayal of the role of blues music in the lives of African Americans. But this is where he goes wrong: It is obviously true that most important jazz musicians are African Americans, and of course their music reflects their lives, just like all great art does. So it is true that most jazz does reflect the lives and sensibility of African Americans. But by extrapolating this fact so as to state that the art form itself somehow *must* reflect African Americans' lives in order to be authentic is, I believe, a profound mistake. The novel does not have to be written by Britons—the "inventors" of the novel—in order to be authentic. Nor do composers or performers of "classical" music have to be Germanic. When someone who is Germanic composes a work of classical music, naturally it reflects his or her life on one level or another. Jazz is no different in this regard. And therefore it is malleable in every sort of way, including what Murray calls its "accents." Does Phil Woods not play with the right "accents"? Or Zoot Sims? Pee Wee Russell? Very few, if any, prominent jazz musicians, black or white (at least from a pre-Marsalis generation), would agree with such a statement.

In addition, Murray's theory ignores the fact that for most of its existence, jazz has been kept alive mainly by its white fans. Go into any jazz club or to any jazz festival and it becomes obvious that without white jazz fans such venues could not exist. In addition, jazz musicians have survived at times only through the support of European and Japanese fans. Every jazz musician knows that his or her music could never have survived with only its black audience. Obviously, people of all races have heard something in this music that is relevant to their lives.

It is also true that some black musicians have complained about whites in jazz, but mostly this is concerning the business end of jazz and the critics. The drummer Art Taylor published a book called *Notes and Tones*, which included his interviews with several prominent black jazz musicians. These interviews are quite different from the usual sort of thing done with white jazz-critic interviewers in that the jazzmen were far more open and revealing since they were being questioned by a colleague. Many white jazz fans were shocked by the expression of anti-white anger in a number of these interviews. But virtually every one of these musicians has worked with and even hired good white jazz musicians at one time or another. For instance, the great drummer Philly Joe Jones, in his interview with Taylor, was particularly outspoken. But one of his favorite colleagues was Bill Evans, with whom he has played and recorded on several occasions.

As I said before, Murray's book is, more or less, the manifesto of the neoclassicist movement. It is Murray who insists that jazz is simply a somewhat more sophisticated form of the blues, a folk art. It is Murray who says that for music to be accepted as being truly idiomatic "blues music," it has to be part of a limiting tradition, one born only from African-American culture, or rather, Murray's concept of a single homogeneous American black cultural sensibility. It has to swing, therefore, and the blues always have to be present. It is a narrow, tired, and reactionary vision, inherently racialist—toward blacks and whites alike—and ultimately destructive to this music that Murray clearly loves.

If Murray with his manifesto is the Karl Marx of this movement, Crouch is its Lenin. It seems incredible that Crouch, who is so outspoken on the anti-white racism of certain black writers, not only let Murray off the hook but seems to embrace his feelings about jazz and race. How could he not see the huge contradiction?

If you have any doubt about Wynton Marsalis's true feelings toward white jazz musicians, his attitude is clearly laid out in his own words. In 1994 Marsalis published a book with the rather clumsy title *Sweet Swing Blues on the Road*, describing his life as a touring jazz musician. As the diary of a working jazz musician, it is honest and often revealing, and it gives valuable insight into the daily life of a jazzman on tour. In one section Marsalis answers the questions of an unnamed (and probably fictional) interviewer. The interviewer asks why black people are the best jazz musicians. Marsalis answers, "Crouch says 'They invented it.' People who invent something are always the best at doing it."[4] Following this logic, then, only white people could be great novelists, only Europeans great classical composers and musicians, and, for that matter, only Americans could be great baseball players. Edison invented the motion picture. Does that mean that only white people can create the best movies? However, later he equivocates by saying, "Jazz includes everyone. That is further proof of its greatness." But here Marsalis is being somewhat disingenuous if not downright dishonest. Perhaps somebody pulled his sleeve at some point and pointed out that he had a separate career playing music created by white Europeans; if the ability to perform or create art had something to do with ethnic provenance, shouldn't he stick to jazz? But nobody but a racist would ever say such a thing about Andre Watts or Kathleen Battle or Marsalis as a classical trumpet player. Somehow saying the same thing about jazz has become acceptable.

When Marsalis was asked on "60 Minutes" why the Lincoln Center program had never performed works by any white composer, he answered by first stating that he hated to lower himself to the level of such a question, and then said, "Duke Ellington was the greatest composer in the history of jazz. Period." I would venture that most viewers, like myself, were something less than satisfied with this answer.

Yet there is no denying that the bulk of great jazz musicians are black. I think that there are several reasons why this is so, and they have nothing to do with a racist notion of inborn ability. Some of these reasons are quite obvious.

Black musicians had few outlets for their talents other than jazz, due to the racism of most of American culture, including "high culture." Throughout most of this century, black musicians were simply not seen in the concert hall, nor were they accepted as, say, composers for film or even as studio players, which may not be all that creative but which is highly lucrative for a career musician. The entry of blacks into these areas is relatively recent, and it is still on basically a token basis—much to the shame of the music business. But talented white musicians had myriad career possibilities. In fact, since most whites are afflicted to one extent or another with a belief in white supremacy, the number of talented white musicians willing to play a music clearly dominated by blacks was very limited. The sickness of racism made it difficult for many white people to be involved in an art form in which black people have been the most important innovators. And the underlying existentialist sensibility at the heart of jazz arose from the African-American experience. I will discuss this later in the book.

Nevertheless, there have been a number of white jazz musicians equal to the best (although not the very greatest) black jazz musicians. And really, if this were not so, it would mean that jazz is not a great art form, not an art form that goes to the heart of our universal experience, but rather a provincial and very limited art form, a folk art created and truly understood by only one ethnic group, African Americans. If this were not so, jazz fails the test of universality essential to a truly great art form.

Both Murray and Crouch greatly admire Ralph Ellison, the author of one of the most powerful and beautiful of all American novels, *Invisible Man*. Ellison also wrote a number of essays on jazz. To a degree, they have modeled their own careers after this literary titan. Yet Ellison, while writing about the natue of jazz and its connection to the lives of African Americans, nevertheless was very clear in his belief that all races were capable of playing the music. Ellison was quite clear in his belief that jazz could be authentically played by musicians of any race. In his essay on Leroi Jones's book *Blues People*, he brilliantly rips into Jones's contentions that blues music is hermetically black music. At one point Ellison writes, "His assertions . . . are not in keeping with the facts; his theory flounders before that complex of human motives which makes human history."[5]

Marsalis has complained that the reason he has been sniped at for the policies at Lincoln Center is because a black jazz musician has been put in charge of such a program. I hope he gives greater thought to the reason for this sniping. There is no doubt that the impulse to ignore white musicians is an understandable reaction to the many decades that black musicians have suffered due to white racism. The New York Philharmonic, which also performs at Lincoln Center, for many years refused to hire black musicians. They claimed that there simply were no black musicians good enough to meet their standards. But when Art Davis, one of the world's greatest bass players, tried to get a seat in the orchestra, he was given the runaround—and there was absolutely no doubt as to his ability. And black musicians for many decades could not get work doing lucrative studio work, let alone play in white-led bands (with a few exceptions like occasional spots in the bands of Woody Herman and, Benny Goodman). The anger of black musicians is more than justified.

Yet denying the importance of white jazz musicians is wrong, not so much because of the harm it does to white people—which is negligible since most white people (and people in general, for that matter) could not care less what goes on in the jazz world. But condoning one of the basic concepts of racialism—that it is possible to predict any sort of ability based on race alone—keeps the concept of racism alive and well. And those most hurt by racism are, of course, racial minorities.

By spotlighting only black musicians, the Lincoln Center brain trust helps to give solidity to the idea that race can be used as a criterion for ability. By tacitly agreeing with this basic tenet of racism, racists of whatever stripe are empowered. And since there are far more white than black racists, black people lose. Any time racism of any sort is given credence, ultimately black people suffer more than anybody else, at least in this country. "Sure," white racists would admit, "you black folks can play that jazz music better than anybody else. 'Cause you're right: 'Whoever invents something, does it better than anybody else. You're born with those "accents" in your bones.' "

So what does this have to do with the "murder of jazz"? Everything. According to Gene Lees, who was editor of *Down Beat* in the early 1960s and author of a book about jazz and race called *Cats of Every Color*, "The current jazz scene is the most segregated I have seen in my forty-five or so years of association with it. There was segregation in the public, but now there is a kind of segregation within jazz itself. It's ominous." Jazz used to be the most progressive and visionary force in American culture. A return to racial orientation in jazz is reactionary, just as the idea of racial segregation itself is reactionary, whether it comes from a black nationalist or a member of the Ku Klux Klan. The progressive idea that all so-called races are equals, and that by interacting they can grow and gain wisdom, is at the heart of jazz—it lies at the core of jazz's initial creation, its development as an art form, and its role as a positive force in the greater society. Americans cheered the Benny Goodman trio, quartet, and sextet in the 1930s and early 1940s, all of which were racially integrated long before Jackie Robinson joined the Dodgers. It is central to the jazz vision. Just think of the lyrics of one of the earliest jazz songs, "Basin Street Blues": Basin Street is described as a jazz haven where white and dark can meet.

Miles Davis often expressed his idea that integrated jazz groups often produce the best music, that the interplay of different sensibilities gave the music a depth not heard in racially homogeneous bands. Miles once said to me, "Why do they call me racist when my first band was almost all white?" This was true—his first band was the Birth of the Cool nonet, which was dominated by white players, as well as some great black players, too. Ever since then, Miles worked with a long list of important white players, from Lee Konitz to John McLaughlin and David Liebman. Yet nobody was more outspoken than Miles about racism and the perniciousness of white supremacy in America.

I believe that one reason talented black people have been drawn to jazz is because they have recognized the pluralistic vision inherent in jazz—a vision, of course, not very different from Martin Luther King, Jr.'s "dream." In jazz, they could define themselves and redefine themselves every time they walked onto the bandstand. This opportunity for self-realization that is so crucial to the creation of jazz was, needless to say, a powerful attraction for members of a minority that was generally held in such low esteem by the greater society.

Musicians discovered that as they changed, the music changed. And, in turn, the music itself changed them. Jazz was a force for freedom, a visionary art form that offered hope even in the darkest of times. And that was because it was not just a wonderful, life-giving form of music, but it was also a beacon that, despite the fact that it was mostly ignored by the majority of both whites and blacks, still could illuminate the often dark American landscape.

All of this is tied directly to the universal nature of jazz, the fact that it is an art form that was born by the melding of European and African culture, the meeting of Western and non-Western twains. That jazz was first developed by black people is not surprising; if they were to have a future in this country, it lay in the possibilities of the melding of black and white culture, the meeting of the twains of East and West. It was a battle against the myopia of most white people in this country, who clung to the vestiges of a moribund culture that had less and less relevance for life in this New World. The comfort Western culture offered was the lure of empowerment through the myth of white supremacy. Certainly on some level the brilliant African Americans who developed jazz must have seen in the creation of this music a path to their own freedom.

So it is not surprising that those who have reactionary ideas about the music itself would also embrace this "Crow Jim" attitude. They deny the visionary, progressive elements in the music and its culture. Rather, they see the music as a limited, narrow, predictable art form developed by American blacks to reflect the lives of a mythical homogeneous black sensibility. Whites or others might try to play it, but they are simply unable to create authentic jazz.

Jazz *is* African American, but in a much deeper sense than the ludicrous belief that only a single ethnic group can play it authentically. What makes it so profoundly African American is the social and philosophical agenda implicit in this music. The bandstand is the place where the members of a jazz group can explore the possibilities, limits, and consequences of freedom, and by so doing also help liberate those in their audience. These children and grandchildren of slaves burned with an obsession for freedom, and for many years the bandstand was the one place in America where black people could be truly free. When playing jazz, for a few hours a musician could spread his wings and soar, be defiantly himself and ecstatically free. So in this very profound sense, jazz *is* African-American music: More than any other group, African Americans understand know how the impingement of individual freedom is crippling to the soul, and in jazz they devised a music in which that freedom was at its heart, a music whose power could humanize those who may have taken such freedom for granted.

THERE IS ANOTHER trend in jazz, which to some in the jazz world is even more bothersome than that of race. And that is the new obsession with youth. Young players have always brought to jazz vitality and fresh ideas, often revolutionary ideas. And there have been very young players—Charlie Christian, Jimmy Blanton, Fats Navarro, Booker Little, to name a few—who had original styles at a very young age. The difference is that the young players on the current scene sound young, in that most of them have not had the seasoning to develop a genuinely personal style. Rather, their playing is a cobbling of styles borrowed from the great jazz individualists from the past.

Yet in the current scene these young, inexperienced players are getting large recording contracts and headlining at the major clubs while veterans are still scuffling. Joshua Redman, James Carter, Roy Hargrove, and Javon Jackson are but a few of these very young lions. This obsession with youth has become a fad remindful of the bossa nova craze when record companies thought that all they had to do was have whatever jazz musicians were at hand record bossa nova tunes in order to sell records. If the new popularity of jazz was true and deep, naturally the great master musicians who are still with us—Art Farmer, Phil Woods, Sonny Rollins, Gary Bartz, George Russell, Sonny Fortune, and others—would be the ones in the limelight. As the insightful critic Francis Davis put it, "This drooling infatuation with youth is itself a sign that jazz is beginning to show its age. Years ago, *Down Beat* used to review reissues in a column headlined Old Wine, New Bottles. Given the current emphasis on classic repertoire and fresh young faces, most of today's new releases could be listed under Old Blood, New Bodies."[6]

Young jazz musicians used to go through a period of apprenticeship, playing gigs in big bands or small groups led by experienced jazz musicians from whom they could learn the nuances of jazz expression. Instead, most neoclassicists have learned jazz in school, a good place to learn technique but not the subtleties and philosophy inherent in the creation of jazz. In this disposable society, these "young men in suits" (as they are called because of their Marsalis-influenced fashion sense), as the neoclassicists have been called, are in leadership roles before they have developed a mature, individualistic style and have gained the experience—"paid their dues"—to play music with depth and meaning.

One example—who is probably not the worst, just typical of this generation—is guitarist Mark Whitfield. Signed to a major conglomerate, Polygram, he is technically accomplished but has not even come close to an original style. His playing is a predictable meld of the styles of Wes Montgomery and Kenny Burrell—in other words, the jazz guitar style of the 1950s and early 1960s. His compositions are not much more than a series of chords with only a very thin melody connecting them. He obviously has talent, perhaps a great talent. But he needs much seasoning before he should be in a position of leadership. Unfortunately, most of these musicians will not undergo the period of apprenticeship known in jazz as "paying your dues" that is necessary to hone an individual conception as long as they are being treated like "young lions."

Jazz is important; jazz is very important in myriad ways. This I believe with all my heart, mind, and soul. At the center of the creation of jazz lies the deepest issue facing man in this century: the burden of freedom. As I will explain in Chapter 13, "Lighting Out for the Territory," it is by its very nature a truly existential art form, a peculiarly American form of existentialism, and at its best it has been a kind of compass for these tumultuous times.

One thing that I have so respected about jazz is that it eschews sentimentality in its refusal to hold on to the past and that its gaze is ever unblinkingly forward—at least until the last few years. The neoclassicists embrace figures ranging from Louis Armstrong to Thelonious Monk as classic icons now that the innovations of these great figures have become part of the mainstream. But all of these figures were musical revolutionaries who, according to the neoclassicists of their day, were destroying the "real" jazz tradition. The difference was that the neoclassicists of the past were mainly writers and fans. The musicians ignored them and continued to explore the frontiers of the music. We now have in the current jazz mainstream virtually the complete opposite of this situation.

This has been called the "American century," and now that this century is coming to its end, I think it is a good time to assess where the most American music—jazz—has been, what its nature really is, and where it still might take us. Is jazz innately reactionary, a music in which tradition overrides innovation? Is it music for and of one ethnic group, or is it universal? Is it an art of the status quo, or is it, like the dance of the stars in our universe, ever in a state of flux?

3.

The Jazz Age Revolution

IN MY ATTEMPT to offer an alternative vision of the nature, development, and significance of jazz, I start with a few seemingly simple premises: that jazz musicians, despite the unprecedented and unique nature of their art form, nevertheless have the same general goals as artists in other forms of art traditionally have had. I also assume that jazz musicians have always been conscious of what they were doing, that they are not "native geniuses" creating art solely through intuition and a supposedly simple sensibility. And like the art of the novel or sculpture or classical composition, jazz is a form of art that is a blank slate the artist fills in out of the grist of his or her own life and experience. These assumptions may seem obvious; I simply claim for the jazz musician what is assumed to be true of any artist of the modern age.

Saying that jazz is the equal of other art forms in profundity and universality is not the same as suggesting that it can be understood in the same terms as other art forms. Jazz is often misunderstood and confused with other forms of music. Just the expression often used to describe jazz—"African-American classical music"—indicates how deep the confusion lies. The idea that to be taken seriously, music must be either classical or like classical lies in the assumption that Western culture is ultimately greater than any other—and that the body of work known as classical music is inherently the greatest music ever produced.

These assumptions about classical music, and classical Western literature and art, have been used like a bludgeon against those from non-Western cultures—as proof that the West is more civilized than the rest of the world.

Although jazz has been influenced by classical music throughout its development, it has been influenced at least equally by non-Western forms of music. It is more than a hybrid; it is a new form of art, a new *kind* of art, and it must be understood completely on its own terms. Not only is it profoundly American, it is just as profoundly a phenomenon of this waning century.

Innovation is uniquely central to the jazz aesthetic, unlike classical music. This is not to say that classical composers do not innovate, but rather that innovation is not a necessary part of the process in creating classical music. With jazz it is. This should not be confused with the built-in obsolescence of so much pop music—that is faddism, not innovation, and it is driven by the marketplace, not by the nature of the music itself.

Part of the reason that innovation is inherent in the development in jazz lies in the African roots of jazz. Music in Africa was not just entertainment. It was a social force that had direct relevance to the day-to-day lives of those living in a tribe. Music—rhythmically complex drumming—had a direct correlation to language in that it was used as warning or to pull the tribe together. As John Miller Chernoff writes in his book *African Rhythm and African Sensibility*, "[Musicians'] language is a fundamental dimension of their lives which they bring to their music, and people associate the melodies and rhythms with speaking because their speech has meaning in terms of its melodic and rhythmic character. . . . The relationship of drumming to language is one of the most important factors in limiting the freedom of improvisation."[1]

The fact that music was tied so directly to the lives of those in the tribe meant that it had to reflect changes in that society as they happened. The music had to be malleable and flexible, and the musicians playing it had to be sensitive to the lives of their fellow tribesmen and -women.

Using music as a social force was a concept that black people brought with them to this country. Slave songs sung in the fields were a way of communicating the white slavemaster did not understand. And of course spirituals like "Let My People Go," although on the surface supposedly about the Israelites' bondage in Egypt, had a much more immediate subtext for black slaves. This gives us a major clue as to why innovation is so important to jazz: It is a music that also has, albeit far more subtly, a direct connection to the lives and the society of the musicians who play it.

Jazz was born as a voice of rebellion, a rebellion against the Jim Crow laws, which segregated New Orleans society. These laws now affected the large Creole population, which previously did not consider itself black although they were of mixed blood, white, black and/or Indian. As James Collier points out in his book *The Making of Jazz*, forcing the Creoles and blacks together caused a fusion that turned into jazz. The blacks brought the tradition of the blues and the rhythms carried over from their African heritage. The Creoles had the European instruments, knowledge of European harmony, and band repertory. It was this interaction, this true fusion, that brought about jazz.

It should be no surprise that among the first of the great jazzmen were two great black Creoles, clarinetist and soprano saxophonist Sidney Bechet and composer/arranger/pianist Jelly Roll Morton. Morton insisted that he "invented" jazz, but just as in every subsequent major step in jazz's evolution, no one man or woman invented it. However, Morton was the first true jazz auteur, creating works with a jazz band in a personal manner that would serve as a model for such future jazz auteurs as Duke Ellington, Charles Mingus, and Cecil Taylor.

Bechet, on the other hand, although he played for most of his career in the New Orleans ensemble, nevertheless was such a powerful player that he really had more in common with the great soloists from Louis Armstrong on. Even in his earliest days as a jazzman Bechet was a powerful soloist. Bechet toured Europe with a large band called the Southern Syncopators. The great Swiss conductor Ernest Ansermet heard the group and said about Bechet, "There is in the Southern Syncopated Orchestra an extraordinary clarinet virtuoso who is, so it seems, the first of his race to have composed a perfectly formed blues for the clarinet. . . . I wish to set down the name of this artist of genius, as for myself, I shall never forget it—it is Sidney Bechet." This is, I believe, the first time anyone ever characterized a jazz musician as being a genius. And Ansermet also said that the musical road that Bechet was exploring might be one the "whole world might swing down in the future." Ansermet was a genuine prophet. But it was not the genius of Bechet or the innovations of Morton that set off the so-called jazz age.

When we think of the jazz age, we rarely think of jazz itself. Rather, images of flappers and gangsters, bathtub gin, and the fiction of F. Scott Fitzgerald are what most readily come to mind. This is not surprising when it is remembered that in 1927 the first full-length movie with sound was released called *The Jazz Singer*, although there is not a moment of jazz in the film. The film's star, Al Jolson, may have believed that putting on blackface instantly made him a jazz singer, but his style, more rooted in Yiddish and cantorial singing traditions, displayed remarkably little jazz or blues influence. But this is just another example of the confusion about jazz in these early days of its acceptance on a national rather than just a regional basis. Paul Whiteman was known as the King of Jazz, although except for his employment of a handful of jazz musicians—including at one time Bix Beiderbecke and Frankie Trumbauer—the music his band played was sedate and unadventurous light classical or pop dance music. At the same time that Whiteman was being hailed as the king of the new music, Louis Armstrong, Sidney Bechet, Jelly Roll Morton, Fletcher Henderson, and the young Duke Ellington were creating some of the greatest jazz that has ever been heard.

The first jazz group to record—and to set off the supposed jazz craze and the jazz age—was not one of the great black New Orleans groups, but the mediocre Original Dixieland Jazz Band. But this was not so much rank injustice as a failure of vision on behalf of those better musicians. Some of these musicians, such as the legendary trumpeter Freddie Keppard, were asked to record before the ODJB, but turned down the chance for fear of having their best ideas stolen. It would take others who saw the opportunity, and in particular a young genius, to realize the profound connection between jazz and recording.

Say what you want about the ODJB, if nothing else they really did play jazz, unlike Jolson or Whiteman. Sure, it was crude, and it featured dumb barnyard sound effects, but it had at its core the driving jazz message. It was a message that you as much felt with your body as perceived with your mind, something not lost on the guardians of the public's, and particularly the youths', morality. And that message was like an electric current that illuminated the American landscape. The first ODJB records sold over a million copies, an incredible amount for their time (and not so bad even today). As watered down as the jazz message might have been in these initial jazz recordings, these second-rate jazz records changed America as much as did World War I or the mass production of the automobile.

Kathy J. Ogren's book *The Jazz Revolution* is about this era, and it makes clear that jazz itself was one of the main causes of social and cultural revolution in the 1920s. She writes:

> Detractors criticized jazz's musical characteristics—which they dismissed as noise—and its origins in lower-class black culture. Jazz lovers hailed the same sounds as everything from exciting entertainment to an antidote for repressive industrial society. . . . The attractiveness of urban nightlife was embraced by American youth in revolt against what they saw as stuffy prewar society, and their critique joined that of young intellectual dissenters who published an alternative set of beliefs that they hoped would challenge the general confidence in commercial values. Writers and critics like Malcolm Cowley and Ernest Hemingway chose to exile themselves from America and eschew materialism, gentility, and parochialism. Labeled the "lost generation" by Gertrude Stein . . . for them the newest musical sensation—jazz—became the specific symbol of rebellion and what was new about the decade.[2]

Jazz as an agent of change was felt, one way or another, by most Americans, as Ogden points out: "Americans shared a common perception that jazz had transforming qualities that could last beyond the time of a song or the space of a cabaret act. For many Americans, to argue about jazz was to argue about the nature of change itself." It is almost scary how profoundly this applies to the current debate in jazz, although now it is kind of a reverse situation: The neoclassicists refuse to acknowledge the changes in music and society of the last thirty or forty years.

This era was the true beginning of the twentieth century. Before World War I, America was still a secondary power in the grip of a society and culture grounded in the Victorian ethic. The war pushed America into the position of the leading world power, and by the 1920s a number of elements would coalesce to change America's social and cultural landscape, and as Ogren makes clear, jazz was among the foremost.

The shock waves produced by jazz would be felt 'round the world. Among other things, the advent of jazz was the theme music announcing that this would be the American century. This new music, brash, outgoing, with little regard for musical conventions and traditions from the past, was a perfect reflection of the image of America held by the international community. Of course, its melding of black and white, African and European musical traditions and cultural sensibilities was what made jazz profoundly an American statement.

In a way, those who attacked jazz for undermining the morals of

America's youth actually did understand in some crude way the visceral nature of the music. Those churchmen and politicians who thought they detected in jazz the unmistakable sound of sexual license and miscegenation had a point. The surge of rhythm and the brassy, boisterous, ecstatic sound of this music did not deny sexuality but rather celebrated the entire human experience, from the most cerebral (the at times complex polyphony) to the earthiest (the type of rhythm that you felt throughout your body).

Jazz writers have often expressed disdain for those who insisted there was a relationship between jazz and sex. Partially this disdain comes from the suspicion that such a belief arises from racism; the stereotype of black people, after all, depicts them as being "closer to the earth" and as far more sexual than whites. That is one reason so many critics and fans in the jazz world disavow the music's sexuality: it seems inherently racist to claim that at least to some degree sex is an element in the making of jazz. So a clear-headed discussion of sex and jazz has never been encouraged in the jazz world.

Yet denying the element of sex in jazz is simply avoiding reality. I do not state that sex is part of the expression of jazz because the word originally was a slang term for sexual intercourse, or because in its early days jazz was notoriously played in New Orlean's Storyville brothels, though I think those are not irrelevant facts. But I think there are a number of more germane arguments.

Several years ago I interviewed Ornette Coleman for a magazine. Interviewing him was easy because all I had to do was ask him an initial question and he launched into a monologue as hypnotically engrossing as one of his solos. At one point he said that the reason he did not like to play clubs was because the element of sexuality was so strong there that he felt like he was playing his horn unclothed. He felt that playing jazz—spontaneous music based on one's deepest feelings and emotions—was so nakedly confessional that there was something voyeuristic about an audience watching the performance of a jazz player in the intimate atmosphere of a jazz club. There are obvious similarities: In the act of sexual intercourse, as in the creation of jazz, the past and the future are irrelevant; the only thing that matters is the ecstatic here and now. And, of course, the element of sexuality cannot be missed in the playing of jazz: the pushing, irresistible rhythm and the soloist building his solo, spurred on by the other members of the band and the audience too, and finally reaching what musicians call a climax. And perhaps more importantly, the use of vocalized effects, the very *sound* jazz musicians produced on their horns made jazz a music in which sensuality is obviously a powerful part of its aesthetic. A number of jazz tunes refer to the music's sexuality. One of the most popular early jazz tunes was "Jazz Me Blues," and that is just one of the more obvious examples. Duke Ellington was famous for writing music that reflected his intimate life. "Warm Valley" (which is *not* a reference to a geographical valley) is one such example.

Sexuality is part of jazz because the creation of jazz involves one's whole being, mind, body, and soul. Sex is not more important than the intellectual or spiritual elements, but sexuality is acknowledged in jazz as being part of life and therefore having a place in one's art. This idea had great currency in the 1920s when Freud's theory about the magnitude of sex in affecting everyday behavior was being hotly debated. If it was Freud who unleashed the libido, jazz provided the music that it danced to. Of course the Puritan ethic still held sway in America, just as it does to some extent today, despite the assaults of modernity. An art form that dared accept sex as jazz did inevitably raised the hackles of the morals squad.

Although they were correct in perceiving sex in jazz, the fears of those who considered jazz a threat to the moral purity of the young were ludicrously exaggerated and often close to hysterical. But in many ways, their worst fears were justified: Jazz was creating a true social and cultural revolution. Or at least it was a major component of that revolution. Sex was just one element of those fears. The fact that jazz combined this perceived sexuality and also was the musical voice of black people made it especially fearsome to many, and welcome and liberating to others. In Ogren's book she includes a news clip that shows the extent that the fear of jazz had reached. Taken from a 1926 copy of the *New York Times*, it reads:

> The Salvation Army of Cincinnati obtained a temporary injunction today to prevent the erection of a moving picture theater adjoining the Catherine Booth Home for Girls on the grounds that music emanating from the theater would implant "jazz emotions" in the babies born at the home. The plaintiffs realize that they live in a jazz age, declared the suit. . . . "But we are loathe to believe that babies born in the maternity hospital are to be legally subjected to the implanting of jazz emotions by such enforced proximity to a theater and jazz palace."[3]

Obviously such expressions of fear were blown way out of proportion. It is interesting, though, that jazz was perceived as such a real and genunine threat.

The realization that jazz was a very visceral music, that one felt it as well as appreciated it with one's mind, was not far from the truth. Even if it is not dancing, an audience listening to jazz moves their bodies, shakes their heads, and often vocalizes their joy.

The intimacy of this experience explains why jazz has always been best heard in clubs rather than on the concert stage; in the intimate atmosphere of the jazz club, the close communion between musician and audience is obviously more viable. This truly is a liberating experience; the fact that there is a strong sexual element in jazz should be celebrated, not stifled. The fact of jazz's sexuality certainly is not a reflection of the fact that most of the great jazz musicians are black. Probably the two most sensual tenormen in jazz, for example, are Ben Webster and Stan Getz; of course the former is black and the latter white. As long as nobody loses track of the intellectual brilliance and spiritual depth of this music, its sensuality should be allowed to be let out of the closet.

Yet sex was only one part of the jazz revolution of the 1920s. Jazz provided a turning point in American culture. From jazz and along with the careers of writers such as F. Scott Fitzgerald, Ernest Hemingway, and William Faulkner, a new sensibility was born, vital and alive and standing in sharp contrast to the increasingly moribund culture of Europe (with some important exceptions). And the first serious filmmakers were changing the very way we perceive reality.

America was simply in the process of redefining itself. Fitzgerald's masterpiece *The Great Gatsby* is on precisely that subject. In order to win Daisy, the love of his life, Gatsby must completely reinvent himself, re-create himself in order to be acceptable to Daisy and her class. Reinventing oneself in this way is perhaps the essence of the "American dream." Hemingway showed us that a life based on risk was the only one worth living. And Faulkner in his greatest novels, like *The Sound and the Fury* and *Light in August*, explored the often tragic consequences of our freedom. Yet in his magnificent speech accepting the Nobel Prize he insisted that, after all, mankind shall not just go on existing, but prevail.

All of these themes are, of course, close to the heart of the making of jazz. And just as the great writers who emerged in the 1920s and 1930s wrote with a sense of a genuinely American language, jazz redefined the entire concept of music making in a way that reflected the best aspects of the American character: innovative, spontaneous, basically optimistic, and at its best open-minded and tolerant (of course there is another, far less positive, side to the American character, too). What Whitman and Twain had begun, artists in the 1920s were carrying to their logical end—an American culture increasingly divorced from Europe, and particularly from the Victorian Age.

The impact of jazz on this time is incalculable. Jazz loosened up the way people danced and then moved, eventually sang and talked. More than any other factor, jazz melded non-European, in particular African, sensibility with the sensibility carried over from Europe that had still dominated the country. The word *sensibility* may seem vague, but there is no more apt word to use when discussing the genuine sea change that America was going through. Sixty years after the freeing of the slaves, a new, broadened worldview, a radically different perspective on life, was entering the mainstream of American life, or more like *storming* America, creating a true cultural and social revolution that is still ongoing.

The jazz revolution would not have been possible in any previous century because it was so dependent on certain technology of this new age. The fact that both radio and records were becoming increasingly popular by the 1920s was essential for this to have happened. If this technology had not come into being, we can be certain that jazz probably would never have progressed beyond being a folk art.

If it is true what many, including Wynton Marsalis, say about jazz—that it is a reflection of American democratic society—it could never have become that if it were not for all the divergent voices that went into creating it. Because American society contains such great human variety, our culture should reflect the synergy of all these minds and voices. And of course jazz has done exactly that, but it would have been impossible without modern technology.

Don't forget the great difference between jazz and other Western music: When a jazz musician plays, it is a spontaneous event, and the notes of a jazz improvisation are just part of his musical message. The *sound* of the great jazz musicians, absolutely idiosyncratic, as personal as their deepest, most hidden thoughts, is at least as important as the notes. And it is impossible to separate the improvised accompaniment of the rhythm section from the solo itself. Jazz improvisation at its best is a kind of conversation between the soloist and his accompanists. And jazz improvisations are often replies to those of the other soloists. In his autobiography *Beneath the Underdog*, Mingus recalls that one night right before a performance, he was having a deep philosophical conversation with Eric Dolphy. When it was time to go onstage, according to Mingus, the two simply continued their conversation through their improvisation. That anecdote alone should change one's perception of the jazz solo. The greatest jazz performances are a totality that is greater than the sum of its parts. Therefore, sheet music, which is fine for the exposition of all other Western music, is virtually useless for a jazz performance. The only way to hear all that a jazz musician is trying to express is actually to listen to him, and only him, play his improvisation, his spontaneous composition. Some other musician or group of musicians playing the notes of this improvisation is simply not the same thing, not the authentic jazz expression. So the technological revolution of the late nineteenth and the twentieth centuries made it possible for jazz to evolve as a great art form.

From its very beginning there have been those who have confused jazz with older forms of music. In this way it is like the other great art form of this century, film. The earliest movies were really just stage-plays filmed as if the camera were viewing the action from a seat in a theater; the actors were locked foursquare into the proscenium. The earliest film directors had not caught on to the profound difference between theater and cinema. It was directors such as D. W. Griffith and Sergei Eisenstein who discovered montage, close-ups, and other techniques that took film out of the theater and into the world of cinema. Likewise, it took a while before an understanding of the special qualities that made jazz so different from other types of music became clear.

Both jazz and film were born around the beginning of this century, and neither would have been possible without key modern technological innovations. Obviously, the art of cinema would not have been possible without the invention of moving pictures. Less obvious is the fact that jazz would never have grown into a major "fine art" form if it were not for the invention of recorded sound. The elements of jazz might have come into being, but it never would have developed beyond the realm of a localized folk art if it were not for the advent of both radio and recordings.

Neither rock nor any other forms of music are dependent on recording in this way, because they are not based around the primacy of individual sound and improvisation. Yes, it is true that Indian ragas and much other music from various parts of the world also involve improvisation, but it is a completely different type of improvisation from jazz. A musician playing a raga, for instance, must hew tightly to traditional raga patterns, which are handed down from one generation to the next, and he is encouraged to play his instrument within a limiting tradition. On the other hand, the jazz musician has enormous freedom to create his or her music. And unlike raga, and classical music too, there is no traditional or classic way of playing any instrument in jazz. The sound of Ben Webster and that of John Coltrane, who both play the tenor saxophone, are so different that the musicians might as well be playing different instruments. In jazz, there is no ideal way of playing an instrument, or of composing or arranging, for that matter; developing a personal sound and a completely individualistic way of playing, no matter how unorthodox (think of Thelonious Monk or Pee Wee Russell), is the essential trait of a great player.

With this in mind it should be obvious why jazz could not have developed without recordings. Buddy Bolden was supposedly the first jazz trumpeter, but since he was never recorded (at least as far as we know), Bolden's music is really the stuff of legend and conjecture rather than fact. It is quite similar to the old philosophical riddle: Does a tree make a sound if it falls in a forest with nobody around to hear it? Of course, there were many who actually heard Bolden play, but without recordings, memory alone is not sufficient for us to evaluate the playing of a jazz musician.

Here are a few famous examples of the effect of recording on the development of jazz. Bix Beiderbecke grew up in Iowa, far from New Orleans, where the music was for the most part born. When he heard the first records of the Original Dixieland Jazz Band, he connected with the music and was able to listen to it over and over again, picking up the intricacies of jazz that could be heard even in the rather crude ODJB.

In the next decade, a youthful Lester Young heard some of the records that Bix made with his colleague Frankie Trumbauer, and a light went on in his head. Listening to these records over and over again showed him a direction that he followed in creating one of the most seminal and brilliantly original styles in the history of jazz. Again, Young would probably never have had the chance to hear this music especially because Bix and Tram mainly played this kind of jazz in the recording studio. Both of them were sidemen with Paul Whiteman, where they were given only the briefest amount of solo space. And like Bix in regard to the ODJB,

Young could listen to Bix and Tram over and over again, absorbing their subtlety and songlike lyricism.

Push forward a few years to when the young John Coltrane heard Lester Young on the radio. Until then he had only been aware of Coleman Hawkins's style. Young's playing astonished young Coltrane and made him aware that there were all kinds of musical territory to be explored that he had never dreamed of. Hearing Young probably more than any other experience convinced John Coltrane that he wanted to become a jazz musician. It is true he might have heard the Basie band with Young play somewhere in his home in North Carolina. But without the radio it is a lot less likely that John Coltrane would have had the experience that eventually led to the magnificent music he created for us, such as *A Love Supreme*.

With Coltrane, jazz history dovetails. When he became interested in the soprano saxophone in 1960, he went back to listen to the first great master of the horn, Sidney Bechet. Bechet was no longer alive by this time, so of course the only place Coltrane could explore his music was through records. Although Coltrane's style owes little directly to Bechet, by listening to the New Orleans giant, one of the first great jazz soloists—and hearing how he created such a powerful sound out of the small horn—Coltrane was able to make certain connections that gave him the impetus to start doubling on the soprano. Because of Coltrane, tenormen ranging from Zoot Sims to Pharoah Sanders took up the soprano. Bechet was a living influence despite his demise years before. Coltrane often said that he frequently went back to the jazz tradition for inspiration, and so did many savvy jazz musicians. That true jazz tradition can only really be heard on records. No sheet music, no written or verbal description, could convey to Coltrane the true sound of Sidney Bechet's music.

Perhaps one reason the 1920s were the jazz age was that they were the beginning of the modern age of communications. Radio, the phonograph and recordings, and even some of the earliest successful TV transmissions all coalesced in the twenties. It should be no surprise that an art form intrinsically tied to modern communications should reach its first peak at this time.

LIKE ALL REVOLUTIONS, the jazz revolution produced certain figures who led the way, who were at the forefront of the revolution.

Without such figures, revolution can lapse into anarchy, but with the Jazz revolution, there was, fortunately, a genuine genius, one who was able to make all the right connections between the music and his place in time, someone who pointed the way and made sure that this "revolution" was worth the struggle. Of course, his name was Louis Armstrong.

Genius: The Triumph and Tragedy of Louis Armstrong

WYNTON MARSALIS HAS been outspoken in his praise of Louis Armstrong. I find this not only praiseworthy but refreshing, for most young jazzmen pay scant attention to the earlier giants of this music. I think that Marsalis has performed an important service by acquainting the current generation of musicians, and younger jazz fans, with the great pre-bop musicians, Louis Armstrong in particular.

Of course, Armstrong's music fits right into Marsalis's agenda. After all, Louis was a magnificent blues player, and he is the chief inventor of swing. Lovable Louis seems like such a quaint figure now, his music so beautiful, his commitment to the "classic" elements of jazz so complete.

Yet I insist that quite another perspective can be gained than the narrow one of neoclassicism, which champions Armstrong's place in the jazz "tradition." I believe that the Louis Armstrong of the 1920s and early 1930s—the height of his career as a creative musician—has little in common with the neoclassicist jazz musician. Perhaps this is true for the later Louis Armstrong; in the last few decades of his life, Armstrong angrily disavowed modern jazz, continued playing the same music with a tired, bored band of supposed "All-Stars" night after night in places like Las Vegas and blowing solos note for note in exactly the same way as the original recordings. But Armstrong at the height of his genius was quite a different matter.

There are no two ways about it: Armstrong was a true revolutionary, a genius with the hubris to change the very way we think about the creation of music. His innovations did more than change jazz forever. He brought to music a new type of consciousness that can only be called modern. Louis Armstrong, like James Joyce, Freud, Eliot, and Einstein, is a twentieth-century titan, one of the architects of modern culture and modern consciousness. His break with the classic New Orleans ensemble jazz style is as audacious as the innovations of any other twentieth-century cultural rebel like Picasso or Stravinsky.

One interesting note about the early New Orleans jazz bands: The neo-classicists insist that all authentic jazz must swing. But these early bands did not swing at all, in fact the whole concept of swinging did not really exist. For one thing, the music was played in 2/4 rather than swinging 4/4, and the whole rhythmic impetus was different from what would later be called swing. There was syncopation, but syncopation is not necessarily swinging, at least not in our modern understanding of the term (this is one of the problems with this use of the word *swing*—it means different things to different people). For example, certainly the piano playing of Jelly Roll Morton, the self-proclaimed "inventor of jazz," did not swing by any definition of the term. But Morton was a seminal musician who, although he did not really invent jazz, nevertheless gave it direction at this early critical period of jazz's development. But if the neos are right, and music without swinging is not jazz, then even Jelly Roll Morton is barred from the house of jazz, as well as all the New Orleans players in this early period. Jazz would have to wait until the mid-1920s before the concept of swing was born.

Probably the greatest band of the second decade of the twentieth century was King Oliver's, which did not record until 1923, half a dozen years after the Original Dixieland Jazz Band's first recording session. The music of this band, although stylistically past its peak at the point when it was recorded, nevertheless was as brilliant and inventive as that of the ODJB was crude and blunt—at least not in the classic definition of swing.

But besides the music itself, the King Oliver sessions were crucial to jazz in that they were the first time Louis Armstrong recorded. According to legend, the sound of his horn was so loud that the sound engineer—who said that Armstrong's horn was "the loudest sound he had ever heard"—made Armstrong stand several feet behind the microphone. This was during the earliest period of recording, of course, and techniques were quite crude. But despite the problems involved with recording, and the far less than pristine quality of sound that it it produced, the experience undoubtedly ignited Armstrong's genius. Recording, he realized, was more than a temporary fad—it was the future of jazz, the canvas on which a jazz musician could create his art in a permanent form. Recording made the art of the improvised solo viable. The invention of one modern genius, Thomas Edison, gave substance to the art of another, Louis Armstrong.

It was his understanding of the potential of recording that enabled Armstrong a few years later to go into the studio with his own group and begin recording his classic Hot Fives and Sevens, probably the single most important recording project in the history of jazz. These groups were only recording bands; Armstrong did not perform with them in public. But it was on these sides that he played solos of such unprecedented length, rhythmic push (swing), subtlety, melodic continuity, emotional depth, and sheer brilliance that simply through the release of these sides alone he turned jazz from an ensemble form to one where the soloist dominated. Even more crucially, he transformed jazz from a folk art into a "fine" art (in his book *Early Jazz*, Gunther Schuller cites Armstrong's "West End Blues" as the exact turning point).

Before Armstrong, improvisation in jazz was minimal. The short solos that were allowed were often worked out ahead of time, and often were played the same way whenever a tune was played, even by different groups (like the famous "High Society" clarinet solo). The improvisation in the ensembles was also very minimal, more melodic embellishment than improvisation as we have come to think of it.

Ragtime and early jazz conveyed the feeling of spontaneity, even if the music itself was not as ad-lib as it might seem to a casual listener. But the concept of the improvised jazz solo as we think of it now simply did not exist until Louis Armstrong. I must add that Sidney Bechet was a soloist close to Armstrong in the power and detail of his solos (most of which he apparently worked out before playing or recording them). But as great as Bechet was—and he was one of the greatest of all jazz players—Armstrong is unique in the *wholeness* of his improvisations. And the rhythmic thrust of his playing was the first that we could say truly swung. As a soloist Bechet took the New Orleans ensemble to its greatest peaks; Armstrong invented a whole new way of playing jazz.

In many ways, Armstrong's revolution was more audacious than even that of the boppers twenty years later. Although in retrospect these brilliant records seem so perfect and inevitable, to some, like the clarinetist/dope dealer Mezz Mezzrow, Armstrong was killing the "true" jazz. And when Armstrong went even farther in the 1930s and performed as a soloist with a backing big band, the musical reactionaries of their time, such as the critic Rudi Blesh, accused him of leaving the "true jazz" behind. After all, said these classicists of their time, there is an established "jazz tradition" and Armstrong was playing far outside it. If others followed in his footsteps, they feared, the "real" jazz would die.

As would happen throughout the evolution of jazz, both Armstrong's innovations and the reasons that some opposed them had at least some basis in societal parallels. Armstrong, needless to say, was a man deeply affected by the society in which he lived and his own hopes and dreams for that society. Armstrong had only recently moved north to Chicago when he began recording, along with many of his black brethren who sought what they hoped to be a more tolerant atmosphere. I don't think it is hard to hear in the Hot Fives and Sevens and his work of the early 1930s Armstrong's celebration of the new feeling of freedom he was experiencing after having moved north. Undoubtedly Armstrong believed that there he would find at least a modicum of freedom and respect, and maybe even be valued as a human being. In other words, in the North he felt he could express himself as an individual rather than as part of a group in which his singular personality was swallowed as part of an ensemble. For a black man in the South, submerging one's personality by performing as part of an ensemble reflected his status in a Jim Crow society where the individual personalities of black people were ignored. And as well, there was a certain kind of safety in numbers. So Armstrong's stepping forward with the Hot Fives and Sevens and asserting his individuality with such artistry was in itself a powerful statement reflecting the changes in his life since leaving New Orleans. Looking at photographs and especially at the few early films of the young Louis Armstrong is bracing. He bears little resemblance to the lovable Uncle Louis of most of his later career. He is a firebrand, a man filled with creative energy, animated from within by the fires of his imagination. And of course his music bears out the truth of these images. The bursting creativity and visionary innovation heard on Armstrong's Hot Fives and Sevens is astonishing. In its way, it surpasses the creative heights of the two other great jazz geniuses who are often considered ultimate jazz geniuses: Charlie Parker in the 1940s and John Coltrane in the 1960s.

We can only speculate about Armstrong's participation in jam sessions and other live performances, but certainly his solos heard on the Hot Fives and Sevens were the result of a great amount of trial and error. In other words, like other innovators, his discovery and development of the jazz solo was not as sharply sudden as the records seem. Like other recorded turning points in jazz, from Bird and Diz's "Groovin' High" to Ornette Coleman's *Free Jazz* to Miles Davis's *Bitches Brew*, what seemed like sudden innovations were really the result of a long period of hard work and careful, steady progress. Like these later innovators, Armstrong listened, played, pushed, and developed his radical ideas over a period of time.

Jazz probably would have faded away by the end of the 1920s if it had retained its ensemble form, a form that restrained much development and evolution and in which individualism was eschewed in favor of the ensemble. Radical ideas had to be discouraged when one was playing mostly within an ensemble. And an art form that did not allow for fierce individualism (albeit within the context of a group) really ran roughshod against the American grain. So Armstrong's great innovation did more than change the jazz of his time; it made possible all jazz innovations to come.

Listening to Armstrong's solos of the Hot Fives and Sevens period from the vantage point of seventy years later, it is easy to view this music as inevitable. But it was not. Armstrong, as Wynton Marsalis has pointed out, had to know exactly what he was doing, and he pursued his musical vision with an indomitable will.

One can hear so clearly the joy of discovery in Armstrong's music of the 1920s and early 1930s. The development of Armstrong's musical conception from the earliest Hot Fives to the Hot Sevens with Earl Hines and the creation of such masterpieces of American music as "Potato Head Blues," "Weather Bird," and of course "West End Blues" is astonishing in the increasing emotional depth and subtlety of Armstrong's art, as well as the growth in improvisational creativity and formal musical techniques. Listen especially to the playing of the other musicians in comparison to Armstrong. Players like Johnny Dodds were among the best New Orleans jazzmen, but their soloing seems hopelessly rooted in the past. In this way, the Hot Fives and Sevens are remindful of other seminal recordings, such as the small Basie group Jones-Smith Inc., which included Lester Young's first recorded solos, or the Red Norvo 1945 jam session in which a group of swing players jam with Charlie Parker and Dizzy Gillespie. Next to other players, the playing of the revolutionaries seems to have an extraordinary vitality and creative vigor. There was one musician on a par with Armstrong, or at least close to it: the great pianist Earl Hines. And it is especially when they play together, as in "West End Blues" and, even better, the duet "Weather Bird," that new territories of musical thinking seem to be opening up. Armstrong would continue to be a brave music adventurer into the 1930s. And then there came a drastic change.

The man who could improvise twenty choruses in a tune, all completely different, the trumpeter who had changed jazz from a folk art to a fine art, the genius who created a revolution, simply stopped in his tracks. Instead of the musical firebrand, he became a crowd-pleasing entertainer who almost seemed to eschew improvisation in favor of repeating solos note for note over and over again. He started emphasizing his singing over his trumpet-playing, and became a great showman, indulging in often rather bawdy humor, creating an onstage persona not far removed from minstrelsy. This may have been partly due to the increasing problems he was having with his lip, the kind of problems that often affect trumpet players as they get older. And he would lead some superb small bands, such as his group that included Earl Hines and Jack Teagarden in 1940s (however, his All-Stars would greatly decrease in quality in the latter years of his career). But the persona he began to present to audiences is not so easily explained.

"Louis may Tom," said Billie Holiday with compassion, "but he Toms from the heart." Armstrong may not have been really an Uncle Tom, but he was a variation: Uncle Louis. Rather than continue being a hero to black people, as he had been in the 1920s and early 1930s, Armstrong became something of an embarrassment. He was obviously tailoring his onstage persona to pander to the expectations of a white audience.

What happened?

In a way, just as the early Armstrong was a model of other jazz revolutionaries like Charlie Parker, Dizzy Gillespie, Ornette Coleman, and John Coltrane, the later Louis foreshadowed Nat "King" Cole, Wes Montgomery, and George Benson in the decision to pursue wide public acceptance. It is strange that Wynton Marsalis excoriates Miles Davis for being a "sellout," yet never says a thing about Armstrong, who unquestionably made a decision to be a showman rather than a creative jazzman. Miles at least continued to develop his music, no matter what anyone thinks of it, but Armstrong simply simply relinquished his role as an innovator.

This is not to suggest that I think that Louis should be ridiculed for the path he took. After all, being a black jazz star was unprecedented. And after Armstrong got Joe Glaser as his agent, he was encouraged to be an entertainer rather than an innovative jazz musician. Armstrong was brought up with the concept that in order to have any chance of success in America, a black man had to have a white man front for him. Anyone with a bit of compassion can understand why Armstrong, given his background as an orphan, would have gone the safest route. However, I think it should be made clear that this is what he did, and no matter how awed we are by his great achievements, we still must be honest about the course taken by Louis Armstrong.

Being a black musical genius in a racist country was a lonely and difficult course. He had reached unprecedented heights, but as an orphan he had learned the necessity of a safe haven. And the daring of this music must have seemed like sheer hubris. One cannot forget Armstrong's early life when considering the choices he would ultimately make. I think it is possible to be saddened by some of those choices while at the same time having great compassion for Armstrong himself; he did, after all, give us so very much. But on the other hand, believing as I do in the existentialist nature of jazz, I also must believe Armstrong ultimately did make a choice, and we cannot ignore that or its consequences.

The difference between the Armstrong of the 1920s and early 1930s and the Armstrong of the later thirties and onward is this: In the early part of his career, Armstrong was inner-directed, creating music out of his own life, heart, and soul. But his later career was "outer-driven" by his audience, agent, manager, and record companies. I am not saying that he did not still create magnificent music. Everything he did, even the most blatantly commercial recordings, had at least a touch of pure genius. But the firebrand who was such a fecund and inventive improviser and took jazz to places it had never been before was no more. It was a bit as if after finishing *Finnegans Wake*, James Joyce went on to write only greeting cards for Hallmark. Sure, they would have been the best greeting cards ever written, but we had come to expect so much more.

I think that something that Wynton Marsalis said about Armstrong in a video about the trumpet kings of jazz is very important: This was no clown who bumbled onto something through accident and blind intuition. Armstrong was no "noble savage." He was a genius who knew exactly what he was doing, why he was doing it, and the implications of his achievements. This was a man who, in his own words, was "serious about his music."

In his book of essays *The Blue Devils of Nada*, Albert Murray includes an essay about Louis Armstrong called "The Armstrong Continuum." Murray finds Armstrong a great and joyful presence in twentieth-century culture, and he is of course correct. But the essay is amazingly one-dimensional in its refusal to see any gray areas in any aspect of Armstrong's life and career. It is simply a catalog of praise, tremendously simplifying a career and a man who in his own way was as complex as Miles Davis (who greatly admired Armstrong—he once said that everything played in jazz came from "Pops"). Perhaps this is not surprising. After all, if Armstrong is the alpha of jazz trumpet, Miles is the omega. Both men had the extraordinary power to transfix their audiences solely with the sound of their horns. In his essay, Murray writes:

> The worldwide acclaim for Armstrong's genius and the unsurpassed sense of earthy well-being that his music generated everywhere he went seems to have meant very little in the ever dicty circles of the neo-Victorian watchdogs of proper black decorum. To them, apparently, there was no such thing as a genius who sometimes doubled as court jester. In their view, Louis Armstrong was only a very popular "entertainer" anyway. But even so, he owed it to "his people" to project an image of progressive if not militant uplift.[1]

Murray writes as if Armstrong was criticized simply because his onstage humor was too earthy for those uptight "dicty blacks." But Armstrong was not criticized for joking around onstage (after all, Dizzy Gillespie was even more of a jester and could be even more bawdy). The problem is that he adapted an onstage persona that was based in the preconceptions of white audiences about black performers, and he overtly pandered to his mainly white audience in places like Las Vegas after Joe Glaser became his manager. There is nothing wrong, of course, with a great musician who also chooses to entertain his audience with humor. But that is not why he so embarrassed many blacks and progressive whites, and ignoring that he did this is simply avoiding a sad truth about the options available to Armstrong, or at least the truth as he perceived it.

It is interesting that Murray thinks that this onstage persona was the real Louis. The truth is that the lovable onstage roly-poly, eye-rolling, sweating, constantly, constantly smiling and laughing "Satchmo" was not the real Louis Armstrong, a thoughtful and mercurial man. (as others have pointed out, there should be a volume published of Armstrong's collected letters. He was a constant letter writer and these letters give us great insight into the real Louis Armstrong). And it was not just "dicty" blacks who were embarrassed There was little difference between Armstrong's onstage persona and someone like Stepin Fetchit—both played the roles of a white stereotype of black men. Who would not be embarrassed just by some of Armstrong's film appearances, in which he usually played a porter or lackey of some sort, kissing the ass of Bing Crosby or the other whites who were always at the center of the film? How can one not be embarrassed about the short in which Armstrong's actual head, singing, is on the body of an animated ape-man swinging through the jungle? And what about some of his later musical choices, such as playing with Hawaiian, country-and-western, and hymn-singing choral groups?

Yet somehow Armstrong transcends the more embarrassing moments of his career, and even late in his career he was capable of surprising us. In the 1950s he recorded two excellent albums, salutes to Fats Waller and W. C. Handy. And he also recorded *A Musical Autobiography* in which he re-created his greatest recordings with great vitality and a maturity that gave even these re-creations a new depth of feeling.

When Armstrong finally did put down the mask in order to blast Eisenhower and his reluctance to enforce the Supreme Court's decision about school desegregation it came as a complete shock to many Americans. And some blacks, like Sammy Davis, Jr. (hardly an example of a "dicty, neo-Victorian" black man), blasted Armstrong, not for the statement itself, but because Armstrong was playing before segregated audiences on a tour of the South at the same time as he made his remarks, just as he always had, something most black performers no longer would do. And further cause for anger was the feeling that Armstrong had done little to help the cause of black liberation with his Tom act.

Murray celebrates Armstrong's travels throughout the world, entertaining audiences in almost every corner of the earth. But here too there are complexities. Armstrong did much of his traveling for the State Department, who used him, especially on trips to Third World countries, as a way of masking America's racism; condemnation of America's racism had been the source of some of communism's most effective propaganda, especially in Third World countries. Armstrong, smiling, laughing, always happy and uncomplaining, was the image of the American black—albeit a false image—that the State Department wanted to convey throughout the world to counter those pictures of segregation, lynchings, and terrible poverty that much of the world had come to associate with American black people.

Certainly Armstrong was aware of his complicity in this; he had to know that he himself was a tool of propaganda. On the other hand, it is true that he did bring joy to a great many people around the world, and that is what was most essential to Armstrong. And maybe ultimately he was right. Nevertheless, in the context of the times, his role as "jazz ambassador" was troubling to many Americans, and understandably so. Certainly it should have troubled Louis Armstrong—to serve as "goodwill ambassador" especially to countries inhabited mainly by people of color while knowing that even he was treated like a second-class citizen throughout most of his home country.

Listening to Armstrong's development from his early sides with King Oliver, a little later Fletcher Henderson, the first Hot Fives and then the masterpieces of the late 1920s and early 1930s gives us the unique opportunity to follow a genius discovering both the possibilities inherent in the jazz improvised solo and his own emotional and spiritual depths. Regardless of whatever one thinks of Armstrong's later work, there could be little to equal the self-discovery, excitement, and sheer joy created by true innovation. Armstrong hit on some profound truths about the meaning of freedom and was able to translate them into music. Trying to make Louis Armstrong the symbol of jazz as a narrow and limited art form where innovation is irrelevant, as Murray and Marsalis do, is profoundly wrongheaded. However conservative he might have been in later years, at the peak of his career Armstrong was a true revolutionary and a man dedicated to changing jazz far more profoundly than the boppers or even the free jazz movement of the 1960s were. This is the real Louis Armstrong, the hero Louis Armstrong, the one who still believed in the possibilities of freedom.

AS I STATED before, Armstrong gave jazz a future. Of course the immediate future would be the so-called swing era. Since Armstrong more or less invented swing, obviously the musicians of this era—or at least the jazz musicians of this era (much of the music of the swing era had virtually nothing to do with jazz or swing)—were deeply indebted to him. This was yet another aspect of Armstrong's importance to American culture: Without swing music, without all the great big bands of this era, the Depression would have been far more dark and much more hopeless. One thing is certain: Armstrong's celebration of the freedom of the individual and the primacy of rhythm was a beacon in the darkness.

5.

Déjà Vu All Over Again

While considering the views on jazz of the architects of the neoclassicist movement, I had an odd feeling of having come across the same confluence of racial and reactionary views sometime before. It was the composer/arranger Bill Kirchner who pointed out to me their similarity to those of Rudi Blesh, one of the earliest jazz critics. And Blesh was not alone. His views were gainsayed by many on the jazz scene, enough to build a movement of critics, fans, and musicians who were given the disparaging tag "moldy figs."

Besides Blesh, perhaps the two most outspoken members of this movement were the French critic Hugues Panassié and the clarinetist/dope dealer Mezz Mezzrow. Panassié is an interesting case. Originally, after hearing some of the musicians known as the Austin High Gang in the Chicago area, he believed that whites were the most important jazz musicians. However, one of the musicians that he met here, Mezz Mezzrow, eventually convinced him that quite the opposite was true: that *only* blacks could play jazz.

So what about Mezz himself? Milton "Mezz" Mezzrow was of Russian-Jewish heritage, but he considered himself kind of an honorary black man. While serving time in jail and meeting a number of black convicts, he came to the conclusion that blacks had a great attitude toward life, that they were perpetually happy-go-lucky no matter what trouble fell in their path. Blacks, Mezz decided, really knew how to live, how to enjoy life. And, of course, music was just naturally in their bones. He writes in his fascinating memoir, *Really the Blues*:

> The white man is a spoiled child and when he gets the blues he goes neurotic. But the Negro has never had anything before and never expects anything after, so when the blues get him he comes up smiling and without any evil feeling. "Oh, well," he says, "Lord, I'm satisfied. All I wants to do is to grow collard greens and eat 'em."[1]

I am sure Mezz would have been shocked if someone told him that he was guilty of stereotyping, that his belief that blacks all had a similar view of life was racist at its core. He felt so deeply about these things that, as he explains in *Really the Blues*, he decided to give up his status as a white man, move to Harlem, marry a black woman, and, as much as possible, live life as a black man. He even insisted that his race be listed as "Negro" on his passport, which no doubt gave pause to agents every time he went through customs.

In many ways, Mezz Mezzrow was the first hipster, a true "white Negro," to use Norman Mailer's phrase. *Really the Blues* was read avidly by the early beats and had an enormous influence on their lives, ideas, and the supposed beat lingo, virtually all of it borrowed from jazz.

Mezzrow was a master of this lingo, which came out of the jazz world, a hip vocabulary that, as he demonstrates in his book, was almost a totally worked out new language. This language was necessary to Mezzrow in his vocation as a dope dealer. He could have a conversation with a customer almost right under the nose of a cop without giving away the illegal nature of the transaction under discussion. Undoubtedly, the foundation for the "hip" argot goes all the way back to the days of slavery. Back then, slaves had their own coded language in which they could discuss all kinds of matters right under the nose of the slave master. From its beginning, the whole idea of making statements that only those "in the know" can truly comprehend is crucial to the development and nature of jazz.

Mezzrow cut himself off completely from the "straight" white world, and lived his life in a new kind of underground society that was based around jazz. Besides having its own language, this world had its own conception of morality and a burgeoning philosophical and spiritual slant that would be influential on cultural rebels for decades to come.

Mailer's hipsters, the beats, the hippies, and even to an extent the hip-hop subculture, all are extensions of this early jazz subculture. Make no mistake: It is not Mezz Mezzrow who is responsible for this alienated subculture; it was the jazz musicians who even early on felt as if they were part of a separate society that was more compassionate, relentlessly creative, and truly alive than "straight" America. There is no mystery how they developed these feelings: improvising this brilliant music simply forced them to be more aware of living life in and for the moment. These feelings brought jazz musicians together, both black and white, and no doubt they are one of the reasons that jazz evolved at such an astonishing pace.

Mezz considered himself mainly a musician who just dealt pot on the side. But his talent was very limited. He only seemed to be able to play blues, and every time he played he seemed to be simply making a slight variation on the same basic solo. However, he became very popular with jazz musicians since he sold the best marijuana in Harlem. His smoke was so good that *Mezz* began to be used as a term itself meaning marijuana, especially very good marijuana. Louis Armstrong, who greatly enjoyed Mezz's goods, used to send out greetings to his dealer over the radio, which only other musicians in the jazz subculture would understand. He would say, "Just want Mezz to know how much I dig his Mezz, yeah, man!" Sounded like nonsense to the average American listener, but to those in the know, Louis was celebrating the state of feeling absolutely no pain.

Reading between the lines of Mezzrow's book, his story becomes rather Nabokovian: He was always invited to recordings and jam sessions for what he wanted to believe was his value as a musician. But it was painfully obvious that the musicians (including Louis Armstrong and Sidney Bechet, two of Mezz's favorites) had another, very obvious, reason for wanting him there.

Mezzrow was a true reactionary; he believed that only the original New Orleans style of jazz was the authentic music and all the post-Armstrong innovations had little to do with the "true jazz" tradition (sound familiar?). I find it interesting that Mezzrow was so convinced that only early, mainly ensemble jazz was the real jazz because in many ways it fits into his stereotyping of blacks. Like so many whites, Mezzrow believed that blacks were more "natural" than white people, that they were "closer to the earth," not filled with all those sophisticated ideas, just simple beings, like animals in the field, or insects, for that matter. In other words, they were not profound enough or didn't have the ability to deal with complexity demanded by composition or, for that matter, a lengthy improvised solo. But working in an ensemble, they had sort of a collective genius, kind of like a beehive. This kind of imbecility I believe is what lay at the heart of Mezzrow's—and many other whites'—ideas about jazz. Certainly, Mezzrow meant well, and he believed that he was a true friend to African Americans. But any type of stereotyping—any fostering of the belief that people of a particular ethnic group are homogeneous, all share the same sensibility, the same view of life—is simply a form of racism or, if you will, racialism. To Mezzrow, the original jazz was genuinely "earthy," as "natural" as a watermelon ripening on the vine.

Mezz's feelings about jazz might have had little weight, but through the French critic Hugues Panassié, his narrow ideas gained an international covey of acolytes. When Panassié first discovered jazz, he thought that the white players were the great jazz musicians. One of the musicians whom he mistook for being a jazz genius was Mezz Mezzrow. On a subsequent trip to America, Mezzrow showed Panassié the error in this thinking, introducing him to the music of Sidney Bechet, Armstrong, Tommy Ladnier, and others. Panassié's views changed 180 degrees, but remained just as narrow: Now, *only* black musicians could play authentic jazz. The reason? Unless they were perverted with those sophisticated white ideas, "the Negro was purer and closer to nature than whites."[2]

And like his guru, Panassié developed a sentimental fervor only for the "real jazz," a phrase he would use as a title for one of his books on the subject. Panassié had some very odd ideas on what was and was not the real jazz. Although after he was indoctrinated by Mezz Mezzrow he had disdain for almost all white jazz musicians, including Benny Goodman, Artie Shaw, Bud Freeman ("strange") and Pee Wee Russell ("tiresome"), his enthusiasm for Mezzrow as a musician is enough to make one wonder about his ability to distinguish the difference between great jazz talent and mediocrity. He wrote:

> "Mezz" Mezzrow assimilated the style of the (great Negro New Orleans) clarinetists so perfectly that one would think he had originated in New Orleans. In fact, Mezzrow's claim to fame is that he plays the blues better than any other white musician. I am not speaking of clarinetists only—he plays the blues in the same way of the great Negro musicians."[3]

Panassié's opinions of some black jazz musicians—including some of the greatest of all jazz musicians—were even more bizarre. He had such a limited view of jazz that, quite like the leaders of the neocrowd, he was unable to appreciate those who did not fit into his narrow parameters. Here is what he writes about one of the very greatest of all jazz musicians, somebody who most critics, and musicians, and fans would agree is probably equal to Armstrong or Charlie Parker in improvisational genius and sphere of influence: Lester Young: "Frankly, I do not understand the reason for [Lester Young's] fame. His sonority is small and frankly ugly, and in the lower registers frequently reminds one of an automobile horn. His melodic style is overdecorated and often too choppy [!]. He affects queer phrases which have no continuity."

So much for the musician who was dubbed "the President" of the tenor sax. In his book *Real Jazz,* Panassié saves his sharpest scorn for the musician known as "Little Jazz," Roy Eldridge:

> Imbued with notions of progress, [Roy Eldridge] attempts to do things which no other trumpet player has ever attempted. Likewise, instead of playing naturally he forces himself to use all the resources of his virtuosity to create strange phrases and audacious harmonic relationships . . . his music *does not swing* [Panassié's italics]. And the fact that many musicians have an exaggerated admiration for him is undoubtedly because they are dazzled by his difficult technical tricks. Roy Eldridge does not swing easily and nonchalantly as do the great jazz musicians, his playing is enervated and that enervation even appears in his exaggerated vibrato.[4]

It comes as no surprise that Panassié has little use for white jazz musicians, even declaring some, like Benny Goodman, as not really being jazz musicians at all. (Again, the similarity to many of the pronouncements of the neo–brain trust is eerie.) Bix Beiderbecke? I am certain that Albert Murray would nod agreement while he read: "Bix Beiderbecke . . . was never able to assimilate the spirit of the Negro musicians, which is the only true jazz spirit. He had a rare freedom and profound sense of jazz. And it is surprising that instead of conforming to the language of the Negroes, he should have turned more and more as the years passed toward an emphatic and precious phrasing and a sonority which was certainly lovely but too honeylike." I find it interesting that Panassié concedes that Bix had "a profound sense of jazz," because this is something that he himself obviously lacks. If the true idea of freedom is at the heart of jazz, then the idea that one must conform to any one sort of sensibility should be repugnant. The fact that Bix does not sound like the great black players means that he was playing out of his own life and sensibility and not trying to emulate someone else's. This is the essence of jazz if anything is.

About fourteen years after publishing *Real Jazz*, Panassié, along with Madeline Gautier, wrote *Guide to Jazz*, a book similar to Leonard Feather's *Encyclopedia of Jazz* or the *Grove Dictionary of Jazz*. Since the publication of *Real Jazz* in 1942, the bop revolution had taken place in the mid-1940s, and by the time of the publication of Panassié's *Guide* in 1956, it was long over and the modernists now dominated the mainstream—modern jazz was now accepted by nearly everyone on the scene, except for Hugues Panassié. Bop and post-bop, to him, simply were not jazz, just as free jazz and fusion are not jazz to the neos. It is amusing to read Panassié's entry for Charlie Parker: "An extremely gifted musician, Parker gradually gave up jazz in favor of bop. . . ." And he writes similar things about Dizzy Gillespie, Bud Powell, and even Miles Davis.

It may be difficult to imagine a critic more reactionary than Hugues Panassié, yet Rudi Blesh was exactly that. In his history of jazz, *Shining Trumpets*, he insists that only one kind of jazz was the authentic music: the original, black New Orleans style. All jazz beyond that is a mongrelization of the pure jazz. And so he excoriates jazz musicians from Louis Armstrong (that is, Armstrong's post–Hot Five work) to Fletcher Henderson, Jimmie Lunceford, Duke Ellington (whose work is described as "ridiculous and pretentious hybridizing"), and Count Basie, none of whom, he insists, really played jazz.

Blesh's views arise out of two factors: One, like Panassié and Mezzrow, is a view of African Americans that makes them a totally homogeneous group all with the same sensibility. The other is his obviously leftist politics. He continually describes New Orleans jazz as revolutionary. This is true, in that the advent of jazz was a culturally revolutionary event. But with Blesh, it is obvious that his concept of "revolutionary" is strictly Marxist. Of course, communism's views on art are at least as narrow and single-minded as those of the far right.

To Blesh, the "murder of jazz" took place when whites began to interfere in the "natural" music making of the blacks and began to commercialize this once-pure music out of capitalist greed: "Commercialization was a cheapening and deteriorative force, a species of murder perpetuated on a wonderful music by whites and misguided Negroes who, for one or another reason, chose to be accomplices to the deed." There is, of course, more than a grain of truth in this statement. Of course, there have been throughout jazz history those who have commercialized jazz and who have corrupted the music. There still are (Kenny G., for example). But the diluted jazz has never completely destroyed the music that is generally agreed to be genuine jazz. And much of what Blesh considers "corrupted jazz" is considered by most in the jazz world to be some of the greatest achievements in the history of the music: Louis Armstrong's post–Hot Fives and Sevens work, Fletcher Henderson, Duke Ellington, Count Basie, Benny Goodman, and of course all modernists. He insisted that the original New Orleans jazz, with its collective improvisation, was the only authentic jazz, and even that the continued creation of this particular jazz—although only this kind of jazz—is "revolutionary."

It is not hard to read between Blesh's lines and assume that he is speaking from a leftist perspective; he does make some interesting points, a few of which are tangential to what this book you are reading now is about. For example:

> What happened to jazz is a little laboratory test, if you will, of democracy. "Giving the people what they want" in this case at least, consists of planning a product that can be put together by hacks, that can be profitably sold to the people and then, amidst an advertising campaign unrelenting and continuous, can be unobtrusively substituted for what the people already wanted and had. As long as this is a diffused process arising more or less as the end result of a social-economic system, it may be accepted by the many and resented or feared by the few and is seldom seen in its full implication. A case can be made for the nationalization of the resources of human spirit, for the taking of, buying and selling of art, for the subsidizing of artists, and the preservation of artistic values, uncontaminated and undistorted, for all the people.

In other words, the government should decide what the "true" art is and should nationalize it in order to "keep it pure." Well, Blesh has a point: if government ran jazz, it probably never would have evolved from its earliest style. Fortunately, jazz musicians have throughout the music's history (at least until the last ten or fifteen years or so, when critics have had so much influence) been the ones who have determined the evolution and development of the music.

Blesh strongly denounces white racism and the oppression of blacks throughout *Shining Trumpets*, to a degree that is bold for the time (the late 1930s, early 1940s) in which he wrote his book. Of course, it has to be noted that at the time when he wrote his book, few whites other than those far on the left expressed such outspoken outrage at America's treatment of blacks. But that does not mean that such leftist whites did not have their own stereotypes of African Americans, stereotypes that fit neatly into their social and political worldview. And Blesh was unfortunately no different. In *Shining Trumpets* he writes about the black sensibility at the heart of the "true jazz":

> It was a . . . point of view, a way of looking at the world innocently, directly, and imaginatively. Like the primitivism of children, it sees without veils and records in its own peculiar, powerful, magical symbols. This helps explain the easy adaptability of the Negro to Western ways and the ease with which he adopts elements of arts foreign to him.

I am sure that Blesh, who obviously looked upon himself as a great supporter of African Americans, would be shocked that anyone would dare to accuse him of racist stereotyping. But it must also be pointed out that these beliefs have much to do with his view of the nature of jazz—that it was a collective, intuitive art form, uncorrupted by the egotism of Western art. In other words, he saw jazz as the perfect model of the Worker's Paradise, where the workers, stripped of those corruptive Western notions of sophistication and individuality, are happy to contribute in a collective enterprise.

In Ralph Ellison's masterpiece *Invisible Man*, the black narrator is befriended by a group of white Communists. At first he believes that he has finally found a group of whites who are willing to treat him with respect. But he gradually comes to realize that he is just as much a stereotype to them as he is to most other white people. And he also realizes that he is being exploited for his role of the "ultimate victim" of capitalism. To these leftists he is still an "Invisible Man," not a flesh-and-blood human being. The left in the 1930s and 1940s considered jazz the "people's music," although most of them knew little about it. Blesh did, yet his rigid beliefs, both about the nature of art and that of African Americans, led him to conclusions totally antithetical to the true nature of jazz and the true social and cultural revolution—one very different from the Marxist concept of revolution—that was unleashed by the advent of jazz.

It is interesting and instructive to note the similarity between the views of Mezzrow, Panassié, and Blesh and I guess what you could call the architects of this current neoclassical generation of jazz musicians, Marsalis, Crouch, and Murray. Two things have changed. The most obvious is that the first group is white (despite Mezz Mezzrow's insistence to the contrary) and the current group is black. The other difference is that the first were of the left and this group is definitely on the right. Yet both think in rigid, narrow terms, aesthetically as well as socially. Such rigidity in and of itself runs counter to the very nature of jazz.

I think that the parallels—these rigid judgments—are no coincidence. Over fifty years may separate the ideas of these men, and a great deal of water has gone under the bridge, in terms of our society as well as for jazz. But certain things remain the same. Certainly race and racism are still dominant issues in our society. And so is the type of totalitarian thinking that insists on dictating in the most limited terms what is or is not authentic, whether politically or in terms of art. The great lesson that anybody who has been involved in the world of jazz over a period of years should learn is that such rigid distinctions never hold up, thanks to the continual musical curiosity and constant search of the best jazz musicians. Is it any more foolish to declare that Duke Ellington and Count Basie do not play authentic jazz than it is to say that Miles Davis no longer played jazz because he used electric instruments? Or to ban one of the greatest of all modern jazz composers, George Russell, from performing simply because he uses an electic bass? Or to say that Cecil Taylor, who has been active in the jazz world since the mid-1950s and has recorded with jazz musicians ranging from Kenny Dorham and John Coltrane to Archie Shepp and Jimmy Lyons, is not a jazz musician? No matter how you feel about Taylor's music, if jazz is supposed to be a true reflection of American democracy, his voice, or that of the "electric" Miles or the musicians of the AACM, have a right to be heard. It is similar to that concept at the heart of our democracy: "I may not agree with what you say, but I will fight to the death your right to say it." Substitute *play* for *say* and I think this concept is just as applicable to jazz. Of course the same thing was true fifty years ago; Panassié and Blesh may not have liked Roy Eldridge, or Duke Ellington (in fairness, Panassié did respect Duke, unlike Blesh), or Lester Young, or the bopper, but they suffered from tunnel vision when they insisted that these great musicians were not authentic jazz players. The parallels with this current era are obvious.

6.

Swing and Its Discontents

IN A RECENT piece about the 1990s jazz scene written by a supposedly knowledgeable critic for a major Canadian newspaper, the current jazz scene is compared with that of the swing era.[1] Once again, this is either a case of gross jazz history revisionism or, quite simply, the writer needs a remedial course in jazz history.

During the swing era of the 1930s and early 1940s, jazz, or swing, as it was called, was by far the most popular music in the country. During the height of the swing era, every night of the week one could hear, on network radio broadcasts, the leading jazzmen of the day, from Ellington and Basie and Lunceford to Goodman and the Dorsey Brothers. And incidentally, it was not just big band jazz; the Goodman trios and quartets and sextets and such combos as the John Kirby group and Artie Shaw's small groups were almost as popular. Swing records dominated the recording business (although it is true that much of the music was really more pallid pop music than jazz—certainly not unlike today, when the best-selling jazz albums are by Kenny G. and Spyro Gyra) and jazz performances were jammed with young people, many of whom followed the bands with much the same enthusiasm that teenagers today exhibit for Metallica or the Smashing Pumpkins.

How can that possibly be compared to today's jazz scene, where a year or so ago the biggest star of today's jazz mainstream, Wynton Marsalis, had trouble filling the tiny jazz club the Village Vanguard? And as we shall see, in terms of creativity and innovation, comparing the current post-Marsalis generation of jazz musicians to those of the swing era is an idea that belongs in a jazz version of *Alice in Wonderland.*

The swing era has been so glorified through the prism of nostalgia that it is difficult to assess its true place in jazz history. However, I think that a close study of the jazz of the 1930s makes it clear that beyond the romance of this era, for jazz this was a time of feverish innovation, of tremendous change, growth, and rapid evolution.

That rapid evolution becomes clear by listening to even the best jazz of the mid-1920s, like the Armstrong Hot Fives and Sevens, and much of the jazz of the mid- or late 1930s or the early 1940s, such as Basie or Lunceford or, of course, the Ellington big bands as well as the small-group work.

The swing era was actually a time that produced the same kind of iconoclasts and dyed-in-the-wool innovators who had changed jazz in the previous decade and who would change it even further in the next one. As I will try to make clear, the jazz tradition was as much that of change and evolution in this "golden age" of classic jazz as it would be in every other period (with the exception of the present one). This evolution was a natural outgrowth of the innovations of Sidney Bechet, Earl "Fatha" Hines, Bix Beiderbecke, and of course Louis Armstrong. These musicians were the "John the Baptists" of the swing era, prophets of the new music. Equally as important as these figures is Fletcher Henderson, who first envisioned the kind of jazz band that would set off the swing era. To the moldy figs, the music of the swing era, even that of Basie or Ellington, was heresy, far from the true jazz tradition. To them, the big band era heralded the death of jazz.

Once again, if one believes in this straitjacketed concept of a so-called jazz tradition, the moldy figs were right. If New Orleans jazz was the definition of that tradition, then the 1930s big bands had little in common with them. The most obvious difference between them was that New Orleans ensembles were notable for their polyphonic ensemble interplay while the 1930s big bands featured arrangements and solos. There are several other differences, but I think the point is clear: The big band jazz of the 1930s was almost as revolutionary as Armstrong's development of the improvised solo form, though without Armstrong there never would have been the big band era.

The whole concept of swinging itself really comes from Louis Armstrong. He taught whole bands, particularly Henderson's (of which he was briefly a member), how to swing. And I believe it was that rhythmic message more than any other aspect that so enthralled Americans about this music during that period.

Armstrong is not the only key figure whose work of the 1920s led to jazz's swing era. The other great soloists, like Sidney Bechet and Earl "Fatha" Hines, were also crucial innovators. But most important were those big band pioneers of the 1930s, such as Fletcher Henderson, Don Redman, Glen Gray (whose Casa Loma Orchestra was an early, but hard-swinging, jazz band) and the youthful Duke Ellington.

The Depression 1930s were of course a dreadful time in America (and throughout the world, for that matter), an era when the Dream seemed to be going all wrong. The whole country fell into a deep funk, like somebody suffering on the morning after a night of partying and alcoholic high jinks. That must have been exactly the way it felt; a kind of retribution of the "Roaring Twenties."

It was that way in the jazz world, too, in the early 1930s. During that period, it looked as if jazz were finished, an artifact belonging to a happier, more celebratory age. With the legalization of alcohol, a whole way of life centered around clubs, speakeasies, and gangsters disappeared suddenly. And whatever one may think of these vestiges of Prohibition, they were conducive to jazz. Not because jazz needs the association of "sin," but simply because it is in the loose, intimate atmosphere of clubs that jazz thrived.

Needless to say, clubs are imperfect. Many people go to clubs not to hear the music but rather to drink and socialize, and they are often indifferent and insensitive to the music. But there is no other venue where a jazz musician can have the close relationship between himself, the other musicians, and the audience. Clubs have always been conducive to jazz creativity and to the relaxed atmosphere where a musician feels free to explore his or her music and move it forward. Certainly neither the concert hall nor the dance hall has ever been a place where jazz musicians can comfortably "stretch out," the first because it is too formal, the latter because playing music that is best for the dancers may inhibit the jazz musicians from being more adventurous.

With the Depression, clubs disappeared because most Americans lacked the money to go nightclubbing as they had done in the 1920s. The places where jazz could be played rapidly vanished, but other things were on the mind of the nation.

Nevertheless, jazz refused to die. Jazz musicians during this period stubbornly stayed committed to their art form, although tales of their suffering during this period due to lack of work—and this was true for both white and black jazz musicians—are now part of jazz legend.

Yet even during this bleak period just after the start of the Depression there was still some great jazz made. Armstrong continued to produce masterpieces, even though he often used a band whose sound was based on that of his idol, Guy Lombardo; jazz musicians have always had the ability to hear musicality in places that defy our comprehension.

During this period Armstrong recorded one of his masterpieces, "Knockin' the Jug," with a racially mixed band that included, among others, his friend and frequent colleague the great Texan trombonist Jack Teagarden. And there were brilliant obscure sessions like those of Billy Banks. Banks was a so-so singer, but in the early 1930s he recorded with a remarkable racially mixed band that included Fats Waller, Tommy Dorsey, trumpeter Red Allen, and Pee Wee Russell. Some listeners, including the British poet Philip Larkin, consider these Banks sides the "hottest" jazz ever played, and they are marvelously vibrant and constantly inventive sessions. The fact that both the Banks and the Armstrong sessions were racially mixed was of little concern in the jazz world, at least in the confines of the recording studio. After all, jazz musicians of different races had been sitting in with each other since the New Orleans days. Armstrong once said to Teagarden, "I'm a spade, you're an ofay. We both got soul. Let's blow." Undoubtedly, the spectacle of black and white musicians playing jazz together during the swing era that was enjoyed by both black and white fans certainly had some positive effect on paving the way for the civil rights advances of the next few decades.

The swing era was mainly the age of the big band, but not all big bands of the time played jazz. However, there were a number of bands that played a sophisticated, often complex orchestral music that was entirely true to the genuine "jazz spirit." The big bands of the 1930s were playing jazz that demonstrated a musical depth and virtuosity only dreamed of in few big bands of the 1920s. So while it had appeared that the jazz revolution had come to a halt with the beginning of the Depression, jazz arose from its supposed demise and continued forward as it would do throughout its history.

Some of the bands that are most associated with the swing era, like Glenn Miller's band, played excellent dance music, but played a very watered down kind of jazz. These bands emphasized ensembles over solos, and there was little feeling of true spontaneity. There were hordes of bands during this era that played what was called "sweet" music by fans and was labeled "Mickey Mouse" by musicians. These bands—Guy Lombardo's band is an example—played a prettified music with virtually no jazz content at all and are now basically the stuff of nostalgia and sentimental reveries about a more innocent time.

But the greatest bands, at least from a jazz point of view, like those of Benny Goodman, Jimmie Lunceford, Cab Calloway, and especially Duke Ellington and Count Basie, played music that is still exciting and emotionally stirring even to modern ears. We don't weep nostalgic tears over these great bands; their music is still a living force.

FOR THE PRESENT time, and for the purposes of this book, the concept of orchestral jazz needs to be reexamined in the light of the repertory bands such as the one led by Wynton Marsalis at Lincoln Center. Do they have a claim on legitimacy, or are they distorting those elements that make orchestral jazz unique?

The idea of orchestral jazz has always been a complex one. Since jazz—great jazz, at least—is for the most part improvised, how can large bands really convey the jazz message? Yet if jazz cannot be played on a grand scale, and is limited to the small groups, that greatly narrows the possibilities of this music. Jazz composers and arrangers have grappled with this question in various ways, and the music of Ellington, Basie, and Goodman presented different methods of dealing with this central problem with the specific nature of orchestral jazz.

With Goodman, we must automatically think of Fletcher Henderson, because Henderson's arrangements were the staple of that band, and many of Goodman's other arrangers used Henderson's model for their own variations. As we have already noted, Henderson had unsuccessfully led his own big band in the 1920s. Whether he was simply ahead of his time or was just a victim of racism is difficult to suss out. But credit Goodman with the good taste and vision to appreciate Henderson's arrangements. Henderson did not invent the makeup of the classic jazz big band. However, by combining his elegant conception with a roiling sense of swing (learned from Louis Armstrong when he was briefly with the band), and utilizing some superb soloists (such as Coleman Hawkins), he created the big band sound that was the blueprint for much of the swing era.

The story of Goodman's success has become an American legend; Hollywood even made a corny movie called *The Benny Goodman Story* that starred Steve Allen as the clarinetist. But for our purposes this much should be remembered: Goodman had been appearing on a radio show broadcast from New York City. There was another band on the program, a "sweet" band, and Goodman's band performed in the later segment. There seemed to be little interest in the "hot" music the band loved to play on the East Coast, but they were unaware of the impact they were creating elsewhere. In California, which of course is in an earlier time zone, young people had been picking up on Goodman's music and becoming increasingly enthusiastic about it. Many of them began to develop new kinds of dancing, "jitterbugging," that was inspired by "hot" jazz.

The Goodman band went on a tour that was largely unsuccessful and depressing to the high spirits of the band. They chiefly had to play tame dance music to make their employers happy rather than the "hot" (that is, jazz) style they loved. This is just what they did when they played California. The crowd seemed totally uninterested in their music. But Goodman, believing that his band was doomed anyway, decided to let it go out playing the music it loved. Of course, as soon as it started playing "hot"—genuine jazz—the crowd exploded, much to Goodman's astonishment. This explosion is usually described as the ignition for the swing era.

There is much that is significant in the story of Goodman's eventual success. Jazz was still so revolutionary that most of the venues that the Goodman band played absolutely would not tolerate any band playing "hot." It is simply great luck that Goodman found an audience—young Californians—who wanted to hear and dance to this music before he folded the band.

Despite the fact that back in the 1920s Fletcher Henderson first explored many of the concepts associated with the Goodman band, nevertheless the jazz big band was still an avant garde idea in the mid-1930s. The musicians in Goodman's band, which included some excellent players besides Goodman himself (Harry James, Jess Stacy, Gene Krupa), wanted to play and explore this music whether or not they had an audience. It was simply the confluence of the right band playing the right music for the right crowd at exactly the right time that launched the Goodman band as a commercial success and touched off the swing era.

I realize that in the eyes of some, Goodman and his band were white imitators of black music, exploiting the innovations of great black musicians such as Fletcher Henderson and composer/arranger Don Redman, making them palatable for the white audience. There is no doubt that Goodman and his musicians were influenced by the great black musicians. But it is also true that at its peak this band took on its own personality and developed a sound that was its own. Every musician is initially influenced by the great players who preceded him or her. But once they have digested and internalized that influence, the best jazz musicians develop a style that is their own voice, their own vehicle for expressing the truth of their lives.

Certainly this could be heard in the playing of Goodman himself: when he reached his mature style there was no mistaking him for anybody else, black or white. The same was true for other members of the Goodman band such as Jess Stacy and Harry James (a genuinely great improviser who has been admired by most important jazz trumpetmen, including Miles Davis). Even when playing Fletcher Henderson's arrangements, the band had a unique sound, not just a whitened version of one of Henderson's bands. All you have to do to confirm this is listen to records of Henderson's band and the Goodman band.

By the way, Henderson was tremendously grateful to Goodman both for providing him with a good income and for getting his musical ideas heard. Once again, what the majority of jazz musicians care about most is the music itself.

The birth of the swing era could not have happened without the advent of radio. For young people in the gray world of the 1930s, listening and dancing to this "hot" music was a reaction to the tameness of so much American life as it was reflected in those sedate dance bands that played "acceptable" music. The jitterbug's dance was wild and highly sexual, an explosion of pent-up energy after the years of the Depression. Of course, Goodman would eventually hire black musicians like Teddy Wilson and Lionel Hampton; although they only appeared with Goodman in small groups, not the full band, this was still unprecedented, and the presentation of black and white musicians obviously enjoying playing together and challenging one another on the bandstand was a turning point in American life.

Goodman may have seemed like a nice Jewish boy on the outside, but there was a strong rebellious element in him. He openly embraced black music and the musicians who played it, and that alone (sad to say) alienated him from most of those, friends and family, whom he had grown up with. But it is his use of Fletcher Henderson's arrangements that is probably his most important contribution to the development of the big band. By playing these arrangements he gave a voice to one of the key innovators in the history of orchestral jazz. But I think it is important to understand that Henderson's take on jazz composition was not terribly different from that of the model of classical music. An arranger/composer wrote charts, detailing what every instrument should play (except for those sections where there were solos), and those charts, like the compositions of a classical composer, could be used in any band that had the instruments required. In other words, the arranger/composer was an omnipotent figure whose works were meant to be played the same way every time they were performed—with the exception, and not an unimportant one, of those sections where there were solos. It was Benny Goodman who made the world hear Henderson's genius, and for this alone we are in his debt. Of course, he was also an absolutely brilliant clarinetist and improviser, at times even a daring one. He has almost been taken for granted in recent years and that is too bad; he and his bands and groups created some of the greatest jazz ever heard.

Henderson's approach was the classic one, and for the most part it would be followed by most jazz composers. But there were two other approaches, both of which reached their peaks in the swing era, that perhaps were created with the most revolutionary ideas inherent in the jazz aesthetic.

The less radical one was Count Basie's band of the 1930s and early 1940s. Basie's band was originally that of Bennie Moten, one of the great figures in early Kansas City jazz. Kansas City jazzmen were a special group, a tight brotherhood of musicians who loved to jam all night long and into the day. In the 1930s, Kansas City was a wide-open town, filled with raucous speakeasies, brothels, and gambling dens. Jazz always seemed to thrive in such an anarchic atmosphere: New Orleans's Storyville, Chicago when it was truly a "toddlin' town," Kansas City, and the constant chaos of New York. It is not because jazz or jazz musicians are decadent or dependent on vice. But rather, it is in a loose atmosphere that jazz musicians feel relaxed and unpressured, and in which they feel as if they have the freedom to let their music take them wherever it goes. Also, in these cities there were plenty of the kind of clubs that are most conducive to the playing of jazz. And with jazz, the only way for the music to evolve is not through theories or even practice, but in the existentialist situation of musicians defining themselves in the moment by playing the music with other musicians in front of an audience.

As Basie recounted in his autobiographical *Good Morning Blues* (co-written, incidentally, by Albert Murray, who did a superb job), Moten hired Basie to sit in on piano. Basie was heavily influenced by the stride style, but he began to eliminate everything that was extraneous from that style, paring it down to an almost Zenlike simplicity. He caught on to the fact that with a big band, a pianist might be more effective with a highly streamlined, understated style. After all, he could hardly compete with all those horns, so his strategy was to make the ear of the listener fill in the blanks that his style left, to intrigue his audience with just the perfect few notes or a simple chord.

After Moten died from a botched tonsillectomy, Basie took over leadership of the band. It was a band that, after a few changes in personnel, had a panoply of brilliant soloists, each one a great individualist and one of whom was one of the greatest innovators and improvisers in the history of jazz. His name was Lester Young.

But Lester Young was hardly the only great soloist in the first Basie band. The band also included tenor saxophonist Herschel Evans (whose playing was superb but more in the Coleman Hawkins–influenced mode of most tenormen of this time), trumpeters Harry "Sweets" Edison and Buck Clayton, trombonists Dickie Wells and Benny Morton, and singers Helen Humes and Jimmy Rushing, and, of course, Basie himself. It was an astonishing array of brilliant talent.

Basie's laid-back, minimalist approach to piano playing was indicative of how he ran his band. Basically, his style was laissez-faire, giving the musicians tremendous leeway. Most arrangements were simple affairs, often "head" arrangements, which means that the musicians in the various sections of the band created the arrangements rather than having an arranger write them out. This was not a band to look for brilliant writing. The main idea was to provide driving encouragement for the series of solos that were really at the heart of these pieces. At its height, the Basie band defined swing like no other band ever had. This had much to do with the All-American Rhythm Section, one of the greatest in jazz. It was made up of Basie, Walter Page (whose legendary Blue Devils served as a key influence on Basie and his band), the rhythm guitarist Freddie Green (who just played steady rhythm guitar, never taking any solos), and the key innovative drummer Jo Jones. This rhythm section seemed to reinvent jazz rhythm in its own terms, and rhythm sections from there on would never be the same. The innovations of this rhythm section were a key to the birth of modern jazz; in particular, without Jo Jones alone, the discoveries of the iconoclastic bop drummers, such as Kenny Clarke and Max Roach, would have been impossible. Jones played steady rhythm on the cymbals and accents on the snare and bass drum, a technique that Clarke and Roach would take even farther.

The Basie-ites probably hit their height in the early Kansas City days. It was not truly a big band then; rather, it was something in between a large combo and a big band. When the band hit the "big time" Basie was encouraged to beef up the sound and added extra horns. But this killed some of the pure spontaneity and streamlined swing, although the band remained a magnificent unit. By the mid-1940s the original band no longer existed. While Basie would always have fine players, he would never again have such an array of solo talent as well as a band whose members were so close in sensibility and musical persuasion that they could improvise arrangements that were keyed to the soloist. Later bands were more in the Fletcher Henderson mode: The musicians were far superior at reading and playing the arrangements that were written for the band by composers and arrangers such as Quincy Jones and Neal Hefti, meaning that head arrangements were no longer created by the band. In many ways, the later Basie bands were tighter than the original one, more virtuosic as far as playing intricate charts, but the freewheeling spontaneity of the greatest Basie band was gone forever.

All of Basie's bands were enjoyable on one level or another, but the great band was of course the original one. For one thing, this band truly embodied the spirit of jazz, a musical environment where each musician was given tremendous freedom, even when it came to creating what were more or less "arrangements." It was in this environment that Lester Young felt free to play and explore a style that was considered highly iconoclastic at the time—and that had powerful ramifications for modern jazz—and Jo Jones was free to reinvent jazz drumming.

In the 1950s, Basie rerecorded many of the pieces he had originally recorded with the first band. His band at the time was far more proficient at playing arrangements, but they simply could not recapture that spirit of the original recordings. That is because, like all genuine jazz, this music was created in and for the moment, and it reflected the lives and times of the musicians playing it. Time travel only exists, alas, in science fiction. Hearing these new versions with different musicians, the simplicity of the music just sounds one-dimensional; its depth came about because of the souls of the musicians who created it at that original time. Yet this lesson seems lost on many of the repertory bands being heard these days. This music is simply so different from classical music that, for the most part, it just cannot be played in a repertory situation. A band of young musicians playing charts based on the Basie band of the 1930s and early 1940s is in a musical Twilight Zone.

....

PERHAPS NO IMPORTANT jazz musician has created more perverse and confused perceptions than Duke Ellington. Because he is generally considered the greatest of all jazz composers, his music is a favorite of repertory bands. After all, if you can't perform Duke in a repertory situation, who else is there?

Well, the truth is you really can't perform Duke—not if you want to re-create his music in any form that might be called authentic. And as we shall see, this is precisely because Ellington understood the nature of jazz on such a profound level. Ellington's music now may seem familiar, a body of work that, despite its amazing variety, nevertheless is finite and therefore safe from our current vantage point. There is no longer any chance of Ellington's music going in new directions. But while he was alive Ellington saw no boundaries of any sort in his art. As a musical thinker and composer, nobody was as dedicated to renewal and redefinition as was Ellington.

Duke Ellington has lately become somewhat controversial because of a book by James Lincoln Collier that appeared a few years ago, and an angry essay in response by Stanley Crouch.[2] In his biography of Ellington, Collier attempts to bring Ellington's reputation down a peg or two by demonstrating that many of his compositions were not really composed by him. There is a nugget of truth in this contention, but basically his point is irrelevant once we come to understand how much Ellington was imbued with the jazz aesthetic.

Ellington is one of the most crucial figures in jazz, and in many ways he is the best litmus test for the differing views on the nature of jazz now in contention. Wynton Marsalis has repeatedly called Ellington the "greatest jazz composer," and Crouch has even called him the "most American composer." Terms like *greatest* and *best* have long beleaguered the jazz world, though one would think that anybody who understands the nature of jazz—that is, the fact that it is such a personal, idiosyncratic expression—would eschew such terms. For too long jazz has been treated at times like a form of athletics rather than an art form. Far too often, musicians are admired for their speed or agility rather than the depth of the music they create. Certainly we do not admire Louis Armstrong because of his ability during his youth to show off by playing a series of shattering high Cs, but rather because of his melodic invention and the beauty of his tone. The competitiveness in jazz that is encouraged by the jazz magazines trivializes its nature. There has never been such a thing in classical music; there has never been a poll for "best violinist" or "best cellist" or "best pianist" or "best composer." Actually, it would make a little more sense for classical music than for jazz, since there are certain traditional standards for the playing of classical music. But jazz is supposed to be the expression of the individual—one is supposed to find a personal way of creating music through his or her instrument. Is Oscar Peterson better than Thelonious Monk? Other than the fact that both men play jazz on piano, there is absolutely no way to compare the two, and certainly not in terms of relative quality. They both play what they feel and have created styles that best give expression to those feelings. Such popularity contests are pointless and intrude a competitiveness into jazz that is irrelevant and unhealthy.

And this competitiveness has taken its toll. One of the most famous examples is Sonny Rollins. Rollins had been the hot tenorman on the scene until the late 1950s, when some critics and fans proclaimed John Coltrane as the new king of the tenor. Rollins was so shaken by this competition with his good friend Coltrane that he went into hiatus for a lengthy period of practicing and study that lasted until he felt confident to return to the scene. When Crouch or Marsalis calls Ellington "America's greatest composer" or the "most American composer," they are apparently asserting that Ellington is "greater" or "more American" than, say, Aaron Copland, Charles Ives, or Samuel Barber, as well as such key jazz composers as Thelonious Monk, George Russell, and Gil Evans (whose arranging was really a form of composing or recomposing). Again, what is the point of making such a claim? One of the things jazz should teach us is that all true artistic expression is relative—there is no such thing as "best" or "greatest" or certainly "most American" if the work is on a similarly high level. And Ellington is sui generis, one of a kind, and it really is virtually impossible to compare him to anybody else. Crouch is right, of course, in that Ellington should be as respected as any composer of this century.

Perhaps Crouch goes overboard as a corrective to the dismissal of Ellington as a serious composer by the cultural establishment. The fact that the Pulitzer Prize committee refused to give Ellington even a "special" award that was recommended by their nominating committee makes one's blood boil and shows how ignorant and, let's face it, downright racist the culturally elite can be.

This *can* be stated: No jazz composer has been as much admired by those familiar with jazz as Ellington. Because of that, he is probably the most performed composer among jazz repertory bands. But because Ellington's music is so deeply saturated with the true jazz spirit, because Ellington understood the nature of jazz on such a profound level, it is virtually impossible for any band to play authentic Ellington.

Why is that? Ellington has been described as a jazz player who improvises with an entire band, and that is correct. When he started out, he did not have great ambitions. He led a "sweet" band that played sedate music that was popular at social affairs. But after he heard the great reedman Sidney Bechet and the trumpeter Bubber Miley, his imagination was fired by the new music. Almost instantly he grasped the essence of jazz and understood its power. It awoke his genius, and he started on the road he would follow the rest of his life. The controversy over Ellington is based on this: According to some, he was not really a composer. He did not even write many of the melodies for which he is credited. And after all, when he attempted long, complex works, like his 1940s tone poem "Black, Brown and Beige," he fell on his face. Collier goes out of his way to prove that Ellington was "lazy," stealing themes from his own musicians. Collier implies that Duke spent too much time enjoying himself, primarily with women, to be as committed to music as a serious composer should be. Perhaps Collier should read a modern biography of Mozart.

Anyway, this notion is contradicted by the sheer enormity, and diversity, of Ellington's music. Ellington must be understood as being the most quintessential jazz composer in the history of the music. He understood the nature of the music better than anyone until, arguably, Miles Davis. If there is one musician who proves that there is no such thing as a limiting, straitjacketed jazz tradition, it is Ellington, which makes it so ironic that he is such a hero to the neoclassicists.

Actually, Ellington is a tradition unto himself. Like most of the great jazz musicians, he was not enamored of the word *jazz*, nor of the constraints that were placed on musicians by those who believed in the jazz tradition. He continued to evolve and change until the day he died, but the changes in his style had little to do with whatever was happening in the jazz mainstream at the time. Even in his earliest days, his music sounded like nothing else that was being played during the 1920s. In the 1930s, he won a number of fans caught up in the swing era, although his band played music totally different from the kind of big band music that dominated that period; in the 1940s, he ignored bebop, although harmonically his music could be just as sophisticated as that of the young turks of the time, and in some cases, such as his "The Clothed Woman," far in advance; according to some (like Crouch), he reached new peaks in the 1950s and 1960s, but his music had nothing to do with cool jazz, hard bop modal, or free jazz, the directions jazz took during those decades. Ellingtonia was simply a world unto itself.

As for the contention that Ellington did not actually write a number of the most famous themes he is credited with, these melodies, in themselves, are the least part of his genius, whether or not he wrote them. It is how he used these melodies and "played" his band, the *sound* he created, that is the epitome of his genius. Ellington understood that personal expression was the key of jazz. He did not look upon his band as a collection of horns and reeds, but as a group of individual styles and sounds that he manipulated (in the best sense of that word) to create his musical world. In his book, Collier asks why Ellington did not hire any white players, such as Stan Getz or Zoot Sims or Chet Baker. The answer is not that he was racist—Ellington was anything but that. When Boyd Raeburn, a white bandleader, was no longer able to support his band, Ellington lent him the money to do it. And Ellington offered high praise for a number of great white players. However, as Stanley Crouch rightly states, those white musicians did not have the particular sound he needed, despite their great abilities as jazz musicians. As I pointed out earlier, there is such a great difference between Getz or Sims, both of whom were originally influenced by Lester Young and, say, Ben Webster or Paul Gonsalves, who at different times played in the Ellington band, that they might as well be playing different instruments. Duke wanted a certain kind of thick vibrato, a particular tone to fit in with the rest of his reed section and produce the sound he needed. The sound of Getz or Sims would never have fit into Ellington's conception.

When Ellington wrote one of his concertos, it was not a "Concerto for Trumpet," which a classical composer would do, but a "Concerto for Cootie" (his trumpeter Cootie Williams). Ellington was constantly experimenting, working with his band to develop and explore the possible tonal colors that this particular group of jazz musicians created. That was the essence of his genius.

I once saw a film clip that showed how literally true that statement is. Ellington was not at the piano but was in front of the band, although so close to the band that it was obvious that he considered himself as much a part of it as any of his musicians. And he was not "conducting" it so much as he was dynamically shaping the music. Billy Strayhorn, who worked closely with Duke, collaborating on compositions, writing his own pieces (including the band's theme song, "Take the 'A' Train"), and occasionally sitting in on piano, describes Duke's leadership of his band this way:

> Ellington's concern is with the individual musician, and what happens when you put their musical characteristics together. Watching him on the bandstand, the listener might think that his movements are stock ones used by everyone in front of a band. However, the extremely alert may detect a flick of the finger that draws the sound he wants from a musician. By letting his men play naturally and relaxed, Ellington is able to probe the intricate recesses of their minds and find things not even the musicians knew were there.[3]

Newcomers to the Ellington orchestra were often confused because the band never followed whatever was written on paper. They might start at one point, jump to another point, somebody other than the original soloist may solo, then they might go back to an earlier point, and so on. In other words, this was truly a jazz orchestra at a very profound level. A performance by Ellington with his orchestra was as much an existential act of creation, in the moment, as any soloist improvising.

Therefore a repertory band playing Ellington's scores as he supposedly wrote them is not really playing his music. This was music that was incomplete until Ellington and his musicians performed it, the same as for any small group of jazz musicians.

Repertory band re-creations of Ellington's music may sound fine, and serve as an introduction of sorts to the work of this genius. And they may even be performed with more technical élan than that of Ellington's musicians, since Duke chose them because of their personal sound and style, not necessarily because of their ability to read or to play charts. But it must be made clear that these performances bear little relationship to how Ellington made music with his band. It is true that at almost every performance he played a lengthy medley of his hits—after all, this is what many in his audience came out to hear. But Duke himself no longer had any interest in these pieces. Playing his hits was the price he had to pay so he could then perform his and his colleague Billy Strayhorn's new work, improvising with the band, creating intricate big band music in the moment. What an extraordinary musician.

In his autobiography, Mel Tormé writes about the time he was booked to sing for a week at New York's now defunct Basin Street East with the Ellington band also on the bill. It was decided that Torme would be accompanied by the band. But when they tried to play Tormé's arrangements, they sounded like a bad high school band, although they had played brilliantly with Ellington himself.[4] These were no slick studio musicians. These were idiosyncratic, improvising jazz musicians. André

Previn once remarked, "You know, Stan Kenton can stand in front of a thousand fiddles and a thousand brass and make a dramatic gesture and every studio arranger can nod his head and say, 'Oh yes, that's done like this.' But Duke merely lifts his finger, three horns make a sound, and I don't know what it is." What it is, of course, is Ellington's manipulation of the sounds and styles of a group of highly individualistic jazz musicians.

So if you want to hear Ellington—authentic Ellington—there is only one possible way to do so: listen to his records. Like all great jazz musicians, Duke's true canvas was the records he made, not whatever he wrote on sheet music. Even if a band could be put together with musicians who sounded exactly like those in one of the Ellington bands, without Duke leading the band, molding its sound, it would still not really be "Ellingtonia." And the proof of this is the music created by Ellington mainstays, such as Johnny Hodges or Cootie Williams, when they recorded on their own. Much of it was fine—these were superlative jazz musicians, after all—but, again as Crouch points out, none of it reached the level of creative brilliance that was true of so much of the music of Ellington's own bands as well as the occasional small group that he led. Of course, if a group or band wants to use a tune associated with Ellington, that is one thing. But claiming that, say, one of the current repertory bands plays authentic Ellington is to ignore what is unique about jazz and to make the obviously false assumption that Ellington is simply a great composer like any other composer, for example, Bach, Stravinsky, Copland, and the like.

Ellington is a magnificent composer, one of the greatest of this century. But to understand him means understanding this other kind of aesthetic, this jazz sensibility.

Late in his life, Ellington was frequently asked why he continued to tour with his band, why he didn't stay home and compose there and just give occasional concerts. After all, he had enough money and a continuing income from song royalties, and life on the road, especially when you perform mainly one-nighters, was often harsh and exhausting. Of course, anyone who truly understood the nature of Ellington's music would never have asked such a thing. He composed with his orchestra, for those individuals in his band. For him to continue being creative he had to have his band, much the same way that a pianist needs a piano or a violinist needs a fiddle.

In his last days, Ellington performed a number of "sacred concerts," often in churches. The communion of souls that had always been at the heart of his music had made him a deeply spiritual man. The deepest realms of life have always been part of jazz. Although Ellington's music could be frankly sensuous ("Warm Valley," "A Drum is a Woman," for example), that deep spirituality was always in his best music, just as it is prevalent throughout all of the greatest jazz.

Perhaps the sacred concerts arose out of his own experiences as leader of his band, his discoveries concerning composing from a jazz perspective. Of course I do not really know, but maybe Ellington came to have a vision of God as being One who is an improviser, rather than being omnipotent, like the role of the classical composer. A jazz conception of composition; a jazz conception of God. That is, an existentialist God who, like a jazz musician, is constantly defining and redefining Himself, who improvises His work with and through us, His Creation ceaselessly unfolding in a universe of endless becoming.

THE JAZZ REVOLUTION continued in the 1930s, not only through the development of big bands, but also with the appearance of several key jazz innovative soloists. The birth of bop in the mid-1940s did not occur in a vacuum; it was a natural progression from the innovations of several of the leading 1930s soloists, who in turn were developing out of the innovations of Armstrong, Earl Hines, and Sidney Bechet.

Coleman Hawkins, for example, developed a style of great harmonic sophistication. His greatest recordings of the 1930s, such as his classic version of "Body and Soul," had great harmonic sophistication. His style, with its deep vibrato and its roiling arpeggios, seems prescient of Coltrane's "sheets of sound" in the late 1950s. Hawkins's style *was* the way to play jazz on the tenor saxophone in the early 1930s and virtually every tenor player used this style as a base on which they developed their own personal variation. Chu Berry, Ben Webster, Herschel Evans (who was the other tenorman in the same Basie band in which Lester Young first become famous) all worked out their own styles, albeit styles created out of the Hawkins tenor vocabulary.

If Hawkins had done nothing else but what he accomplished by the early 1930s, namely creating a style of playing the tenor saxophone that established that instrument as a dominant jazz voice, he would have been considered one of the great jazz musicians. But Hawkins was more than that; in many ways he was emblematic of all jazz musicians, and he stood as a model that others would follow. For Hawkins never stood still; he always remained open to whatever new ideas were arising in the jazz scene. He never slavishly followed fashion; rather, he discovered ways of using these new ideas to broaden his own style. He remained identifiably himself to the very end. But in the 1940s, unlike many of his generation, he welcomed the boppers and hired them, including Dizzy Gillespie, Fats Navarro, J. J. Johnson, and even Miles Davis.

A little over a decade later, when a new generation of tenormen with innovative ideas emerged, he listened and played with them, and developed his own style even further. In the early 1960s he recorded an amazing session with Sonny Rollins. Rollins was exploring free jazz at the time, which for him meant playing music of even greater abstraction and unpredictability than his earlier playing. On this date, with a rhythm section that included the ever avant garde pianist Paul Bley, he played some of the weirdest jazz ever recorded, not just playing outside the chord changes, but also outside anyone's expectations of what is considered normal music making, even by someone like Ornette Coleman himself (whose music is actually quite logical). Yet Hawkins was not thrown by the bizarre nature of Rollins's playing, and even sounds eager to meet Rollins's weirdness with his own somewhat earthier variety of bizarre improvisation. It is a fascinating record to say the least. And once again it displays how rooted Coleman Hawkins was in the true jazz tradition of continual flux and growth.

Roy Eldridge, as we have already noted, was such a daring soloist that the moldy figs like Rudi Blesh virtually wrote him out of jazz. But Eldridge's burning brilliance would be the main influence on a young trumpeter who first started playing professionally in the late 1930s, John Birks "Dizzy" Gillespie. Eldridge was such an inventive and fiery soloist that he never sounded dated, although his style did not change much with the advent of the modern jazz era. He even recorded with Gillespie in the 1950's and easily held his own. At his best (when he is not showing off his high notes) Eldridge was simply one of the most compellingly exciting musicians in the history of jazz, to the extent that he was even nicknamed "Little Jazz." But to some, strangely enough, Eldridge's daring placed him outside the true jazz tradition. Think of it: a jazz tradition without Roy Eldridge! Without the man called Little Jazz!

One more comment about Eldridge: He insisted that he could tell the difference between white and black jazz musicians. The critic Leonard Feather took him up on this claim and subjected Eldridge to a special racially oriented blindfold test in which he listened to records and was not told which musicians were playing. Eldridge completely failed to guess correctly in virtually every case (perhaps others should be subjected to such a test).

In the 1930s, Eldridge often played on records and in clubs (like those in the burgeoning Fifty-second Street scene) with the tenorman Leon "Chu" Berry. Berry was killed in an auto accident early in the 1940s, but he made his mark on jazz. He was an important influence on Charlie Parker, who in some recently found recordings can be heard before he gained fame playing tenor sounding much like Berry. Parker loved Berry's playing so much that he named his son Leon after the great tenorman.

Billie Holiday, for me the greatest of all jazz singers, made her first records in the 1930s, usually with the brilliant pianist Teddy Wilson. Holiday understood the idea of a "jazz singer" probably better than anybody before or since (with the obvious exception of Louis Armstrong). She improvised, but she did not greatly distort the melody and never resorted to scat singing. She simply had a way of turning any song she sang into as personal an expression as any jazz musician's improvisation. She changed the course of American song (her influence can be heard in virtually every pop singer that followed, even a singer who is not always thought of as being a jazz singer, such as Frank Sinatra) and influenced jazz instrumentalists, too, with her ability to caress a melody, and to make everything she sang swing.

And frequently accompanying her in the early peak of her career in the 1930s was the man she dubbed "Pres," short for "president of the tenor sax"—Lester Young. As an innovator, Young is virtually on a par with Armstrong or Charlie Parker, although he is rarely granted such eminence. Yet it is virtually impossible to imagine all the developments of jazz from the late 1930s on without him. In many ways Young is a father of the bop movement; while growing up in Kansas City, Bird was transfixed by the playing of Young, to the extent that he knew by heart most of Pres's greatest solos on disc. Cool jazz directly stems from the Lestorian sensibility—virtually to a man, the players in this movement had styles derived from that of Young. Interestingly, the honks and riffs of the rhythm-and-blues tenormen, a style that would seem 180 degrees removed from "cool," were also derived from certain aspects of Young's style. And as we have previously mentioned, the young John Coltrane was electrified by listening to Young on the radio, and decided to become a musician because of Pres's inspiration.

If anybody rebelled against a so-called jazz tradition it was Lester Young. By the mid 1930s, there was only one style of jazz tenor saxophone, and that was the one developed by the so-called inventor of the tenor sax (not literally, of course) Coleman Hawkins. But Lester Young, influenced by Bix Beiderbecke and Frankie Trumbauer, wanted to play with a light, airy sound, with only a very dry vibrato, and his approach was completely horizontal—melodically inventive, dancing through the harmonies of a tune like Fred Astaire would if he could play the saxophone.

Rhythmically, Lester played just behind the beat, never stomping on the beat like Hawkins, often sounding like a man walking on clouds. Listening to Young's earliest solos on disc, recorded with a small group from the Basie band, few listeners will find much that is startling in his style. That is because Young's imitators have become so ubiquitous, and not just among tenor saxophonists, that to modern ears his style seems anything but extraordinary. But back in the 1930s, Young was looked on as a raging iconoclast. And he was: by the time he arrived on the scene there was a definite tradition for playing jazz on the tenor saxophone and Young would have none of it.

There is a wonderful story about Young concerning the period when he played in one of Fletcher Henderson's early 1930s bands. Henderson's wife would drag Young down to her cellar where she had a record player so he could hear her Coleman Hawkins records and grasp the "right" way to play jazz saxophone. But Pres was well aware of the Hawkins style and respected it. It was just that he needed to play a style that reflected his own mind, heart, and soul. Young's style and innovations were a result of his musical personality. In order to play the music he heard in his mind, he simply had to ignore any supposed tradition or whatever was thought at the time to be the proper way to play the music. Young loved melody above all else, and this is what dominated his style, the other elements falling into place so Young could, in his words, tell his musical story.

In a way, he was perhaps the original discoverer of "harmolodics" and therefore the musical antecedent of Ornette Coleman—that is, to Young, the creation of melody was everything and harmony was at best a secondary consideration. In hindsight it is virtually impossible to imagine post–swing era jazz history without Lester Young. But once again, thosewho insisted that he was not part of the jazz tradition were actually correct if one has a narrow and straitjacketed vision of that tradition.

Lester Young was a unique man whose individuality was sometimes so extreme that it entered the realm of eccentricity. Take, for example, even the way he spoke. His inventiveness extended beyond music; he developed his own hip lingo some of which become part of American vernacular, but much did not. For instance: "Bing and Bob" meant the police. "I've got eyes" meant that he desired to do something. He called most musicians "Lady"—for instance, Charlie Parker was "Lady Bird," Fats Navarro was "Lady Fats," and most famously, Billie Holiday was "Lady Day."

One more interesting and significant thing about Lester Young was that he profoundly believed that a jazz musician must be constantly developing and changing his style, that improvising was itself the motor of change. After World War II, there were many in the jazz scene who thought that Young had deteriorated as a player. He had been through a disastrous tenure in the army in which, after marijuana was found among his things, he was arrested and sent to the brig where he was harshly treated by racist guards (they treated Young especially viciously after finding a picture of his white wife). Young was a true innocent, a profoundly innocent man who had lived in his own world of music, pastel dreams, and gentleness. He had of course run into racism before, but because of his talent he was able to live a relatively peaceful life. So his terrible experiences in the army affected him deeply. It is those experiences that generally came to be accepted by many writers and fans as the cause of the supposed deterioration of Young's style.

But Young himself insisted that he was not deteriorating, rather he was doing what any jazz musician must do if his playing is still spontaneous and constantly inventive: He was changing and growing. As Young put it, in his own inimitable way, "I try not to be a repeater pencil. I'm always loosening spaces, and laying out to somewhere, and something like that." As usual, many in the jazz community simply could not accept change—to them it was deterioration.

As Lewis Porter states in his excellent study of Young (*Lester Young*, Twayne Publishing), "For these writers, as for many fans of the early Young, the problem is largely that the style changes. Many people who loved the early style simply could not accept that Young would change in any direction." But Lester Young was deeply responsive to the spirit of jazz in his ability to grow and change constantly, to redefine his style as he changed as a man. From the vantage point of the present, Young's straddles eras in the history of jazz, from the swing of the 1930s to the boppers of the forties, to the cool jazz of the fifties and the free jazz of the 1960s. And besides his towering importance to the development of jazz, Young also produced a body of work that in its entirety—including his work of the 1950s—is equal to that of anyone else in jazz.

THE GREAT PIANIST Art Tatum was almost as much of an iconoclast than Lester Young, having developed a style that really did not fit into any conventional stylistic slots of jazz piano or jazz itself. As has been pointed out by most critics, Tatum's finest playing was his solo work, not that of his group settings, where he always seemed hemmed in. Previously we have stated that jazz centered on the individual improvising in a group context. Here is an inarguably crucial figure in jazz who doesn't even fit those broad parameters! In addition, there is virtually no blues in his work (nor did he play the blues very often, and when he did, it was rather reluctantly).

But you can drum Art Tatum out of the jazz tradition only over the screams of indignation of every jazz pianist who followed him, and many other musicians, too. Charlie Parker got a job washing dishes at a club where Tatum was playing just to be able to listen to the great pianist. And there is no doubt that Tatum's harmonic daring was one of the great inspirations not only on Bird but for the entire bop movement. In many ways, Tatum's career bears a parallel to that of Cecil Taylor, in that both men were stylistically so unlike other jazzmen and so advanced, such fierce virtuosi that their best work was probably when they were free of any constraints, that is, when they were playing solo.

In the late 1930s, another innovator and brilliant soloist appeared: the electric guitarist Charlie Christian. He was not the first jazz musician to play electric guitar—that honor probably falls on Eddie Durham, who played electric guitar on Lester Young's magnificent Kansas City Six sessions for the Commodore label. Christian gained local fame in his hometown Oklahoma City. He was "discovered" by John Hammond, who induced Benny Goodman to hire the guitarist. According to legend, Goodman at first refused even to listen to Christian after seeing how funkily he was dressed. But Hammond got Christian into a Goodman performance where he played a twenty-minute solo on "Rose Room," a favorite jam tune of the time. Each chorus was more brilliant than the last, and of course Goodman was overwhelmed and immediately hired him to play in his sextet.

I think it is probable that there was another reason why Goodman was not initially enthusiastic about hiring Christian: At the time, the amplified guitar was still an exotic instrument, thought of as more a kind of gimmick than a viable instrument. In other words, it was the exact attitude that neos now have toward other electric instruments. Christian's style had a bluesy lyricism similar to that of many players from the Southwest, in particular Lester Young (whose playing, incidentally, was loved by Benny Goodman).

This similarity becomes clear in the only recordings that were made by Young and Christian together. Young reorganized his previously records-only Kansas City Six group for John Hammond's famous "Spirituals to Swing" concert at Carnegie Hall (all of which was recorded and later issued). Christian played electric guitar in place of Eddie Durham, and the few sides recorded are remarkable examples of southwestern swing at its height. It was Christian who convincingly proved the legitimacy of the instrument. He was able to get a round, full-bodied tone out of the electric guitar, and his improvisations were hypnotic in their swing and inventiveness.

But Christian's iconoclasm went beyond playing, and making acceptable, an instrument that had formerly been thought of as not in the jazz tradition. He felt limited and hampered playing with Goodman, and when he was in New York, after playing with Goodman downtown he would go uptown to Minton's, a club in Harlem where he would jam with the burgeoning young turks of the early 1940s, including Dizzy Gillespie and Thelonious Monk (Charlie Parker was not yet a part of this scene). Christian was an early contributor to the birth of bop, and he undoubtedly would have been far more than that; he probably would have become one of the most important modern jazz musicians if he had not died of tuberculosis in 1942 at the age of twenty-six. This was an enormous loss for jazz. He never even recorded under his own leadership. Except for a few odd sessions (one being an amateur recording of a jam session at Minton's), all of Christian's recordings are as a sideman with Goodman. Yet based on the few sessions he did record, he still remains one of the seminal jazz innovators. Without Christian we would not have had the major modern jazz guitarists: Kenny Burrell, Tal Farlow, Wes Montgomery, Barney Kessel, Jim Hall, and George Benson. Christian was another player who broke through the envelope of the so-called jazz tradition, which even then, during the swing era, had been tattered and ripped asunder by the soaring imaginations of the great jazz musicians of that time.

....

EVERY ONE OF these soloists—with the exception of Tatum (who was sui generis if there ever was such a thing)—played under the leadership of a big band leader, either in the band itself or, like Christian, in a small group led by the star that would spell the big band. The above is scarcely an exhaustive list of the great jazz musicians and bands who emerged in the 1930s. We are not attempting, of course, a formal history of that decade or of jazz itself. But what must be noted is that the musicians of this decade redefined jazz as a reflection of their lives in the here and now, just as virtually every generation did, before and after (excluding, for the most part, this current jazz generation). They expanded the music's vocabulary, broke with the so-called tradition, explored new musical territory, and played music that came from the core of their lives.

There are many reasons why innovation has been so constant and rapid in jazz, but perhaps one of the most important is the nature of improvisation itself. Most jazz musicians tend to repeat themselves, to create licks and clichés that fall easily into place. The philosophy behind true improvisation is that genuine spontaneity makes the musician constantly creative, but it is often easier just to play well-worn ideas and "run the changes" (playing notes that fit the harmonic structure without really developing a structured melodic logic—what Lester Young would call a musician's "story"). Miles Davis would often talk about taking a musician who was comfortable playing in a certain context and putting him in a very different musical situation in which he was pushed to eschew his easy licks and clichés and discover fresh ideas from parts of his mind and soul previously unexplored. That has always been the most beneficial effect of innovation: challenging the soloist to think in new ways and to dig deeper into his or her soul for musical truth and "stories" that illuminate that moment in all our lives. By the early 1930s, Louis Armstrong was so influential—on every player, regardless of instrument—that jazz was in danger of becoming stale from the lack of fresh ideas. The innovations of Hawkins, Young, Basie, Ellington, Tatum, and Christian renewed the life of the music until the time came when another generation would take the music even further.

Those changes were the advent of modern jazz and were known as the bop revolution. But they were really a continuation of the ideas of the more advanced thinkers of the jazz of the 1930s. As stated previously, there are only two elements that make up the true jazz tradition: finding one's individual voice and the continuum of change: flux, growth, evolution, advancement. And in jazz, change and innovation always gave those who played or listened to this music a sense not only of freedom but also of hope, hope for a life that was genuinely free, unencumbered by the detritus of ignorance and moral blindness, and was filled with the kind of bravery that led to change in terms of both music and society. Jazz at times almost seemed to be a music in which hope was made manifest, and this was never more so than in the musical revolution of the 1940s.

7.

Jazz Redefined:
The Bop Revolution

THE LATE DAVID Chertok, compiler of probably the world's greatest collection of jazz films, was a friend of mine. He was a wonderful man, generous with his time and his treasure trove of films. When I went to visit him, he would let me look at films of any jazz great that I wanted to see, everyone from Sidney Bechet to John Coltrane. Being able to see the great jazz musicians playing, especially those who had died before I had a chance to see them perform in person, was always a moving and often an instructive experience. A jazz musician's persona is so intimately bound to his or her style of playing that being able to actually view them in performance always added dimensions to my knowledge and feeling for their music. David liked all of jazz (except for fusion), but that had not always been so.

He had been a jazz lover since he was an adolescent in the 1930s. However, he had not been able to follow the developments of the music during the 1940s because of the recording ban during the early years of that decade and later because he was recruited as a soldier and spent most of the war years fighting overseas. So he did not have any inkling about the latest changes in the music until after the war was over. And when he heard the new developments in jazz he (along with a lot of other jazz fans like him) was shocked. He hated bop, couldn't stand it. It seemed shrill and cold, just a lot of fast notes, weird harmonies, and bluster. He felt as if the music he loved had betrayed him in some way. It would take a few years, until the early 1950s, for him to finally "get it" and grow to appreciate the new music and even love the playing of the greatest boppers. His was not an unusual experience.

This was true even for those who became interested in jazz decades later. When I was a kid and first getting interested in jazz, I received a copy of the Verve album *The Essential Charlie Parker* as a gift the first time I subscribed to *Down Beat*. I did not know much about Parker except that I had seen his name mentioned in very intriguing ways in *Down Beat* and in the album liner notes I so avidly read. But upon first listening to the record, I found much of Charlie Parker's music much more difficult to fathom than, say, that of Miles Davis or Mingus or even the John Coltrane of *Kind of Blue* or *My Favorite Things*. And when I heard him on the radio, Parker's solos on "Ko Ko" or "The Hymn" just seemed like flurries of notes played with a tone that seemed so abrasive to me after I had become accustomed to the smooth, insouciant tone of Dave Brubeck's alto saxophonist, Paul Desmond.

I think it was the pieces with strings that first opened my ears and heart to Parker's musical world. I realized that his short but perfectly constructed and emotionally compelling solo on "I Didn't Know What Time It Was," and especially his more stretched out solo on the masterpiece version of "Just Friends," had a concentrated beauty and a remarkable sense of form. From there I was able to listen to the small-group sides and fully appreciate them—and to grow to love them to the point of obsession.

After I "got it," Parker's music entranced me. It seemed so perfect that he had been given the nickname "Bird," although I would learn that the reason for the name supposedly came from an incident in which Parker took a chicken that had been inadvertently run over by the tour bus, cooked it, and ate it. If this legend is true, then it was a wonderful example of serendipity: Parker's music had a soaring quality to it; his notes seemed to flow ecstactically free from Earth's gravity. But there were those who simply never "got" Bird's music and remained staunch in their refusal to accept as authentic jazz the thrilling music of the boppers.

Around the same time as the bop revolution there was another movement in jazz, although it had been brewing (as we have seen) since the 1920s: the jazz revivalist movement. What had been the views of a few musicians like Mezz Mezzrow, and critics like Rudi Blesh and Hugues Panassié, became in the 1940s a full-blown movement, including a sizable segment of the jazz audience, in reaction to music of the late swing period and bebop. Those involved in this movement insisted that only early New Orleans jazz was authentic and that the more progressive forms of the music, especially bop, had little to do with the "true" jazz tradition and were not really jazz at all. They were nicknamed, nastily enough, *moldy figs* by their detractors. The figs rediscovered musicians of the New Orleans style who had long been sunk in obscurity, most notoriously Bunk Johnson, and elevated them to jazz gods. Never before had there been such a clear-cut dividing line between those who believed that jazz was progressive, visionary art and those who maintained an undeniably reactionary stance toward the music. With the advent of bop, these two conceptions about the nature of jazz became more than sharp disagreement and at times became quite a bitter internecine feud within the jazz world, one that destroyed a number of old alliances and friendships. The parallels with the current situation are obvious.

Of course, bop eventually triumphed. The modern innovations of the boppers gained an inextricable foothold in the mainstream of jazz, and the music never looked back. It was really a remarkable victory: It was not just a victory over the moldy figs who vigorously opposed it, but also over some older jazz musicians (such as Louis Armstrong), who at least initially were vociferously bitter in their reaction to it, those critics who routinely panned bop records, and fans like Dave Chertok who, hearing bop right after the war felt, at least at first, that jazz had deserted them and had lost whatever had attracted them to the music in the first place. And it was also a victory over the working conditions: cramped, smoke-filled clubs, lousy pay, and of course late hours, drugs, alcohol, the vagabond life of the jazz musician (making a settled family life almost impossible), police crackdowns. What a miracle that despite all of this, a music of such intricacy, boldness, and enduring beauty was created and prevailed!

Needless to say, David Chertok was not the only jazz fan who had major problems with the advent of bebop. His perspective was that of a fan who had been too close to jazz to notice that the music he loved was in a state of constant growth and change, and really always had been. From our own perspective fifty years later, many elements of the bop movement seem inevitable. We can clearly see from the playing of the most progressive jazz players from the swing era in what direction jazz was headed. Of course what was unpredictable was the way those elements would be put together into a style by the new generation of jazz musicians; in other words, the way the music actually sounded was caused by the idiosyncratic sensibilities of the young people who were playing it.

More plainly put, the music was a personal statement based at least as much in the actual lives of those who played it as it was in the historic, inevitable musical change that coalesced in the bop movement. Although the moldy figs screamed that bop was either the death of jazz or really not jazz at all, it was, of course, simply jazz continuing to renew itself, as it always had since its earliest days, "lighting out for new territories."

I THINK THAT there are some serious misconceptions about bop. One such myth is that it was not until bop that improvisers based their solos on the chords, creating completely new melodic lines. But that is not true—jazz improvisers had been creating new melodic lines based on the chord structure for years before the bop era.

Another myth is that jazz had not used sophisticated, modern harmony until bop. That is not true either. Ellington, for one, had been creating music, especially in the band he led in 1940 to 1941 (the [Jimmy] Blanton–[Ben] Webster band), that was quite bold in its use of chromaticism. Just listen to pieces like the great "Ko-Ko." It has nothing to do with bop (including the Charlie Parker masterpiece of the same name), but Duke had been more than willing to break through jazz's harmonic envelope. And one can hear a number of jazz musicians from this period who were harmonically quite sophisticated. There is a famous recording of the tenor saxophonist Don Byas in a duet with bassist Slam Stewart at a famous concert in New York's Town Hall in which he pushes the harmonic envelope as far as he can, falling just a few paces short of the advances of the boppers. And then there are some who insist that they heard Art Tatum using flatted fifths in some of his more daring roiling arpeggios.

But bop was more than a continuation of the innovations of musicians from the swing era. At its heart, bebop, like the jazz that had preceded it, was a reflection of the sensibilities, lives, and times of the young people who played the new music. Bop was not just a style that these musicians "tried on," it was an expression of their lives as young black men (and a handful of white men, too) in the America of the 1940s. It was created not just as a product of the change in the music itself, but also of the great changes winding through American society, particularly the way this change affected young African Americans.

After a terribly destructive war, the horrors of the Holocaust, and the beginning of the nuclear age, it should be no surprise that a music created in reflection of this era would have a sound that was intense, unpredictable, dazzling, and iconoclastic.

It was music meant to slap its audience awake, to shake them up, not to lull them into dreamy reverie as did much of the music of the swing era. It is interesting that this current generation of neoclassicist jazz musicians has been labeled the "young lions" or "young turks." Decades earlier, the boppers were referred to in these terms. This is further proof of how confused the current jazz scene really is. Young turks or young lions implies those who are brashly pushing forward, men and women filled with the gumption of youth and involved in a revolution. If anything, the neoclassicists are counterrevolutionaries; everything about their movement works to prevent jazz from continuing to move forward. They are 180 degrees removed from the spirit of the young boppers.

ALTHOUGH INITIALLY THERE were many established jazzmen who had resented the boppers (probably because they couldn't play the new music), there were at the same time progressive-minded players who had been in the vanguard of jazz in the previous decade and who were fascinated by bop. For example, Coleman Hawkins played and recorded with several of the boppers, including Dizzy Gillespie, Fats Navarro, and even Thelonious Monk (giving Monk his first opportunity to appear on records). His own playing changed in the mid-1940s; his improvising took on a rhythmic complexity that he had previously eschewed. When one listens to Hawkins's recordings of the mid- and late 1940s, the unmistakable influence of Charlie Parker can be heard in every aspect of the veteran tenorman's style.

Lester Young also hired many of the young lions, preferring the energy of the young musicians he called the "kiddies." As we noted previously, his playing changed and developed, but it did not really become boppish, although Young, rightly, considered himself modern.

Some older musicians were initially shaken by the virtuosity of the boppers. But the idea of there being a major conflict between generations of jazz musicians is greatly exaggerated. As a perfect illustration, there is a famous story about the first time the great tenor saxophonist Ben Webster heard Charlie Parker play. Bird was jamming at one of the Harlem clubs that welcomed the boppers, playing tenor rather than his usual alto saxophone. After listening to him solo, playing with such fluid rapidity all over the instrument, Webster walked up to Bird and pulled the horn out of his hands, saying, "The horn's not supposed to be played that way." But then he went all over town telling every musician he saw about the young genius he had just heard do things with a sax nobody had ever heard before. Webster himself once had been known as a fierce player; his most famous solo, at least in the early part of his career, was a burning improvisation on "Cotton Tail" when he was in Ellington's band in the early 1940s. Webster greatly admired the boppers and wisely decided not to try to compete with them. Instead, he went in the opposite direction: He developed a style based on his huge, beautiful sound, playing with a tone whose vibrato was so full and warm it seemed almost like a physical presence with which he seemed to caress every note. He is best known now not for the red-hot solos of his early years but instead as probably the greatest player of ballads in jazz history—some of the most sensuous "boudoir" music ever created.

As for Ellington himself, the bop movement barely seemed to affect him. He was already leagues ahead of everybody else, and in his own inimitable way always would be. He had created his own musical world, one with its own idiosyncratic musical architecture and a sense of life, its pains and pleasures, quite unlike that of anybody else. Undoubtedly, this concept of a musically self-contained world within a world would be adapted by the man called the "high priest of bop," Thelonious Monk.

THERE ARE OTHER myths about the birth of bop that deserve to be relegated to the trash heap of musical pseudo-history once and for all. One of the most popular is that the boppers created bebop as a music that the white man could not steal.

There is a degree of truth in this popular theory. In the swing era, the most popular swing bands after that of Goodman were probably the kind of bands led by Glenn Miller, the Dorsey Brothers, and Artie Shaw. The music that most of these swing era bands played was a diluted form of jazz, a type of music that can be compared to what is called "lite jazz" these days; in other words, they were the Kenny G. and Bob James of their time. Much swing music had little of the vitality and none of the innovative vision that was true of jazz at its greatest. It was jazz watered down for a primarily white middle-class audience, and its popularity must have troubled the younger generation of fiercely committed jazzmen, most of whom, though not all, were black. The vital message that "authentic" jazz conveyed was lost when the music was so diluted.

However, the popular theory that the primary catalyst behind the creation of bop was resentment of all white jazz musicians, creating a music "that they could not steal," is one that is easily punctured by one looming fact: The first genuine bop group to play on "Swing Street," Manhattan's Fifty-second Street, in 1944 was co-led by Dizzy Gillespie and the great bassist Oscar Pettiford and included the white pianist George Wallington.

Fifty-second Street, "Swing Street," was at this time the center of the jazz world, and the appearance of a bop group served notice that a new generation of progressive-minded musicians were now a legitimate part of the jazz scene. It was a manifesto of sorts—which means that if the whole idea for bop was "creating music the white man can't play," it was rather strange that a movement based on such a consideration would launch its debut in the heart of the jazz world with a white musician in such a central role.

Even more importantly, in the second wave of modern jazz musicians, there were many white boppers, most of them greatly respected by the black innovators. Charlie Parker's favorite pianist, for instance, was Al Haig. And after Miles Davis left his band, Bird chose Red Rodney, a fine white trumpet player, to replace Davis at a time when every young bop trumpeter, black or white, vied for a chance to play in Bird's group. White drummers like Stan Levey and Shelly Manne were quickly accepted by the boppers for their deep understanding of those complex bop rhythms. The great drummer Max Roach, who has often expressed quite vehement feelings against racism, was a great admirer of the blind white pianist/composer Lennie Tristano, the pianist who was one of the key fathers of cool jazz. And the boppers warmly welcomed to their ranks young white jazz writers like Leonard Feather and Barry Ulanov, who helped crusade for the new music against often fierce opposition. And the first group Miles Davis ever led was a nonet that had far more white players than black (a fact that Miles mentioned whenever he was accused—quite wrongly—of being racist).

However, once again all the key innovators of bop were black. And also once again, the changes in jazz reflected changes in American society, in particular changes in the lives of African Americans. It is not hard to see how World War II affected such change. After fighting against a racist regime in Europe, young black men looked toward the endemic racism of their own country, for which many had been willing to sacrifice their lives. They returned home feeling as dedicated to bringing about social change in America as they had been to the defeat of Germany and Japan.

I think from the perspective of the end of the 1990s, it is clear that this century is divided by the World War II. After that calamitous war—

and the horrors associated with it—the world and in particular America would never be the same. And jazz, always so plugged into the moment, had to reflect that great change in order to remain valid. And it did.

Incidentally, according to Max Roach, World War II was the cause of a very specific, pragmatic effect that led to the birth of bop. Because of the war, there was a 20 percent surtax on any entertainment that included a singer or a dancer. But there was no surtax on solely instrumental music, for some reason. Therefore, many clubs were open to jazz groups or for informal jamming as a way of presenting entertainment without having to pay the surtax. With all the gigs available, young visionary musicians felt free to experiment.

However, the whole idea that the boppers got together in some kind of conspiracy to create a "modern" jazz has little basis in fact. The Harlem club Minton's is usually characterized as the place where the boppers worked together to "invent" bebop. That is not how any art, and in particular jazz, has ever evolved. According to participants like Thelonious Monk and Dizzy Gillespie, the advances wrought by the boppers happened in almost a casual way, just as a function of the jamming and experimentation that were freely allowed in the loose atmosphere of Minton's. In particular, many of the harmonic advances came about as a way of separating the sophisticated and skilled musicians from the pretenders. According to Dizzy, "No one man or group of men invented modern jazz, but one of the ways it happened is this. Some of us began to jam at Minton's in Harlem in the early 1940s. But there were always some cats who couldn't blow but who would take six or seven choruses to prove it. So on afternoons before a session, Thelonious Monk and I began to work out some complex variations on chords and the like, and we used them at night to scare away the no-talent guys. After a while, we got more and more interested in what we were doing as music, and, as we began to explore more and more, our music evolved."[1]

It is also important to note that the man who was the epitome of bebop, Charlie Parker, did not even jam at Minton's in the early days of bop's evolution. So, as Dizzy himself makes clear in his autobiography, *To Be or Not to Bop*, it is impossible to pinpoint one particular place or even the musicians who were completely responsible for the advent of bebop. Too often jazz history is presented as a series of Great Men and, of course, it is far more complicated than that.

When Bird and Dizzy met in 1939, while Dizzy was traveling through Kansas City playing in Cab Calloway's band, they were both amazed at the similarity of the advances each had made despite the fact that they had been completely unaware of each other. This was long before they had developed their mature styles, when they were just intuitively feeling their way toward what would eventually become bebop. According to most jazz histories, when Dizzy started jamming with Monk at Minton's in the early 1940s, he was able to advance his music further because Monk was the key harmonic architect of the bop revolution. At the same time, Kenny Clarke had taken the techniques of Jo Jones even farther, creating a style of drumming that was perfect accompaniment for bop horns. There were other contributors: Charlie Christian, trumpeter John Carisi (probably the only white player who regularly jammed at Minton's), trumpeter Joe Guy, and other musicians, many of whom are now obscure.

I find it fascinating that there was such a widespread feeling of restlessness among younger jazz musicians in the late 1930s and early 1940s, a feeling among numerous musicians throughout the country, most of them unaware of each other, that a new kind of modern jazz was about to come into being. For instance, drummer Kenny Clarke dates his "discovery" of what would be the style of drumming that eventually dominated jazz back to 1937. Clarke thought that jazz drumming had become, in his term, "monotonous," and he developed a style that increased the musicality of the drums, gave them greater presence in the ensemble, and gave the soloist greater freedom to explore the complex rhythms that were so crucial to the bop movement. At the same time, Dizzy Gillespie, who initially was a Roy Eldridge acolyte, was beginning to evolve his style, which can be heard on recordings of Gillespie from the late 1930s (perhaps most famous is the Lionel Hampton piece "Hot Mallets" from 1939 in which Dizzy takes a solo that is just a breath away from his mature style).

Charlie Parker could pinpoint exactly when he made the key discovery that led to his innovative style:

> I was jamming in a chili house on Seventh Avenue between 139th and 140th. It was December, 1939. Now, I'd been getting bored with the stereotyped changes that were being used all the time at that time, and I kept thinking there's bound to be something else. I could hear it sometimes but I couldn't play it.
>
> Well, that night I was working over "Cherokee," and as I did, I found that by using the higher intervals of a chord as a melody and backing them up with appropriately related changes, I could play the thing that I'd been hearing. I came alive.[2]

This statement deserves close consideration. I find it very revealing that Parker says that after finally making this key musical discovery, he "came alive." He doesn't say that his musical path was now certain or that his music had finally come to life—it is *he* who has come alive. In other words, for Parker, his life and music are completely interwoven, and he does not separate one from the other; his life is his music and his music is his life. Unlike so many of today's jazz musicians, Parker did not view music as a career or as his springboard to success. One of today's most prominent young jazz musicians has talked openly about his hopes that eventually he will gain enough fame to go on to the real big time and maybe have his own TV talk show. In my wildest fantasies, I cannot imagine Bird harboring similar ambitions.

On a more technical level, Parker came alive because he discovered a way of creating melodic ideas without the limitations of the conventional harmonic conception of that period. So it was this sensation of new freedom that made him feel as if he had come alive, and which accounts for the feeling of actual flight that we feel when we listen to Bird's winged solos.

It is also interesting to note that just as Kenny Clarke described the drumming of the period as having become "monotonous," Parker refers to the harmonic limitations of 1930s jazz as "stereotyped." This feeling—that the jazz of the swing era had run its course and was no longer fresh and inventive—was obviously a widely felt one, uniting the young generation of musicians.

Parker, of course, did not know Clarke, or Dizzy, or Thelonious Monk, or even Charlie Christian. Yet all of these musicians were working toward what eventually would coalesce into bebop or modern jazz. At the same time, Jimmy Blanton was overhauling the playing of bass for the jazz ensemble in his work with Duke Ellington. Blanton gave the bass a much more central role, playing far more melodically than bassists previously had been doing, to the extent of creating a feeling of contrapuntal swing with soloists. Blanton, like Christian, died at a tragically young age, passing away a few months shy of his twenty-fourth birthday. Oscar Pettiford was the bassist who in the 1940s adapted Blanton's innovative style into the anchor of the bop rhythm section.

Was it simply coincidence that a saxophonist, trumpet player, guitarist, bassist, and drummer were all working in parallel directions? And that when their individual innovations coalesced synergistically it produced a style that redefined jazz by 1945? So when David Chertok returned from World War II he heard genuinely new jazz, which seemed to have come out of nowhere. But that is because he was a fan. This was not true for musicians plugged into the jazz scene.

In his autobiography Miles Davis talks about how while still a teenager in East St. Louis in the early 1940s, he and many of his musician friends were so anxious to play what even then they called "modern" music. This is before either Miles or his friends had heard Bird or Dizzy, in person or on record. It was as if this entire generation of jazz musicians was somehow aware of the music that Parker described in the above comment: music that existed in his mind and—until that night in 1939—had lain just outside of his reach.

By the time the Billy Eckstine band, the first modern big band, whose personnel included Bird and Diz, among many other young modernists, came to St. Louis in 1944, Miles knew of both Parker and Gillespie, though he still had not heard them. When Miles was hired by Eckstine to replace a missing trumpetman, the young trumpeter (he was eighteen at the time) was so astonished by what he heard that he could not concentrate on the music he was supposed to play. Parker and Gillespie had taken the ideas Miles had thought to be modern to musical areas so far advanced both in their audacity and their musical power that Miles knew he had to make their music the center of his life. The rest, that is in terms of Miles's career, is music history.

So there was unquestionably in the air by the early 1940s an impetus for change that was felt throughout the jazz world. However, I am not saying that the explanation for the great spurt of evolution jazz was undergoing was mystical or supernatural. One has to remember how different the jazz scene was back then from the way it is now. The world of jazz was a tight one, in which musicians traveled around the country—mostly because of their being employed in big bands—sitting in and jamming with local musicians, gossiping and spreading the word of the latest developments. Miles became aware of Bird and Diz initially because of hearing about them from musicians who were in bands traveling through St. Louis.

This mood among younger jazz musicians for making their music more modern bears a similarity to the end of the 1950s, when a number of musicians were thinking of various ways to make jazz improvisation more freely melodic and less hamstrung by the kind of complex harmonies that were the hallmark of bebop. There was no doubt: Change was in the air, and there was a collective desire among the jazz musicians of this generation to redefine their music in a way that was almost an exact parallel to the way they were reacting to the great changes in their lives. This was music that demanded serious focus and respect, that could not be condescended to or ignored. At its greatest, it was music of such force and power that, if you listened to it carefully, its visceral message of airborne freedom and delirious embrace of the present moment was emblazoned on your soul, and your life was inalterably changed.

If you want to have a sense of the "shock of the new" that was bebop, there are recordings that to a degree deliver the sheer exhilaration that at least some jazz fans felt hearing bebop for the first time. In 1945, the vibist Red Norvo put together a group of important swing jazz musicians along with Charlie Parker and Dizzy Gillespie solely for the sake of a recording session. Among the swing era jazzmen are the Hawkins-influenced tenorman Flip Phillips, pianist Teddy Wilson, and Norvo himself, one of the most adventurous and open-minded musicians of the swing era. On most cuts the first few solos are played by the swingers—Norvo, Phillips, Wilson, Stewart. They all acquit themselves superbly, swinging hard and justifying their reputations. But when Bird and Dizzy follow, the effect is bracingly physical.

When I listen to these sides the almost palpable electricity generated by Parker and Gillespie—particularly in comparison with the swing era players—makes me always feel as if I am almost levitating, soaring above the earth in miraculous flight. Even if you know absolutely nothing about the revolutionary harmonic or rhythmic conceptions being employed by Bird and Dizzy, you can feel on the most visceral level the new kind of energy that they had brought to jazz. This was recorded at the very nascence of modern jazz, but these sides make it obvious why this energy so quickly conquered the jazz world. Like Louis Armstrong's Hot Fives and Sevens, the boppers were making a statement about the ecstactic nature of freedom, expressing what it *feels like* to be free. For neither the first nor the last time in jazz, this was music as manifesto.

THE BOP ERA is at least one of the periods in which we can observe this great truth: Innovation is a direct result of the key elements of jazz creation—that jazz is the expression of the individual and that it is music that is created in the moment and is constantly spontaneous (in feeling even if not in actuality), or in Whitney Balliett phrase, the "sound of surprise." Our world—our society, our culture—is in constant change. And as it changes so in turn are we changed. Artists are particularly sensitive to this flow of change. Most artists are not ahead of their time, something that is so often said about visionaries. Rather, as the composer

Edgard Varèse pointed out, they are plugged into the present, and most of the rest of us are caught up in the past. This is especially true of jazz musicians, since their music is an art "in the moment." Therefore, as the times in which they are creating change, so must the music change. Innovation is important in all arts and many other areas of life. But with jazz, innovation is *built into its very conception*. And in bebop this truth is made obvious.

Usually when the birth of bop is discussed, the main progenitors named are Charlie Parker, Dizzy Gillespie, Thelonious Monk, and Charlie Christian. Bassist Oscar Pettiford took the innovations of Jimmy Blanton, who revolutionized the role of the bass in jazz, and adapted them to bop. Bud Powell applied the formal and stylistic advances of Bird and Dizzy to piano (Monk's style owed virtually nothing to either).

These musicians were all great individualists, but they were united by certain similarities that acted as a bond between them. They all demanded that their music be taken seriously and be treated with dignity. They refused to play the role of smiling entertainers for white folks. Jazz had always been a music for self-definition, but the boppers were far more up front with their insistence on being treated like dedicated artists and worthy human beings. In the heart of the bop movement we can clearly see the burgeoning of an African-American movement that became increasingly militant about the oppression of black people in America.

Interestingly, a number of boppers began rejecting Western culture, looking toward the East; some of them became involved in the Muslim religion (not the Black Muslims), and a number of them adapted Muslim names. Others became increasingly outspoken about the treatment of black people in America. Clearly these visionaries knew that "Now's the Time" (the title of a Charlie Parker tune) for change, and not just musical change.

Each of these musicians had a particular role in the development of the bop revolution. Christian died a few years before bop really emerged with all its parts in place. Monk was a progenitor of bop, the "high priest of bebop," which was actually a good description of his role as the master theorist behind the movement. When Miles Davis first arrived in New York and hooked up with Charlie Parker, Bird brought Miles to meet Monk. Monk was the best teacher for any young musician wishing to understand this new music on the deepest levels. Interestingly, Monk's own music was not really bebop, at least not the common conception of bebop, and bebop like all labels can be misleading.

Monk developed a style, both in his compositions and improvising, that created an idiosyncratic world quite unlike that of anybody else. He wrote most of his compositions in the 1940s and the early 1950s, only occasionally adding new ones later in his career. It is almost as if he built a world perfect in every piece with his compositions of the 1940s and 1950s, and simply had little or nothing to add. The entire body of Monk's work is perfect within itself—it is as if Monk had conceived his own private universe that had its own set principles and logic parallel to, but quite different from, that of the world the rest of us share. His music is endlessly fascinating, and extremely beautiful in its own strange way.

Monk would not really receive his due until well into the 1950s. He would eventually become such a popular figure that *Time* magazine did a cover story on him, an idea that would have seemed like a bizarre hallucination in the 1940s and early 1950s, when Monk was an underground figure and the stuff of jokes about weirdo jazzmen.

Saying that Dizzy Gillespie's style is classic bebop is only stating that Dizzy, doing the same thing that Monk did—creating a style out of his own idiosyncrasies as a man and a musician—happens to fit under a label. Dizzy's brand of modernism was simply emulated more than Monk's.

If Dizzy is not as revered as much as Parker or even Powell, there are several reasons for this, but few of them have to do with his actual musical contribution. One of the reasons is that Dizzy's music is such a celebration of life, joyous and often humorous with few if any of the dark shadows we perceive in the work of Bird or Powell. Gillespie was never self-destructive, and he was married to the same woman until he died. He was popular throughout his career, and for a jazz musician financially successful. In other words, he had little in common with the cliché of the tortured artist. Dizzy Gillespie records will lift the spirits of anyone who is depressed; his playing is kind of a musical Prozac. And make no mistake, he was as great a genius as any that jazz has produced.

One of the main reasons Dizzy never really got his due is because he was constantly being compared to his colleague Charlie Parker, "the other half of my heartbeat," as he once called him. When writing about the genius who "invented" bebop, critics almost always refer to Charlie Parker. There are several reasons for this. Undeniably, Bird fit the stereotype of the tortured artist: he lived a dissolute, self-destructive life, died young (months shy of his thirty-fifth birthday), and his life and appetites have become an American legend. He has even received the ultimate encomium, a Hollywood movie made about his life directed by no less than Clint Eastwood (a movie with a portrayal of Parker that, according to those who knew Bird, has apparently little to do with the real man). It emphasized Parker's self-destructiveness more than his genius, just as an earlier film—*Lady Sings the Blues*—did for Billie Holiday. As I write, Stanley Crouch is preparing for publication a major new biography of Parker. Hopefully it will clear away the myth that has so long surrounded this man and finally help us to understand exactly what kind of a man Bird was. I have read most of what has been written about Parker and have known colleagues of his. Nobody seems to be able to portray him in all his obvious complexity.

In his history of jazz, *The Making of Jazz,* James Collier states outright that Parker was a "sociopath." Yet many who knew him claim that such a designation is absurd. In the autobiography of his wife, Chan, Parker is portrayed almost as if he were at heart something of a square, wanting to live a normal life but caught up in the pitfalls of the jazz world. He cared deeply about his children, loved opera, and desperately wanted a simpler life. There is a book titled *Bird: The Legend of Charlie Parker,* which is a compilation of anecdotes and reminiscences of Bird by many who knew him. Parker is portrayed here as the ultimate hipster, a man who could shoot more dope, drink more alcohol, bed more women, and even eat more food (these last two quite extraordinary for a junkie, let alone an alcoholic/junkie) than anyone else. He is the beat hero, who insists on living a life of burning passion in order to create music that reflects the madness around him.

Which one is he? I think, obviously, he is both, but probably Chan's portrayal is closer to the ultimate truth. Parker went with Dizzy and some other boppers to Los Angeles in 1945 in order to spread the bop message by playing at a popular L.A. jazz club. When the others left, Parker stayed behind, selling his airline ticket in order to buy dope. But later there was a shortage of heroin and Parker had a nervous breakdown after drinking himself into oblivion and setting his hotel room on fire. He was eventually committed to Camarillo State Hospital. At first he wanted to be released. But after he had detoxified, he began to love his existence there. He worked in the hospital's gardens and even did some bricklaying. He could develop his musical ideas far better away from his usual frantic lifestyle. Parker wanted to study composition with a major European classical composer. He had life under control for the first time in years. Of course, eventually he had to leave the hospital. And soon after was drawn back to his previous mode of life and ineluctable doom.

Parker became a legend very early in his career, and it is that legend that perhaps more than anything else led to his eventual self-destruction. He was expected to conform to a role that he had not necessarily meant to create, but nevertheless he played it for all it was worth. Being a junkie with an expensive habit made him constantly on the make, and if in order to maintain his habit he had to play the role of the ultimate hipster, so be it.

The beats worshiped Parker without really understanding him or his art. Jack Kerouac wanted to write a novel that would be "improvised" just like Parker improvised one of his solos, or at least so he believed; it eventually became his most famous book, that beat odyssey, *On the Road*. Kerouac used a roll of paper on which he could write without ceasing and without being able to go back and change anything (however, the book that was published went through a great deal of editing). But Parker's music was not just plucked out of the ether.

Charlie Parker, despite his disorganized life, had the ability to create solos that were improvisational but which nevertheless had innate structure and form. Listening to some of his alternate takes, I am often amazed by his ability to come up with not only new melodic ideas on each take of the same tune, but also with different structures—all created in the moment. By listening to various takes on tunes, some completely different, we know how devoted he was to truly spontaneous composition. But he was a very disciplined musician; his improvisations were not just a jumble of musical thoughts cemented together only by Parker's passion. Bird mainly listened to classical music, and he had great knowledge of form. Along with the beauty of Parker's melodic ideas, the fact that his solos are such complete musical statements give them an unforgettable power. Many musicians following in his path could invent ideas, but few of them were able to create work of such coherence.

It is also true that for Parker, music was a direct reflection of his being and his experience. Nobody ever put this better than Charlie Parker himself: "Music is your own experience, your thoughts, your wisdom. If you don't live it, it won't come out of your horn."[3] These words, from probably the greatest improviser in jazz history, should be read and reread by those who believe that a concept like jazz neoclassicism isn't at heart an oxymoron.

In one interview, Charlie Parker seemed to agree in essence with the moldy figs. He did not consider his music as being part of the jazz tradition either. "Bop is no love child of jazz," he told a writer from *Down Beat*. When asked to define it, Parker stated, "It's just music. It's trying to play clean and looking for the pretty notes." It is revealing that Bird told the writer that the main difference between bop and jazz was rhythmic: "[Bop] has no continuity of beat, no steady chug-chug. Jazz has, and that's why bop is more flexible."

Parker was being a bit coy. Like virtually all of jazz's greatest innovators, Bird refused to be straitjacketed by a so-called jazz tradition. He wanted to be free—free to explore music and let his curiosity, knowledge, and intuition lead him to whatever new territory was out there. When he was improvising he certainly did not want to have to keep in mind the strictures of a supposed tradition. He wanted to let the music take him in whatever direction it took him. His response to the moldy fig traditionalists was, Fine, if you don't want me in your little jazz world that is all right; I will continue to create the music that is in my mind and heart no matter what anybody calls it.

Perhaps the single most eloquent retort to the whole idea of a limiting tradition came from Charlie Parker. He put it this way: "They teach you there's a boundary line to music. But, man, there's no boundary line to art." Only a revolutionary like Bird could understand the profundity of that thought.

Needless to say, the idea that Charlie Parker was not a jazz musician—even if he said it himself—is ludicrous. His style was very clearly developed out of the influence of the great jazz musicians who had preceded him. Listening to Parker, it is obvious that he had an acute awareness of the great jazz statements of the past, including those of Armstrong, Hawkins, Tatum, and Lester Young.

A few years ago there was an album released titled *Birth of Bebop*. It consisted of a number of mainly amateur recordings principally of Charlie Parker. The most revealing cut is a recording of Parker jamming with a bassist in a hotel room. Bird was playing tenor sax rather than his chosen instrument, the alto, and surprisingly he displays virtually no influence of Lester Young. He does play with a sound very much like that of Chu Berry or Don Byas, and he uses heavy vibrato—and in most other ways his tenor playing seems more in the Hawkins tradition than that of Young. Actually, this should not be so surprising. It is Hawkins and those of his school who had used the greatest harmonic sophistication in their playing. Before Parker, Young and Hawkins—and those saxophonists influenced by Hawkins—were the two stylistic schools for playing the tenor saxophone. One of the great legends of jazz is about the night Lester Young finally "cut" Hawkins in an all-night saxophone duel. The two styles seemed to be 180 degrees different in every aspect. Perhaps bebop—or at least Bird's revolutionary style—was born when Parker combined the harmonic sophistication and bravura of the Hawkins school with the rhythmic complexity and lyricism of Young and then played this musical alchemy on alto sax rather than tenor. That certainly is a logical explanation for how Parker developed his innovative style, one that appeared on the jazz scene only seemingly out of nowhere. And this explanation, of course, makes ridiculous anybody's claim that his music was outside the jazz tradition.

Nobody had a deeper belief in the concept that the primacy of experience is the source for fresh musical creation than Charlie Parker. There is a story in *Bird* (the book) that describes one night when, between sets at a club, a friend found Parker rolling around in the garbage in the back. When asked what he was doing, Bird replied that it was something he had never done before and he needed new experience so he could play with fresh musical ideas. This story might be apocryphal, but even if it is, it is certainly a reflection of Parker's attitude toward improvising. It is no coincidence that one of Parker's most famous compositions was titled portentously "Now's the Time." As messy as Parker's life was, he was always vitally aware of the moment in which he was living and in which he was playing his music; he was our genius of the here and now.

If you doubt this, simply listen to his greatest recordings. There is a passionate immediacy to his playing that still causes goose bumps. I think this is particularly so with the tracks he recorded with a small string section. The string arrangements are not very imaginative and often crowd Parker's improvisations. Yet even when he is only creating obbligatos around the melody and playing little melodic phrases rather than full-out solos, Bird makes each of the songs his own. The at times mawkish string arrangements seem to act as a spur, compelling him to fill every note he is able to squeeze in with deep emotional pungency, even when only playing the melody. This is especially true on the one cut considered a masterpiece, "Just Friends," but it also applies to, say, "April in Paris," which has far less real improvisation. Simply through his expressive tone, his superb phrasing, and his use of perfect grace notes and obbligatos, Parker imbues "April" with a melancholy power that no other performer has ever been able to dredge out of the tune. "Just Friends" belongs in the category of "Ko Ko," a definitive statement for its time—in which we can hear a view of the world that is ecstatic and celebratory to the point of near madness while at the same time filled with a kind of world-weary melancholy and cosmic angst. It is the mood that can be read in Allen Ginsberg's *Howl* and Jack Kerouac's *On the Road*, as well as in Ralph Ellison's *Invisible Man*. It is a report on the madness of twentieth-century existence from someone who has seen deep into the void and has the artistry to express unblinkingly all that he has experienced and sensed.

Bop may have been music "in the moment" of the 1940s, but like all great art, its beauty and truth still resonate today. There is some bop that was sheer faddish nonsense, and that is of little interest now. But the greatest bebop still is powerful music. I think what composer/writer Bill Kirchner recently pointed out to me is true: that in form and essence, bop is pretty boring. It (at least small-group bop, which was the mode in which it was mainly played) consists primarily of a series of solos with rarely any arrangements (the work of arranger/composer Tadd Dameron is one of the important exceptions). But because there were geniuses playing the music—Parker, Dizzy, Bud Powell, Pettiford, Fats Navarro—it is some of the most brilliant music of this century.

WHEN I THINK about the success of the bop revolution in completely redefining jazz, I often wonder if it could have been possible without the existence of "Swing Street," Manhattan's Fifty-second Street. From the mid-1930s to the early 1950s, Fifty-second Street between Fifth and Sixth Avenues was the jazz capital of the world. One could hear almost the entire gamut of jazz styles in the cluster of small clubs, including such legendary jazz dives as the Onyx, the Three Deuces, Jimmy Ryan's, and the Famous Door. Musicians playing in one group would go next door or across the street to observe what their colleagues were up to, and sometimes even sit in. Although the clubs were small, cramped, and smoky, the looseness of the Fifty-second Street scene was especially conducive to jazz and its development.

When Dizzy Gillespie brought the first genuine bop combo to the Street, it was a clarion call to those in the jazz world that a new generation was now in ascendency; it was a manifesto of sorts. Dizzy was playing in the heart of the mainstream of jazz and, like it or not, this house revolt had to be confronted by those in the jazz world. Having a place like the Fifty-second Street jazz hub, where musicians were able to hear virtually any important player and his latest development, could sit in or jam together, learn from each other, and just hang out and gossip (gossip is a constant in the jazz world), was obviously deeply vital for the musical health and evolution of jazz. This current generation cannot be blamed because there is nothing like it in the contemporary jazz scene. But without a place like Fifty-second Street, and the opportunity to play in big bands (young Miles Davis, for example, played in both), there is little chance for a young jazz musician to "pay his or her dues," and to learn, not so much the music itself as how to think and feel like a jazz musician. Because if they did understand this, there would be no phenomenon like the neoclassical generation of jazz musicians dominating the mainstream of jazz now.

However, I also must state that the moldy figs, and those who were not as reactionary as the figs but believed that bop was harmful to jazz, also were not proven to be completely wrong about the effect of bop on the course of jazz. There is no doubt that the audience for modern jazz was far smaller than the audience for the jazz of the 1920s or of the swing era. Despite performances like the Norvo jam, many lost interest in jazz, feeling that the music had become too complex and was no longer easy to dance to. Most of these turned to the singers who were becoming increasingly popular in the 1940s and the 1950s, and eventually, of course, rock and roll and its spin-offs would dominate pop culture.

Looking back, it is a miracle that bebop was born at all. It was created for purely musical reasons, having nothing to do with money. The big record companies did not support the bop movement, and most club owners certainly did not encourage it. All the men who developed bop were working musicians who created their music for the most part in funky smoke-filled little clubs or in after-hours joints or in rehearsal halls or in hotel rooms during whatever time they had off from their regular gigs. They did not create it to be part of a fad, but rather because they were so filled with the spirit of this music and the unrelenting desire to explore new musical frontiers that reflected the truths of their own lives that creating this music was, to use Charlie Parker's expression, an act of "coming alive." The problem with the present generation of jazz musicians is not that it has not produced geniuses equal to Bird or Dizzy or Monk, but rather that the spirit that animates the music of the great jazzmen, that passion and faith in the music, as both an art form and social statement, is virtually nonexistent in the current scene.

Jazz definitely paid a price in the name of progress and increased musical sophistication; about that there is little doubt. And for those who thought that bebop was the ultimate development in the history of jazz, the 1950s would produce not only two major movements, one for each coast of this country, but also the beginnings of a new revolution in the music. Thomas Jefferson suggested that America needed a revolution every fifty years. Jazz took the spirit of this declaration to heart but in the speeded-up atmosphere of the twentieth century produced a revolution every twenty years. And even during those periods *sans* revolution, flux in jazz remained a constant.

8.

The 1950s, Part One: Out of the Cool

By the beginning of the 1950s, the bop revolution was over and the young turks (the original young turks) had won. Modern jazz dominated the music's mainstream, and although there were great players with classic styles who were unaffected (at least in terms of their own styles) such as Louis Armstrong and Sidney Bechet, modern jazz was the dominant style of the jazz mainstream.

Yet by the end of the 1940s, change was once again in the air. The atmosphere was not as revolutionary as it had been earlier in the decade. But among many of the young boppers there was a new kind of restlessness.

Perhaps it was due to the nature of "classic" bebop. "Classic" bop was a limited music, after all. The quintessential bebop group was the jazz band stripped to its essentials: one brass (trumpet), one reed (saxophone), and a rhythm section. Arrangements were perfunctory at best: unison statement of theme by horns, solos, restatement of theme, out; some bop pieces did not even have the playing of a theme but consisted of nothing but a series of solos. Obviously, if the soloists were of the caliber of Charlie Parker or Dizzy Gillespie, none of this really mattered. But as a musical movement, classic bop did leave something to be desired. Certainly these concerns must have been on Dizzy Gillespie's mind when he put together his big band in the 1940s. And it had definitely been on the mind of Tadd Dameron, who wrote some of the best bop compositions and arrangements.

The first movement that evolved out of bop is called the "cool" or "West Coast" jazz movement. Whether or not "cool" or "West Coast" are completely apt descriptions of this movement, it was a true movement that arose out of the desire of a number of musicians to play modern jazz in a different way than hard-core bebop. Cool jazz began developing in the late 1940s and flowered by the early 1950s. It is called cool because it supposedly was laid-back—usually played behind the beat—and smooth, and West Coast because it was centered in California. Both terms were misleading. Much of this jazz was red hot and its true roots were on the East Coast rather than the West. However, there is enough truth in those rubrics to make them convenient when discussing this era in jazz.

The fact that cool jazz emerged in the early 1950s is not surprising. It was an era that was on the surface calm and optimistic, but beneath that surface were jitters caused by anti-Communist witch hunts and the fear of nuclear war. After all, these were the early years of the Cold War, a period in which it was clear that everything around us could be literally blown to dust within the space of minutes. In addition, there was the alienation of an increasingly large number of young people toward an American society they perceived as increasingly hollow and conformist (a popular word of the 1950s). Despite the victory over the forces of evil, it was clear that the world was now an even more dangerous place to live in then it was during World War II. In addition, post-Holocaust, all bets were off concerning mankind's basic nature and we continued to be plagued by racism and intolerance.

The beginning of the cool jazz era is usually assumed to be the advent of a nine-piece group led by Miles Davis that was created in the late 1940s and had a very brief existence. The band only played one important gig, but they recorded a number of pieces that eventually would be released on an album titled *Birth of the Cool.* Until recently there was not much controversy about this group and its music or about the cool jazz movement. Cool jazz was accepted as a legitimate style, albeit one that many critics contended had its limitations. But the neoclassicists have decided that the cool jazz movement really wasn't authentic jazz at all, and at best was just an anomaly, a footnote to jazz history. Why? Because according to Stanley Crouch and those who agree with him, cool jazz eschewed both blues and swing, so it could not be classified as authentic jazz.

In Stanley Crouch's essay about Miles Davis, "On the Corner: The Sellout of Miles Davis" Crouch touches on the Davis nonet and the cool jazz movement in general:

> Davis's nonet of 1948–50 . . . largely inspired what became known as "cool" or "West Coast" jazz, a light-sounding music, low-keyed and smooth, that disavowed the Afro-American approach to sound and rhythm. Heard now, the nonet recordings seem like little more than primers for television writing. . . . The pursuit of a soft sound, the uses of polyphony that were far from idiomatic, the nearly coy understatement, the lines that had little internal propulsion, all point to another failed attempt to marry jazz to European devices.[1]

Here is another case of the neoclassicist agenda skewing the history and development of jazz. One example is Crouch's line that the music of the nonet heard from a current perspective sounds like the score of a TV show. There is some truth in this, but that is because those who write music for television and movies have ransacked jazz for decades now. One can hear pseudo-Ellington, -Basie, -bebop, -hard bop, -Coltrane, and others in various sound tracks. That, needless to say, takes nothing away from the original work.

Crouch also implies that all the music played by the nonet comes from white arrangers, especially Gil Evans. The music of the nonet was composed and arranged by several musicians, including John Lewis—an African-American pianist/composer and one of the founders of the Modern Jazz Quartet—who is responsible for several sides. Evans arranged only two sides.

Most important, though, is the contention that the music owes little in terms of rhythm and sound to black music. Crouch ignores the fact that the drummer on these sides was either Kenny Clarke or Max Roach, two of the greatest African-American drummers in jazz history. Perhaps Crouch's statement that the music was influenced by a European aesthetic is correct, but so what? The use of such unusually dense tonal colors may be associated more with classical music than jazz, but that is why these sides sound so fresh and original, even now. However, Crouch is wrong about the use of polyphony. There is very little polyphonic writing of any sort on these sides. As we see again, jazz is an unlimited art form that is wide and deep enough for the expression of any sensibility, even a supposedly white or European one. Here we have a perfect example of jazz usually assumed to be among the greatest ever recorded, denounced by one of the key theorists of neoclassicism because it does not fit into a narrow concept of jazz tradition.

One more thing: Virtually every critic, musician, and fan I know—yes, both black and white—loves and admires these sides. A few years ago

Gerry Mulligan, one of the original participants in the *Birth of the Cool* sessions, rerecorded these arrangements with some of the same players as well as others not on the original session. These arrangements and tunes stand up incredibly well, and in this era of such conservative music making, even sound iconoclastic and vigorously fresh.

So for the purposes of this book, the cool jazz movement and its value both in terms of the actual music it created and its influence on the jazz that followed are of special interest. It serves as a way of illuminating what the great differences are between those who, throughout jazz history, have insisted on the idea of the primacy of a supposed jazz tradition and those who feel that the only limitations of the true jazz tradition are the limits of individual expression, no matter what a musicians' ethnic background is, and the human capacity for change and growth.

HOW, THEN, DID cool jazz come into being? Was it just a bunch of white guys watering down bebop? Or was it something else far more complex with its roots deep in jazz history? As with virtually every twist in the course of jazz history, there is far more here than meets the eye.

Actually, the first cool jazz musician might arguably be Bix Beiderbecke, who like the coolsters played with less vibrato and with a songlike lyricism in contrast to the blues lyricism of Armstrong and those influenced by Louis. As we have seen, to Armstrong this different approach of Bix's did not diminish his respect for Beiderbecke or stand in the way of the two trumpeters musically communing with each other.

But the true fathers of the cool jazz movement were some of the greatest African-American innovators—in particular Lester Young, who as we have already seen was fascinated with the style of Bix and his colleague Frankie Trumbauer. An entire generation of tenormen worked with the musical vocabulary established by Young. But more importantly, the lyricism and smooth sound of his horn as well as his relaxed rhythmic conception are at the heart of the cool ethos. The influence of Young on Charlie Parker is especially obvious in such classic Bird sides as "Cool Blues," "Yardbird Suite," and the great ballads, like "Embraceable You" and "Out of Nowhere" (and all the sides with strings), was another seminal influence on the cool movement.

Miles Davis's trumpet style was also important, especially to such cool trumpet players as Chet Baker, Shorty Rogers, Jack Sheldon, and Tony Fruscella. Early on, Miles decided that he could not play like his idol, Dizzy Gillespie, and so he carved out a style in which the dynamics are much "cooler" than those of Gillespie, more melodic and less brassy to the extent that some critics accused Miles of trying to make his trumpet sound like a saxophone. Miles was, by the end of the 1940s, in a perfect position to point the way toward the cool.

Specifically, the advent of the Miles Davis nonet is revealing in how it illuminates the thinking and creativity of the young musical thinkers of the bop era. The characterization of boppers as hipsters who spent all their time drinking and shooting up heroin that is much beloved in novels and in Hollywood may have a degree of truth in it, but overall it is a slur against these committed and intensely creative jazzmen and -women who were so dedicated to their art. By the late 1940s, there was a group of young musicians who regularly talked out many of the new ideas that were beginning to blossom in the modern jazz world. The place was the one-room apartment of composer/arranger Gil Evans in Midtown Manhattan (near Fifty-second Street). In this little basement flat, a kind of jazz Bloomsbury discussed, argued, dreamed, and eventually planned ways of expanding the potential of bebop. Among the group, besides Evans himself, was Miles Davis, composer/arranger/baritonist/ Gerry Mulligan, composer George Russell, the singer Blossom Dearie, drummer Max Roach, and at times, the group's true guru, Charlie Parker.

Jazz, like any cultural phenomenon, can advance in a number of ways. We tend to think of innovation, at least in jazz, as something that happens through intuition, curiousity, and musicians' need to find an individual expression. But in this case, it came about because of a group of musicians meeting together and discussing their latest ideas and working out musical concepts. Out of this group, at least indirectly, came many of the elements that led to the cool jazz movement and later, to the use of modes, and eventually free jazz.

There were so many ideas in the air at this time that this gathering of geniuses needed a central place just to try to sort them all out. The concept of taking bop in new directions was the focus of their discussions, and the focus of their creative energy. Gradually, their talk turned toward the idea of actually putting together a band that had some of the freewheeling looseness of a bebop combo combined with the ability to play arrangements with interesting tonal colors (it is interesting that this concern can be traced in Miles's music from this, the first band he led, right up to, and definitely including, his great "electric" period of the 1970s.

Miles loved the sound of the Claude Thornhill band, for whom Evans had written some fascinating modern jazz charts. The Thornhill sound was unlike anything else in the big band era, thick clouds of sound that seemed to move at a glacial pace. But how could a relatively small group produce such a lush sound?

The musicians who gathered at Evans's apartment put together these ideas—a new, more melodic type of bebop, perhaps less aggressive rhythmically, more like the playing of Lester Young; the particular sound of the Thornhill group; and the idea of using a minimum of instruments in order to capture the spontaneity of bop as well as the tonal richness of a band like Thornhill's. They finally decided on a nonet as a way of realizing their concept. The instrumentation alone was innovative, using French horn and tuba, which, except for Thornhill's band, had never been utilized in a jazz band before. The nonet's instrumentation was trumpet, trombone, French horn, tuba, alto and baritone saxes, and piano, bass, and drums. Nothing like it had ever been heard before in jazz.

Miles became the de facto leader of the band, and as I stated before, this band was a definite reflection of Miles's musical sensibility. But even Miles acknowledged that just as important were the composers and arrangers, Gerry Mulligan, John Lewis, John Carisi, and Gil Evans (who collaborated with Miles on one piece, "Boplicity"). The group only played one real gig, but it recorded an album's worth of sides for Capitol Records. When the records were first released, they were virtually ignored by most critics and fans. Only some musicians—as usual, far more tuned in than anybody else—perceived how wonderful and important this music was.

When the sides were released on an LP under Miles's name called *Birth of the Cool*, it led to the myth that Miles Davis personally "invented" cool jazz. Of course, the music on that album was a group effort (though Miles should be given his due for putting the ideas into pragmatic action as well as for his superb soloing). In addition to that, these sides were not the sole cause of the cool movement. Once again, the innovations that have been labeled cool jazz are the result of the work and concepts of many musicians.

Almost at least as important to the nascence of the cool movement as the Davis nonet was the work of Lennie Tristano and those who played in his groups of the 1940s and early 1950s, including altoist Lee Konitz, tenorman Warne Marsh, and guitarist Billy Bauer. Tristano lowered the dynamics of bebop in favor of intricate improvisation that at times seemed to owe as much to Bach as it did to Bird. It is instructive to note that Tristano made the musicians he trained—such as Konitz, Marsh, and Bauer—memorize and be able to play, note for note, improvisations of

Lester Young and Charlie Parker. So the cool movement was deeply rooted in the jazz continuum.

Perhaps the most important breeding grounds for West Coast jazz musicians were the big bands of Woody Herman and Stan Kenton. Art Pepper, Stan Getz, Zoot Sims, Lee Konitz, Jimmy Giuffre, and Shorty Rogers were just some of the cool or West Coast players who emerged from these bands. Maybe it is difficult to associate the loud, brassy Kenton band with the pastel sounds of the coolsters. But Kenton encouraged his arrangers, such as Bill Holman and Bill Russo, to experiment with jazz forms, bringing in at times classical elements and intricate orchestrations. The Four Brothers of Herman's band were white saxophonists, all of whom had been deeply influenced by Lester Young. Stan Getz was one of the Brothers, and his incandescent solo on the Herman band's "Early Autumn" is what first brought him fame and was an early example of cool improvising.

IT IS HARD to ignore the fact that one reason many have a negative attitude toward a movement that produced a fair share of fine music is that it is the only jazz movement that was dominated—or rather, is usually *assumed* to be dominated—by white musicians, although the movement actually also included a number of important black players.

But once we go beneath the skin and closely examine the actual music made during this era, we are led to an astonishing conclusion: cool jazz sowed the seeds for the free jazz movement of the 1960s.

On the face of it, this proposition may seem absurd. After all, cool jazz is supposedly soft, and pastel pretty and gentle, and mainly played by white musicians. On the other hand, free jazz is angry, cacophonous, roiling, and mainly played by black musicians; one seems to be the polar opposite of the other.

And to many critics and fans, they were. But musicians have a very different sensibility from that of most fans and critics. They hear music on a different level. What is called cool jazz was really just another stage in the evolution of the music. The music did, for the most part, have lower dynamics than bebop and had a songlike lyricism. But quite a bit of so-called cool jazz was highly experimental and to a degree served as the early burgeoning of the jazz avant garde movement that exploded in jazz throughout the 1960s.

As important as cool jazz was to establishing the avant garde movement, its ultimate worth is the large body of brilliant jazz that was made—by both black and white jazz musicians—during this era.

The cool jazz movement cut a far wider swath than is commonly thought.

A few years ago Ted Gioia published a book titled *West Coast Jazz*, which completely blows away all the myths about this jazz movement. The truth is that there *was* an important jazz movement in the 1950s that was not unjustly called cool. But all the rest—that it is all soft, smooth, shallow music closer to classical tradition than that of jazz and played only by white jazz musicians living in California—is simply not true.

The idea that this music did not swing is especially ludicrous, no matter how you define swing. On many of the most important cool albums, Shelly Manne was the drummer, and Manne was always one of the most swinging drummers in jazz. The great black drummers Frank Butler and Chico Hamilton also routinely played with West Coast groups and frequently recorded with many of the prominent cool jazzmen.

It is also untrue that all cool jazz was lighthearted and conveyed nothing but pastel emotion. Any survey of the principal cool jazzmen should make clear the great range and depth of the playing of many of them. Alto saxophonist Art Pepper was unequivocally one of the most prominent musicians of the West Coast movement, and he is considered by many to be among the greatest players on his instrument regardless of "school." Although his tone was very similar to that of many of the cool altoists—that is, it bore the influence of Lee Konitz more than Bird—he played with an incendiary passion that in itself gives lie to such criticism.

Pepper was an untrained musician, but his instincts and ear were superb and his constant invention, and depth of feeling, clearly made him a great jazzman. Pepper was a man beset with demons throughout his life, and his struggle wrestling with these demons can be heard in every note he played. In the last period of his life, after years spent in prison, he seemed to wrench the notes out of the horn rather than just play them; his music took on a ragged beauty that was truly a "cry from the heart."

Another West Coast alto player who was also a passionate improviser was the greatly underrated Sonny Criss, who happened to be black. Yet, despite his ethnicity, Criss played with a silvery smooth tone not unlike that of Pepper or such a typical West Coast jazzman as Bud Shank. Like them, tonally he owed as much to Lee Konitz as he did to Charlie Parker. However, his improvising was far more blues-tinged and earthier than that of most other West Coast alto players.

West Coast trumpeter Chet Baker—probably the quintessential cool trumpeter (after Miles, of course)—battled with demons similar to Art

Pepper's throughout most of his career. In the early and mid-1950s, he was truly a golden boy with a horn whose good looks and undeniable talent seemed to indicate that he would reach the greatest heights of stardom. His style, like most of the cool trumpetmen, was based in the vocabulary created by Miles Davis, although Baker had a wispy sound all his own. His playing had a surface prettiness and he was always inventive, but in his early years his music lacked much depth. He took up singing and with his Californian blond good looks became, for a short time, a hit with swooning teens. But his indulgences caught up with him and he spent the rest of his life constantly on the run, living mostly in Europe, fleeing authorites in one country after another, just holding on from gig to gig.

In the late 1960s, during the course of a drug deal gone wrong, he was badly beaten and his teeth were knocked out, which would spell the end of a career for most trumpetmen. But Baker learned how to play with false teeth, not an easy task; it was like learning how to play the horn from scratch all over again.

In the last few years of his life, Baker's music gained an emotional depth that was often devastating. He recorded "promiscuously," to use Sonny Rollins's term, and naturally many of his albums from this period were nothing but a quick money fix. But on several of the albums from this period, the one-time golden boy played a music in which he turned regret into sublime art. Every languid note seems imbued with nostalgia and ennui. At its best, and despite the fact that he had no chops left, really (he was never a technically accomplished trumpet player), Baker's music had a dark beauty and melancholy yearning that was simply unforgettable. Even his singing, once so sunny and shallow, now had a ragged eloquence that at times was devastating. All Baker had left was his heart, and in his last several years he wore it on his sleeve. His latter-day music is some of the most emotionally riveting jazz ever heard.

Baker definitely could swing; if he couldn't, certainly Charlie Parker would never have hired him and have expressed so much enthusiasm for him, telling East Coast trumpeters that they had better watch out when Baker arrived on the scene. For the most part, West Coast jazz swung hard. Shorty Rogers—whose music is often thought of as the paradigm of West Coast jazz—led groups ranging in size from small combo to tentet and big band. The influence of the Davis nonet is quite distinct in his music, but so is the influence of Basie; swinging was always a basic consideration for Rogers.

Gerry Mulligan, who was of even greater importance to this movement, always swung hard regardless of whether he was playing in a small group or in his marvelous Concert Jazz Band. Mulligan was a neoclassicist in the best sense of the word; his music always reflected earlier jazz styles while always remaining personal and often forward-looking and innovative. This was certainly true of his classic pianoless quartet with Chet Baker; as progressive (a popular phrase back then) as this group was, it also constantly seemed to resonate echos that were eerily but unmistakably reminiscent of early New Orleans ensemble jazz.

AS I HAVE already stated, not all of the West Coast jazz musicians were white; Buddy Collette, for instance, was one of the key innovators of this style. He could play just about any reed he could touch. Collette had a decidely cool tone on saxophone and clarinet, and his style had a songlike lyricism similar to that of most of the cool players. There were other important black players who were part of the West Coast movement: Hampton Hawes, bassists Leroy Vinnegar, Curtis Counce (who led a popular boppish combo), and Jimmy Bond (a frequent colleague of Chet Baker and Art Pepper), and, most interestingly, Chico Hamilton.

Hamilton was the drummer in the first Mulligan quartet, but his importance to cool jazz was primarily his own group. Hamilton's group, more than any jazz combo on the West Coast, was the archetype of cool jazz to the extent that its music at times seemed coy and precious. The instrumentation of the Hamilton quintet included cello, guitar, and reeds (usually flute). It was true chamber jazz, although there is no doubt that the group could also swing hard. Hamilton used some of the best jazz musicians on the West Coast, such as guitarist Jim Hall and reedmen Buddy Collette and Paul Horn. Some of the arrangements were a bit fey, the bowed cello creating an atmosphere quite unlike that of most jazz performances. But, like the Modern Jazz Quartet, the Hamilton group found a large audience. I believe the reason was that these groups offered more intricate arrangements than that of the typical bop group. Putting the anarchy of improvisation into arrangements that tighten and direct the flow of the solos is bound to create more accessible music than music that is simply a series of lengthy improvisations.

Undoubtedly Hamilton's most interesting and exciting version of his quintet is when Eric Dolphy, a few years later one of the prophets of the free jazz movement, was in the group. Even though Dolphy's style was still in its formative stages, it is already recognizable: forceful and continually leaping through octaves, almost visible in its palpable energy. So the question is this: Is the Hamilton group with Dolphy really cool?

Hampton Hawes was a major jazz pianist who spent most of his career in California. Nobody would say that Hawes's earthy, feverishly inventive playing is cool—but then again, pigeonholing styles, black or white, East Coast or West Coast, cool or hot, is almost always self-defeating and irrelevant. Hawes's playing was wonderfully funky, and most likely was a key influence on one of the central figures of the hard bop movement, Horace Silver, yet he had a central place in the West Coast jazz scene.

Was Gerry Mulligan really cool? He made a series of albums in which he "met" everyone from Johnny Hodges and Ben Webster to Thelonious Monk, all of whom greatly respected Mulligan (and vice versa). Stan Getz is often labeled the ultimate cool tenorman, but he referred to himself as "an old-time stomping tenorman," scarcely our image of a cool jazz musician.

Actually, if the cool movement produced only one musician, Getz, that would be sufficient for it to be considered an important stylistic movement; that is how great a player he was. Getz's main stylistic influence was Lester Young, but more than any of the Young acolytes Getz forged his own style, one that was far more harmonically complex and bop-oriented, and with an unforgettable sound all his own. We have already seen that John Coltrane—of all people—said, "Let's face it, we'd all like to sound like [Getz]." In the last several years of his life, the jazz world took Getz for granted. Now, a few years after his death, I think it has become increasingly clear how great a jazz musician was Stan Getz. His playing was not just pastel prettiness. Like the man himself, there were many sides to his artistry; going through his recorded legacy, the range and depth of his playing over a career that lasted almost five decades is astonishing.

In the jazz world, Getz's reputation as a nasty s.o.b. was probably as well known as his ability to play some of the most beautiful music ever to come out of a tenor saxophone. Tenorman Zoot Sims once said about him, "Stan Getz is a nice bunch of guys." Getz was the walking definition of mercurial: pleasant and even loving one minute; vicous, nasty, and insensitive the next.

Some people said the same thing about Miles Davis, that he was mean-spirited and even cruel. Certainly there were those sides to Miles. But underneath it, to those who came to know him, and to understand how profoundly sensitive he was, it was clear that his reclusiveness and hostility toward strangers were caused not by his arrogance toward the world, but rather by a high-strung sensibility that made him vulnerable as well as amazingly aware and insightful.

In the new (at least as I write) biography of Getz,[2] we are presented with a full, three-dimensional portrait of the great saxophonist. Some of the stories about Getz's behavior—particularly his treatment of the women in his life and of his children—curdle the blood. Getz could be vicious, both physically and verbally, to the extent that some of his children had difficulty forgiving him even in the last days of his life when he was dying from cancer. But in the biography, Getz emerges not as a monster but as a deeply troubled, emotionally scarred man who happens to be a genius of jazz. And it is clear that his beautiful music was a reflection of his best self, the one that emerged after he freed himself from his demons. Music for Getz was not just a profession; it was his salvation.

Getz was a true prodigy, playing professionally with the great trombonist Jack Teagarden at age fifteen. Teagarden taught the young Getz how to pass the long hours traveling from gig to gig: by drinking oneself into oblivion. After joining Woody Herman's band, Getz graduated, like many in the Herman band, to heroin addiction. When high or drunk he was the horrible monster so notorious throughout the jazz world. But the rare times when he was straight he was quite a different person, and he was deeply ashamed of the terrible things he had done while high. He repeated this syndrome until the last few years of his life, when he finally freed himself of his addictions. Those who got to know the sober Getz were amazed at how different he was from his reputation as a monster. There was an inner sweetness in him, possibly the innocence that had been smothered ever since he went touring—and drinking—with Jack Teagarden while still a boy.

Can monstrous human beings produce beautiful art? Of course they can, and many have. But jazz, at least from my perspective, makes more demands on the true character of the musician than other arts. After all, a jazz musician cannot hide behind his art when he performs—all he has are his musical skill and the gist of his life when he creates his music. Maybe I am being a Pollyanna, but I do not believe that the real Stan Getz was the drunken monster. And the reason I feel that way is his music. If I am right about the nature of jazz—that it reflects the inner life of the musician playing it at that moment in time—then it cannot be so that a monster could create such exquisite and continually moving music, music with such depth of feeling, such poetry, as that of Stan Getz.

THE IMPULSE TO play a cooler version of bop did not exist only on the West Coast. Some of the most important music that can be labeled cool jazz was played by East Coast jazzmen. For instance, trumpeter Tony Fruscella played in a style that was definitely cool, but he worked mainly out of New York. He recorded some sides and one brilliant album for Atlantic but then got caught up in the worst elements of the jazz world. Vibraphonist Teddy Charles was always experimenting with his music; in the 1950s he often worked with Charles Mingus's "Jazz Workshop." He formed his own tentet that was among the most adventurous groups of the fifties. Charles had a working knowledge of modern classical music, and that influence can be heard in his most experimental music. Was it cool? Only in a very free sense of that term.

For that matter, quite a bit of Charles Mingus's music of the early fifties was to a degree cool, in that it combined complex arrangements obviously influenced by classical music of modern vintage with elements of jazz. Among his colleagues in exploring this kind of music was Teo Macero, who besides being a composer would go on to become one of the most famous A&R men in jazz, recording many of Miles Davis's classic Columbia albums.

The group that perhaps best reflects the cool aesthetic was neither a West Coast group nor white. It is the Modern Jazz Quartet, a group often praised by Stanley Crouch and with whom Wynton Marsalis has recorded. In many ways the MJQ is the ultimate cool jazz group. Its dynamics are low, and their music is famous for its subtlety and intricate nuance. More than any other group in the history of jazz, it utilizes aspects of classical music—counterpoint, suites, fugues, and at times even symphony orchestras.

Perhaps one reason the MJQ has lasted so long is because of the inner tension of the group. The MJQ's musical director and pianist, John Lewis, has long been fascinated with the melding of European classical music with jazz and was one of the chief architects of the Third Stream movement, which did just that. His goal was to utilize more formal structures for small-group jazz, creating a kind of jazz chamber music. But the leading soloist in the group, Milt Jackson, is one of the funkiest musicians in jazz, and his love of the blues and gift for free-flowing melodic invention have been constants in jazz since he first became known during the bebop era. Lewis's arrangements for the group are seen by some as an imprisonment of Jackson's free-flowing improvisation. Yet it is interesting to note that the MJQ truly are such committed improvisers, unlike some jazzmen who just play variations of previous solos. This can be tested by comparing various live and studio versions of classic MJQ pieces like "Django," Lewis's moving tribute to the great gypsy guitarist, or Milt

Jackson's famous blues "Bags Groove." The solos from performance to performance are completely different, often varying greatly in mood and structure. It's almost as if structure induces the improviser to ad-lib more freely and make his own statement within the often intricate arrangement.

By now the still extant MJQ has outlasted every jazz movement since bop. And they are still playing wonderful music; Milt Jackson is still the greatest vibraphonist in jazz, and John Lewis, besides being a vastly underrated composer and arranger, is also one of the most subtle and inventive—and criminally underrated—pianists in jazz. The MJQ demolishes all attempts to limit and define jazz according to school or in regard to ethnicity. In addition, they prove that the musical conception that lay behind the cool jazz movement was as valid as any other in the history of jazz.

The notion that the coolsters could not swing is torn to shreds in a set of recordings by a group led by Shelly Manne. Recorded live at the now defunct San Francisco club the Blackhawk (where a few years later Miles Davis would record) the group, which included tenorman Richie Kamuca, British pianist Victor Feldman, and black trumpeter Joe Gordon, swung as hard as any group in its time. It was the Jazz Messengers of the West Coast (more about them in the next chapter). The music is hard-swinging, melodic, and deeply felt, everything one could want from jazz. Yet this is certainly West Coast jazz, a type of music that, at least according to Stanley Crouch, is only a pale shadow of the true jazz.

Probably the heart of West Coast jazz was that of the Lighthouse All-Stars, a group that regularly performed during the 1950s at an L.A. jazz club called the Lighthouse. Led by the club's owner, bassist Howard Rumsey, the group included at various times key West Coast musicians, including reedmen Bud Shank, Buddy Collette, Jimmy Giuffre, Bob Cooper; trumpeters Conte Condoli, Chet Baker, Hampton Hawes, Shelly Manne; and trombonist Frank Rosolino. The group played straight-ahead jazz, swinging as hard as any group on the East Coast. Musicians from the East enjoyed sitting in with the Lighthouse All-Stars; for example, both Miles Davis and Max Roach were recorded during stints with the band. They made numerous albums, and while the music is for the most part basically jam sessions, nevertheless there is a joyous innocence to this music that is rather unlike anything else in jazz.

THERE IS ONE aspect of the Birth of the Cool band, and especially the way it came into being, that is highly relevant to this book. The "jazz Bloomsbury" that gathered in Gil Evans's apartment was in many ways the seed of the avant garde movement that would reach its zenith in the 1960s. The participants—Miles, Evans, George Russell, the composer John Benson Brooks, Gerry Mulligan, John Lewis, Lee Konitz—were all involved to one extent or another with innovations that would lead to the next jazz revolution of the sixties.

And these were not the only ones. Certainly one of the most popular jazz musicians to arise out of the West Coast jazz movement was Dave Brubeck. Brubeck was the first modern jazz musician I listened to, like many jazz fans. However, once I got "hip" and started listening to Miles, Coltrane, Mingus, and the others, I confess that I became a full-fledged jazz snob. Because the Brubeck quartet with alto saxophonist Paul Desmond was probably the most popular small group in modern jazz history, I, like so many jazz fans, decided that Brubeck was too popular to be any good. Only a few years ago did I go back to listening to him, and I was surprised—there was much that was really remarkable about his music, and that of his sidekick Desmond. And more than that, Brubeck was an innovator who took the music in important new directions.

If anyone familiar with the course of jazz heard that in the early 1950s there emerged from northern California a white jazz group (although in the late 1950s the bassist Gene Wright joined the quartet for the duration of its existence) that was truly modern, and enormously popular, he or she would probably assume that the pianist was a Bud Powell acolyte and that the altoist played in the mode of Charlie Parker, like virtually all modern pianists and saxophonists. But he or she would be dead wrong.

When Brubeck first emerged in northern California during the early 1950s, his style was unlike anybody else's but harmonically it was at least as modern as bebop, and at times it stretched into the far realms of tonality. Perhaps this is because Brubeck was largely self-taught, and a basically intuitive musician who, despite the accusations about his supposed classical music tendencies, never even learned how to read music. I think the fact that Brubeck grew up living on a ranch in northern California, far away from the hub of jazz, had much to do with his individuality as a musician. Like Bix Beiderbecke, he had to create his own tradition from which he could build a style. Desmond, too, had a modern ear harmonically, but his playing, with a sound that he described as being like a "dry martini," had no discernible Charlie Parker influence. His style was among the most liltingly lyrical in all of jazz. Brubeck had studied with the polytonal composer Darius Milhaud, and his playing at times reflected Milhaud's concepts of tonality long before such improvising became ubiquitous. In sum, the music of the Brubeck Quartet was without doubt modern jazz, but it was not influenced by bebop, at least not overtly. In the 1950s, that made Brubeck and Desmond, as strange as it may seem given their huge popularity, avant-gardists.

Brubeck took the concept of true spontaneous improvising very seriously, unlike many jazz musicians who played solos with only the slightest of variations from night to night. Comparison of different versions of Brubeck performances makes clear that not only are Brubeck's solos different in each performance, but also that even their basic style is varied. His playing is anything but cool; Brubeck has often been accused of being heavy-handed and not swinging. And there is at times much truth to this. There also seem to be more than a few traces of the musical conservatory in Brubeck's playing and along with that the influence of a number of twentieth-century classical composers. He too often pounds out block chords, producing thick, choked music that seems to thud out of the piano, bludgeoning the listener like a physical attack. This often seems an attempt to appeal to those in the audience who mistake such sweaty bombast for deep emotion. His playing is also often unconnected to the rhythm section, almost as if he and the bassist and drummer are playing in two different groups. The interplay between soloist and rhythm section is what swinging is all about, and that interplay is essential to the tension necessary for jazz improvisation. But in other performances, on the same tune on which he had previously been pounding out those pretentious block chords, he will improvise with bluesy funk or maybe a light, lyrical impressionism. And although this may seem the height of eclecticism, Brubeck's playing is always recognizably personal and inimitable.

The fact that Brubeck seemed unafraid of not swinging was alone a major revelation to young iconoclastic musicians like pianist Cecil Taylor and reedman Anthony Braxton. Taylor has often cited Brubeck as an early, and very important, influence, as has Braxton (who also greatly admired Desmond). Despite the overbearing nature of much of his playing, it must be noted that only a handful of musicians of his generation took the chances Brubeck took: polytonality, polyrhythms, the ferocity with which he sometimes attacked the piano, the willingness not to swing at times (certainly all matters of particular note to the young Cecil Taylor—who would later be attacked by critics for many of the same reasons that Brubeck was criticized).

The Brubeck group often used counterpoint and attempted modal improvising early on. But Brubeck's most famous innovation was rhythmic. It is interesting that a musician routinely criticized for being unable to swing brought important rhythmic innovations to jazz, innovations inspired, incidentally, by Brubeck's listening to African music (although he is often accused of being overly influenced by the European classical tradition). Brubeck pointed out that jazz had been stuck in straight-ahead 4/4 for far too long, and his study of African rhythms revealed to him the great complexity and variety of rhythm that jazz had long eschewed. This concern was the basis for Brubeck's most famous album, *Time Out.* Upon the initial release of this album, many critics accused Brubeck of gimmickry, using meters such as 9/8 and 5/4 (as in the big hit, Paul Desmond's "Take Five") for the sake of novelty rather than serious innovation.

Brubeck was not the only musician in the 1950s to experiment with meters and polyrhythms. So did Charles Mingus, pianist/composer Randy Weston, and Max Roach (who put out an album in which every piece was played in 3/4). But for Brubeck, expanding the rhythmic parameters of jazz was a crusade, and for a while it looked as if these innovations had taken hold. The most dominant jazzman of the 1960s, John Coltrane, frequently used varied meters, and his drummer, Elvin Jones, was a master of polyrhythms. During the free jazz and fusion era, all kinds of various meters were routinely heard, greatly expanding the possibilities of the music. But nowadays in the neoclassicism era, where swinging in its most obvious mode is of primary importance, these gains have largely been forgotten and jazz's rhythmic frontiers closed off. As Bill Kirchner has said, "Jazz is right back to ching-ching-ca-ching."

Brubeck is scarcely the only connection between the coolsters and the free jazz musicians of the 1960s. For instance, the first "pianoless quartet" was not that of Ornette Coleman's classic group but that of Gerry Mulligan. Ornette wanted to be free to create melodic lines without the tyranny of harmonic structure; by eschewing piano, Coleman was freed of the instrument that traditionally guided the soloist through that structure. Mulligan's music was not as free as Ornette's, of course, but he had a similar reason for not using the piano: to give soloists the harmonic room to stretch out and to make possible devices such as counterpoint between the primary instruments (saxophone and trumpet).

Certainly Ornette had to be aware of Mulligan's very famous, and popular, quartet. Coleman spent several years on the West Coast, after all, which was where the Mulligan group was based. And it is simply untrue that Mulligan did not understand the implications inherent in the pianoless quartet. In interviews he often spoke of the freedom it gave each soloist, and of how the form permitted both lead instruments the chance for the interplay and counterpoint that helped make them so popular.

A few years after the breakup of his first quartet, Mulligan put together a sextet that was also pianoless. This group, my own personal favorite of all of Mulligan's combos, was even more adventurous than the quartet, often indulging in group improvisations or pairing off soloists in a manner not very different from many of the improvisational tacks taken by the World Saxophone Quartet, a basically free group that formed in the 1970s, which included some of the most adventurous saxophonists in the jazz scene of the time (and of course had no rhythm section at all). Both groups—the Mulligan sextet and the World Saxophone Quartet—updated the idea of ensemble improvisation that was the core of the earliest jazz. While it was true that the Mulligan sextet did not have nearly the harmonic freedom of the WSQ, nevertheless it created a freewheeling atmosphere that was quite adventurous for that time.

When we think about it, there should not be much mystery about the similarities between the free jazzmen and the coolsters. Both came out of Lester Young, who, as we have seen in a previous chapter, was the first "harmolodic" improviser. In other words, he played pure melody with little concern for creating music with deep harmonic texture. Almost all the cool players also wanted to play pure melody and were profoundly influenced by Young. For instance, Paul Desmond's style has been compared by Gene Lees, quite rightly I believe, to Young's clarinet style, both in terms of sound and ideas. Desmond himself, when asked why he remained with Brubeck for so many years, explained that most bop pianists would not give him the harmonic room to develop his long, lyrical melodic lines; Brubeck knew how to make him sound right even when his connection with the chords of a tune was tenuous at best.

As the next chapter explains, this desire to cut through the thick harmonic jungle of so much modern jazz is what led to the first steps toward free jazz. This was true of modality, originally conceived for jazz by George Russell (and used by him in a piece as early as his "Cubana Be, Cubana Bop" of the late 1940s), which was further explored and advanced by Miles Davis and then taken even farther by John Coltrane. And of course, it was Ornette's goal—his "harmolodic" concept—to "play the music," not the harmonic outline of the music. In other words, to let the harmony fall into place around the melodic line rather than the other way around.

If you continue to doubt the relationship between the cool era and the free jazz of the 1960s (music nobody in their right mind would ever dub cool), consider Lennie Tristano. As already noted, Tristano's music was at least as important to the development of the cool jazz movement as that of the Miles Davis nonet. Tristano taught jazz improvisation as well as playing, composing, and leading jazz groups. Lester Young was so important to his conception that he made all his students memorize Young solos and insisted that they be able to play them by heart on their respective instruments. Young's genius was in the creation of long, lyrical melody lines that often ignored bar lines and which seemed to dance lightly on a tune's harmonic structure. He was certainly not a free jazz player but his singular devotion to melody made him—along with his unprecedented iconoclastic style—both spiritually and technically a forerunner of all the free jazzmen decades later.

But Tristano did seem to understand the ultimate implications of Young's style. In the late 1940s, Tristano recorded two pieces with his working unit, a group that included Lee Konitz, Warne Marsh, and guitarist Billy Bauer, who were completely free. The musicians were allowed to improvise freely, with absolutely no key, no harmonic structure, no regular meter, each player totally on his own. Tristano did not even tell his musicians when or whether to play. The resulting sides are fascinating, but in retrospect really not much more than curiosities. However, musicians knew about them. And as previously stated, Tristano was a powerful influence on the so-called cool jazz musicians, and not just on them. For example, Max Roach was a Tristano enthusiast, as was Charlie Parker. If we do not box in a musician like Tristano, it is clear that his influence is more pervasive than is generally thought.

I am not saying that those two, short, free pieces led directly to the free jazz movement. But I do think that they helped lay the groundwork for the avant garde jazz of a decade later. After all, the jazz world is a small world, and most modern jazz musicians kept abreast of the latest innovations, particularly when they came from someone as respected as Tristano was.

Among them was Jimmy Giuffre, one of the most continually adventurous musicians in all of jazz. His initial style on reeds, and particularly his famous clarinet style, was clearly in the mode we call cool—in other words, more heavily influenced by Lester Young than by Charlie Parker. Giuffre was an important arranger and composer, writing some of the best charts for Woody Herman's Herds of the late 1940s and early 1950s. But Giuffre moved on to explore all manner of jazz creation. Some of his experiments simply did not work, but others produced fascinating music that really deserves to be heard more widely. In this present age, when innovation has almost become a dirty word, Giuffre's adventurous spirit seems more refreshing than ever.

One of Giuffre's experiments that did not work too well is an album called *Tangents in Jazz*. Giuffre assembled a pianoless quartet: his reeds, trumpeter Jack Sheldon, and bass and drums. However, this was not the usual setup of horns with accompanying rhythm section. The drums and bass were part of the front line and never kept time throughout the entire album. If it sounds weird, it was, but as interesting an idea as it was, it just did not work (which is why there was no *Tangents in Jazz Two*). It was the kind of noble failure that any art form needs in order to stay healthy. Giuffre wondered what jazz would sound like if the rhythm section did not keep regular time but rather served a melodic function. He found out: not very good. It had none of the tension and release of jazz at its best, with virtually none of jazz's visceral power to move us. It is a fascinating experiment, but one that just does not work.

That did not stop Giuffre from experimenting, and this time far more successfully. He formed a series of drumless trios, and played a type of jazz that, while unlike virtually any jazz that had ever been created, nevertheless seemed to be evocative of a bucolic vision of earlier times in America, its folk music, country blues, early jazz, long-forgotten songs from childhood, distant trains, and rolling rivers. It was an unusually gentle music, but it was also quite innovative in its conception. Giuffre never got his due, but he has been one of the most original jazz voices of the last forty years or so.

Possibly Giuffre's best groups in this vein had the bizarre instrumentation of Jim Hall's guitar, Bob Brookmeyer's valve trombone, and Giuffre's reeds. Lacking a rhythm section of any sort, the musicians were forced to find new ways to accompany each other and give the music the rhythmic push we call swing. They can be seen playing their music in the classic jazz film about the Newport Jazz Festival, *Jazz on a Summer's Day*.

Later, Giuffre would form a trio with a very different kind of feeling that included pianist Paul Bley and bassist Steve Swallow. The group's music became freer as time went on until it was playing as abstract a form of jazz as has ever been heard. Paul Bley was the leader of the group which was the first version of Ornette Coleman's revolutionary quartet. Much more about that later.

Giuffre had explored free territory early on. He recorded an album called *The Three* with trumpeter/composer/arranger Shorty Rogers, who would gain fame from leading a tentet that played music very obviously influenced by the Davis nonet. The drummer was Shelly Manne, who a few years later would play on one of Ornette Coleman's first records for the Contemporary label (which mainly recorded musicians involved in the so-called West Coast movement). The music was not as free as the brief experiments of the Tristano group in the late 1940s, but it was quite adventurous. What is interesting is that musicians like Rogers and Manne, who are generally thought of as being mainstream players, nevertheless participated in this and several other highly experimental West Coast sessions. And they could turn around and participate in straight-ahead, hard-swinging jazz like that of the Lighthouse All-Stars or Shelly Manne and his Men.

These musicians in particular illuminate the truth about cool jazz, or any jazz movement or body of work: trying to draw tight perimeters around the music of the great jazzmen of any era is a waste of time and an exercise in self-delusion. Cool jazzmen were drawn to jazz precisely because of the limitless freedom of expression that they sensed was allowed in this art form, its openness and encouragement of individual expression. Jazz continued to evolve and prove to be as mercurial as the musicians who created it.

9.

The 1950s, Part Two: Into the Hot

THE LATTER HALF of the 1950s extending to the mid-1960s, is the era in which the music that is so important to the neoclassicists first appeared and reached its greatest heights. It was during the fifties that bebop, which in the 1940s had all the appearances of impetuous youth—prodigious, explosive, unpredictable, at times shrill and overexcited—matured and gained a deeper texture.

The cool movement was an attempt to bring a sense of sobriety and maturity to bop, to filter and restrain its rambunctious spirit and bring forth its inherent lyricism. In many ways it was a "white" movement. It at least seemed to be dominated by whites, and the music often edged closer to European classical music than toward the indigo shades we associate with so-called black music. As we have said before, jazz that leans more in the direction of the music's European roots is just as legitimate as that which leans toward those roots we can trace to Africa. Hard bop was also a movement dedicated to refining bop, but this time through bringing forward elements of black music. These included the darker shades of blues and the heavier, more complex muscular rhythm and the down-home feeling of the black church gospel music that was such an important early inspiration for many jazz musicians.

These elements actually seemed dangerously close to extinction in the cool jazz movement. If the West Coast sound was bop cooled down, this music of the later 1950s once again made jazz "hot." Yet, as with so many issues in jazz, all of these currents are far less cut and dried and far more intricate than they may seem on the surface. For example, vibraphonist Milt Jackson is one of the funkiest musicians in all of jazz whose playing is clearly imbued with the blues. Yet Jackson is one of the founding members of the Modern Jazz Quartet, a group considered by many as being the ultimate cool jazz combo.

Despite these mitigating factors, there is no doubt that cool jazz was at least perceived as a movement by mainly white jazz musicians whose aim was to make bop safe for middle-class white people turned off by the black energy of bebop. Hard bop was certainly a movement of black musicians dedicated to making the music theirs again. When the hard boppers went out of their way to create funky music with tunes that had titles that came directly out of black life—"Cool Struttin'," "The Preacher," "Sonny's Crib," "Back at the Chicken Shack," "Serenade to a Soul Sister"—there is no doubt that this was a conscious attempt to create jazz that was relevant to the lives of African Americans, and to bring jazz "back home."

There is something of a parallel with the beginning of bop here: To a degree bebop was created as a reaction to the watering down of the jazz message also. As I have previously stated, I think cool jazz has gotten a bum rap, not just from Stanley Crouch but from a number of critics who have dismissed cool or West Coast jazz. But it is undeniably true that many East Coast musicians were not happy with the cool jazz movement.

The advent of hard bop was a true indication of the growing mood among African Americans, their insistence on taking pride in their culture and demanding their rightful place as American citizens without giving up their individuality. Jazz, as usual, was a little ahead of the populace in reflecting those ideas. But there is no doubt that hard bop was a movement of great social as well as musical significance.

Musicians playing this music—jazz messengers all, in both upper- and lowercases—were creating within a very particular social environment and place in time. Once again, one cannot separate the music from the times and lives of the musicians who were playing it. The music sounded exactly the way it did because of all these factors, musical, social and cultural. This is one of the reasons why a bedrock pragmatic existentialism is at the heart of the creation of jazz, and why it is one of the most crucial art forms of this century.

Playing the hard bop style outside of the context of this place in time means creating music that has no authenticity. How can it? I have heard some apologists answer that, well, of course Baroque music is still performed, music from hundreds of years ago. Why should jazz be different?

Of course the answer is this: because it *is* different. The real comparison should be with composing, say, Baroque music, because that is what a jazz musician is doing, composing on the spot, in the here and now.

Although the neoclassicists have dismissed the dominant jazz of the early 1950s the cool or West Coast jazz, their attitude toward the dominant jazz style of the latter half of that decade is 180 degrees different; it is the style that the neos have revived and brought back to an artificial life. The neos go beyond merely being influenced by this music. Instead, almost all of their music is wholesale revival of this style. Although Wynton Marsalis himself has moved even more backward in time in order to broaden his music, at heart his music is still hard bop revivalism.

It is interesting that in the 1980s and 1990s there is a revival movement of music from three or four decades in the past, because in the 1950s there was also a revivalist movement of jazz from thirty or forty years before that time. It was the Dixieland jazz revival, an attempt by bands such as the Dukes of Dixieland or the Firehouse Five of young musicians (young compared to the age of the surviving players of the original New Orleans jazz) to play a form of jazz that seemed to have lost its relevance after the Armstrong revolution of the 1920s. The music was much slicker than the original New Orleans jazz and of course the recordings did the music justice. Listening to, say, King Oliver's band of the early 1920s, arguably the greatest of the New Orleans bands, is an experience in patience because of the crude recording techniques.

These bands were very popular, as a matter of fact much more popular than many of the important modern jazz figures of the time. The difference between then and now is that no jazz critic considered this revivalism to be even slightly crucial to jazz history. New Orleans revivalist bands like the Dukes of Dixieland were at best a footnote. After all, everyone understood—or should have understood—that these young, white musicians could capture the surface sheen of New Orleans jazz, but never the nuances or the depth of feeling, nor could they capture that sense of pure spontaneity that was as true for great New Orleans jazz as it was for all jazz since then. The original New Orleans jazzmen, the real ones, lived the music they played, after all. How could some young white guy know what it was like to be black in 1917 or so? Or even what it was like to be a white guy, like Bix Beiderbecke, in 1927? All critics and true fans understood this. And while the Dukes of Dixieland or the Firehouse Five were certainly not doing anything "wrong" in any way, and in fact were capable of being very diverting, nobody who understood the nature of jazz took them very seriously.

I must admit that the neoclassicists' infatuation with late-1950s jazz is very understandable. This was truly a golden age for jazz. Jazz might not have been as popular as it was in the swing era of the 1930s and early 1940s, but creatively the jazz landscape was fertile with brilliant talent, both in terms of exciting young musicians and productive veteran players. And continuing innovation from so many jazzmen made the jazz scene continually vibrant and exciting.

One of the things that made this era so special for jazz was the mix: in addition to the appearance of several great innovators, a number of key jazz musicians from earlier eras were having an "Indian summer" or creative renewal. For example, Duke Ellington often told interviewers that he was "born in 1956," since it was during that year that his career was virtually reborn. The cause of this resurrection was an electrifying appearance at the Newport Jazz Festival in which during a performance of "Diminuendo and Crescendo in Blue" Paul Gonsalves took a fiery twenty-seven-chorus solo that almost sparked a riot. This might have been Ellington's most notorious performance, but it was far from being his most sublime of this period. His creative juices—and those of his colleague Billy Strayhorn—were at least as vital during this period as during any other of his life (a fact that Stanley Crouch, quite rightly, has often pointed out). In addition, during this decade such brilliant players from the swing era as Roy Eldridge, Art Tatum, and Ben Webster recorded some of their greatest music.

But the style that dominated the mainstream of jazz during the latter half of the 1950s was hard bop. I must point out that probably the most important jazz of the latter half of the fifties was jazz that could not be put under any rubric. I am thinking of the seminal music of Charles Mingus, Thelonious Monk, Sonny Rollins, and Miles Davis, among others. As I have said before, the exercise of corralling the creative work of such brilliant musicians into one box or another is self-defeating. But though these were the great innovators of this era, they were also part of the mainstream, and to an extent the music of all of them can be roughly described as hard bop. As I have previously stated, hard bop was to a degree created as a response to the cool jazz movement. I don't believe it was so much the supposed white domination of jazz in the earlier part of the decade that caused the hard bop movement as it was the perception that the music had strayed far from its roots. But once again, nothing, and especially nothing involved with race, is ever so simple in jazz.

For example, the musician often portrayed as the true father of hard bop is, of all people, Miles Davis. Of course, Miles was also supposedly the father of cool jazz. The usual reason for giving Miles credit for this movement is, like *Birth of the Cool*, once again a record. This one, in its original ten-inch LP format, was called *Walkin'*. It included only two tracks, both blues with a group consisting of Miles; the first great bop trombonist, J. J. Johnson; saxophonist Lucky Thompson; bassist Percy Heath; bop drumming pioneer Kenny Clarke; and pianist Horace Silver. It is a classic session, but the only reason it could be considered the "birth of hard bop" is the presence of Horace Silver. Silver's percussive style and funky compositions make him undoubtedly one of the key fathers of hard bop. The music from this session is not really hard bop because of the presence of Clarke. Hard bop drumming was not light and subtle like Clarke's; hard bop drumming was defined first by Art Blakey and then redefined by Philly Joe Jones. In hard bop, the drummer virtually dominated the band, gaining a position in a jazz group that was equal to, and sometimes surpassed, that of any of the front-line instruments.

It is interesting that Silver was "discovered" not by Miles but by Stan Getz, one of the icons of cool. Silver first gained notice through his recordings and appearances with Getz, who was also the first major jazzman to record Silver's tunes. It was when Silver joined forces with the thundering drummer Art Blakey that hard bop was born. They first played together in a group called the Art Blakey Quintet for the sake of a gig at Birdland that was recorded by Blue Note. The trumpeter in this group was Clifford Brown, who would go on to form one of the most important hard bop bands with Max Roach, the true father of hard bop drumming.

Silver and Blakey went on to form a communal band that they would call the Jazz Messengers. I think the significance of this name is obvious. Blakey was a Moslem (though not a Black Muslim), and he viewed this music as a manifesto, a statement of and for the spirit. It was the Messengers who would serve as the model hard bop band. When Silver left to form his own group, their sound would be emulated to the point of oversaturation within a year or two. After Silver left, Blakey took over the leadership, and the band was known as, not surprisingly, Art Blakey and the Jazz Messengers.

If the original Jazz Messengers was the quintessential hard bop group, the one that defined the genre, then it seems obvious that the front line, trumpeter Kenny Dorham and tenor saxophonist Hank Mobley, would be the model hard boppers on their instruments. Yet Dorham's main influence is Miles Davis. The quintessential cool trumpet player, Chet Baker, was also chiefly influenced by Miles. And Mobley's style, which he described accurately as having a "round sound," is just as obviously influenced by Lester Young. It was Young who influenced that crop of cool tenormen who "sounded all alike" to Miles Davis. So maybe the difference between hard bop and cool is not so great after all.

It is Horace Silver who really established the hard bop *sound.* He brought back to modern jazz elements of gospel music and gutbucket blues, which had been lost to jazz since the swing era. The first Messengers album featured a number of his compositions, including such classics of jazz-funk as "The Preacher" and "Doodlin'." Blakey would often play with a heavy back beat in this sort of number, thereby giving the music an earthy feeling of more universal appeal than much modern jazz, with its harmonic and rhythmic complexity. The reverberations of this kind of jazz would be felt for decades to come; certainly the whole era of jazz/funk or jazz/rock fusion of the late 1960s and 1970s is inconceivable without this prior movement.

Silver was a much more inventive composer than he is usually credited as being. His most famous tunes, such as "Song for My Father," "Sister Sadie," and "Señor Blues" are simple, ear-catching jazz/funk. But Silver in his greatest years—the late 1950s—composed and arranged a large variety of fascinating, often quite complex, pieces for his quintet, some of them quite innovative. And as a player he was almost as unique as Thelonious Monk. His piano improvisations were drenched in the blues, played with such percussive force that he almost turned the piano into a drum. But by the early 1960s he began to repeat himself, obviously trying to repeat the success of his most popular tunes.

One of the first musicians to catch on to the implications of Silver's funky music was a pianist named Jimmy Smith. Smith had been trying for years to make the electric organ into an acceptable jazz instrument. The organ had had a checkered past in jazz. While Count Basie and Fats Waller had played some lovely music on the instrument, most other attempts at playing jazz on the organ were thudding disasters. One of the most notorious recording sessions of the 1930s teamed Lester Young and Buck Clayton with an organ player named Glenn Hardman. I am not sure where the producers of this session found Hardman, but it sounds as if it had been at the local skating rink. His playing not only did not swing—by anybody's definition—but its booming presence dominated the subtle interplay of the other musicians on the date like an elephant in a Victorian parlor. Despite the overbearing banality of Hardman's organ, Young and Clayton managed to play some superb solos, but then this was the peak of their careers, and it would have taken a team of wild horses to keep them from playing brilliantly. Nevertheless, Hardman's overbearing organ playing made these sides virtually unlistenable. There had been other attempts at jazz organ by the likes of Wild Bill Davis and Milt Buckner, most of them almost as heavy-handed as the playing of Hardman. But nobody had adapted the complexities of modern jazz to the instrument until Jimmy Smith.

Smith heard in Silver's funky conception a model for the electric organ that would, ironically, recall its place in the black church (especially in such Silver tunes as "The Preacher"), while at the same time enabling it to function successfully as a freewheeling post-bop instrument. Since he was able to play the bass lines with his pedals, his group consisted of himself, a guitarist, and a drummer. Smith was discovered by Blue Note, and he became a sensation. Almost all of his album titles were references to down-home black life, such as *The Sermon, Back at the Chicken Shack*, or *Prayer Meetin'*. This interplay between sacred and profane elements of black culture would reach its height in the pop music of Ray Charles and Aretha Franklin. But it was really heard first in jazz.

Within a few years, Smith was probably the most imitated musician of jazz, with organ trios springing up like mushrooms in clubs throughout almost every urban area in the country. All of them played in the deep-fried, soulful style of Smith, most of them going beyond him in terms of using blues-drenched chords and melodic ideas, as if they were each trying to out-funk the other. Blue Note in particular released organ trio music of Smith and others, continuing long after the clichés of the genre had become almost rote. Frequently horns would be used, especially tenor saxophone. Smith himself led several wonderful jam sessions, which included several musicians, all Blue Note regulars. But these were just slight variations on the basic organ trio—even in the jam sessions, the organ dominated the music, at times overpowering any horn soloist trying to stretch out. But for many African Americans, this music reflected their real lives, on the streets, in the church, in the kitchen and boudoir. Its practitioners made virtually no attempt at innovation; this was, like so much hard bop, meat-and-potatoes music.

It is interesting that there were—at least to my knowledge—absolutely no white organ players, any Smith acolytes, during the height of this style in the late 1950s and 1960s. This music was so wedded to the lives of blacks that a white player of jazz organ seems unimaginable. But in the last few years—surprise, surprise—there have appeared white organ players whose style is grounded in the Jimmy Smith gospel. Joey DeFrancesco is the most famous: By separating the electric organ from its niche deep in African-American social and cultural life, his organ playing seems to ears not familiar with the jazz of the 1950s to be fresh and even innovative. But that is due, once again, to the confusion that is so prevalent in jazz today. This is taking nothing away from DeFrancesco, who has managed to form his own style, like all the better black acolytes of Smith. But the music has far less power here and now, so distant from the cultural atmosphere in which Smith initially developed this style.

Incidentally, in the 1960s, an organist appeared who took the whole organ trio tradition and turned it on its head. His name was Larry Young, and he would be an essential musician in much of the music of the late 1960s and 1970s. Young was as much influenced by Coltrane as he was by Smith, and was without doubt the most adventurous musician who ever attempted to wrangle jazz out of this bull of an instrument. Unfortunately, no one has taken over where Young left off and pushed the organ even further (Young himself died tragically early—in 1978 at the age of thirty-seven). And there can be little hope for such a player to appear in the current state of jazz. Yet Young proved there was a great deal of exploration still to be done of the possibilities of the electric organ in jazz.

In 1955, one of the greatest of all hard bop bands came into being. After Miles Davis, on his own, kicked drugs, he played a brilliant set at the first Newport Jazz Festival. In its wake, he assembled his first classic quintet: Coltrane on tenor; Red Garland, piano; the teenager Paul Chambers, bass; and Philly Joe Jones, drums. Coltrane had not been Miles's first choice; that had been Sonny Rollins, who had joined the Max Roach–Clifford Brown group. What made this Davis group classic hard bop was Jones. His powerful drumming style dominated the group, causing some critics to complain that he was too loud and overbearing. Miles's response supporting his use of Jones revealed some of his deepest feelings about the nature of jazz: "I wouldn't care if he came up on the bandstand in his B.V.D.s with one arm, just as long as he was there. He's got the fire I want. There's nothing more terrible than playing with a dull rhythm section. Jazz has got to have *that thing*. You have to be born with it. If you could buy it, they'd have it at the next Newport Festival."[1] Miles believed that jazz was a great existential adventure. Whether he believed that "hell is other people" I am not sure, but he definitely believed that heaven was a great rhythm section.

Once again, we must separate the truth about Miles's achievements from the myth. Saying that Miles Davis "invented" hard bop, as many have, is, at best, a great exaggeration. The style, as far as it can be really defined, is the product of the imagination of several musicians. But Miles did understand the style, which is why he hired a drummer like Jones.

And more importantly, he realized that this style fitted into the social and cultural currents of the day. Miles always had a remarkable sense of the tenor of the times, and he was constantly on the cusp of change. Miles was of course one of those most responsible for the cool movement of the early 1950s, but he was well aware that it had run its course. And he especially understood the social significance of the new hard bop movement. Being mercurial was a trait that Miles had always enthusiastically cultivated.

Once again Miles put his own stamp on this new style of hard bop and produced music that was as much a personal statement as anything else he had ever done. The idea that Miles Davis invented cool jazz, or hard bop, or any of the later styles, is not only incorrect, it also confuses the nature of Miles's true achievement. It is a product of those who insist on this Parade of Great Men as an explanation for the evolution of jazz. Jazz history is miraculously filled with heroes; the miracle of the consistent growth and innovation of jazz is simply far more complex than that.

Just as Pacific Jazz documented the West Coast jazz movement, Blue Note became the dominant record company for hard bop. The Jazz Messengers and then Art Blakey and the Jazz Messengers produced most of their classic albums for the label. So did Horace Silver and his groups, almost all of which had the now standard hard bop instrumentation of trumpet, tenor, and rhythm. Important hard bop recordings by trumpeters Lee Morgan, Donald Byrd, and Kenny Dorham, and by tenor saxophonists like Hank Mobley, Sonny Rollins, Dexter Gordon (and one classic Coltrane album—probably his first truly great record—the roiling *Blue Train*) were all made by Blue Note. Numerous other hard boppers also recorded for the label.

The story of Blue Note is in itself a fascinating one. It is also of particular significance to this book in light of the current state of jazz, since Blue Note is the label that recorded more of the music emulated by the neoclassicists than any other. Blue Note itself was revived in the last decade, reissuing many of its classic albums, mostly classic hard bop, and recording new music, mostly neoclassicist hard bop. Supposedly the company is "continuing the great Blue Note tradition." But are they? It is ironic that the story of Blue Note illuminates so well what is wrong with this current jazz scene.

The founder of Blue Note was Alfred Lion, a German immigrant who attended the famous first "Spirtuals to Swing" concert of 1938 in Carnegie Hall, shortly after arriving in America. He was particularly stunned by the boogie-woogie piano styles of Albert Ammons and Meade Lux Lewis. He decided that these musicians had to be recorded, and with these early private recordings, Blue Note was founded.

In its earliest years Lion and his partner, another German emigrant named Francis Wolff, mainly recorded traditional jazz. Lion and Wolff were mainly interested in recording black musicians, and this policy would be upheld for decades to come. Their treatment of black musicians was so respectful and generous that Blue Note quickly became a popular label among musicians. During these early years, the owners of Blue Note wrote a kind of credo for their label that exhibited a profound understanding of the nature of jazz: "By virtue of its significance in place, time, and circumstance, [jazz] possesses its own tradition, artistic standards, and audience that keeps it alive. . . . Hot jazz, therefore, is expression and communication, a musical and social manifestation."

The most famous Blue Note recordings of this early period were those of the great New Orleans clarinetist and soprano saxophonist Sidney Bechet. His recording of "Summertime"—a song far outside the traditional repertoire—was a hit and gave Bechet's career a great boost. Blue Note also recorded innovative work by Earl Hines and made one of the first chamber jazz recordings, including the only recording of Charlie Christian playing acoustic guitar.

For outsiders, Lion and Wolff had an amazingly deep understanding of the jazz world, especially considering that they were immigrants. They realized that jazz was a world unto itself, a social structure as well as a cultural one. They also understood that musicians were usually far ahead of fans and critics in their ability to recognize important new players and new directions in the course of the music. By treating musicians with such great respect and common decency, Lion and Wolff were able to become good friends with some musicians who were of great help in their knowledge and understanding of what musicians and new musical concepts were current in the jazz world. Perhaps the most important of these was tenor saxophonist Ike Quebec. Although, partly due to their love of traditional hot jazz, they were at first leery of bop, Quebec convinced them that it was an authentically important development in the music, and he was of great assistance in leading them to some of the most important musicians who were largely being ignored by the major record companies.

Probably Blue Note's most important recordings of the late 1940s and early 1950s were those of Thelonious Monk's first sessions as a leader, in which he introduced many of his greatest compositions. Although at the time Monk was ignored by most fans and laughed at by a number of critics, these sides are now universally considered some of the greatest jazz of the modern period.

But Monk was not the only important musician of this era recorded by Blue Note. They also recorded some of the most incendiary work of Bud Powell, including one brilliant session with a group that included nineteen-year-old Sonny Rollins and bop trumpet genius Fats Navarro. And they recorded Miles Davis in the early 1950s, during a bleak period in Miles's career when he had a major heroin habit and his career was virtually washed up. For many years Miles would cite some of these Blue Note sides as being among his own favorite recordings.

Blue Note treated jazz musicians better than any other record company. It paid them for two days of rehearsal before recording, something unheard of in jazz recording. Because of this extra time, at Blue Note dates musicians were able to devise arrangements of far more intricacy and musical interest than that of most post-bop records of the 1950s, which usually were little more than blowing sessions, a loose series of solos. Prestige was notorious during this period for simply grabbing any jazz musicians they could find and recording them in a supposedly jam session format—which meant that arrangements, and even the tunes themselves, were thrown together in the course of just a few hours. They rarely allowed more than one or two takes, often resulting in less than inspired music making. Prestige, and other jazz labels, often exploited the fact that so many of the jazzmen were junkies and were usually in desperate need of just enough money to score their dope. When Miles was addicted, he would play enough to be paid in cash the money he needed to buy his drugs. If the A&R man wanted more music, he had to hand Miles a little more cash. These sides, and so many created in similar fashion, have been issued and reissued many times in every format from LP to cassette to CD, but Lion and Wolff loved the music and the musicians, and they treated jazzmen like the serious artists they were and are.

Blue Note's commitment to the music even extended to the way it was recorded. By the mid-1950s, working with the great sound engineer Rudy Van Gelder, they established what has been called the Blue Note Sound. Although Van Gelder recorded jazz for several labels, the sound of Blue Note was different, fuller. It had a presence you simply had to hear to understand, a sound that seemed to give extra resonance to whatever music was being recorded. In addition, Wolff was a fine photographer.

His moody photo studies of the various musicians made striking covers that perfectly captured the mood of the jazz world in that era. Jazz fans came to realize that Blue Note records constantly had such high standards that many would buy a Blue Note album even if they had never previously heard of the musician who was the leader. There was a wonderful nexus among Lion and Wolff, the musicians, and the jazz fans, a shared knowledge of what made jazz great that braided them together.

Rarely has a style become as identified with a single record label as hard bop has with Blue Note. The label had virtually a repertory company of musicians, functioning as both sidemen and leaders on various sessions. It was wonderful music, most of it, funky and lyrical, spirited, driving, always intelligent, always moving. If there was little room for innovation, it was made up for by the inventiveness of most of the Blue Note players.

Lion and Wolff's friendship with musicians led them to some remarkable jazz talent. For instance, trumpeter Lee Morgan was still a teenager when he was "discovered" while playing in the brass section of a Dizzy Gillespie big band (although his actual first album was recorded for Savoy). Morgan would go on to record numerous albums for the label, both as leader and as sideman, including a stint in one version of Blakey's Jazz Messengers. In 1963 he would more than pay Lion and Wolff back for their faith in him by recording probably the biggest hit the company ever had, "The Sidewinder." It was an irresistible piece of jazz/funk that reached a large audience that for the most part had never previously heard of Morgan (or ever purchased a Blue Note record).

Blue Note was willing to take all kinds of chances that most record companies never would. Herbie Nichols was a pianist/composer whose music was as idiosyncratic and continually creative as that of Thelonious Monk. But Nichols, like Monk, confused most critics and record producers, and he was usually forced to play with Dixieland bands or other settings that had little to do with his own extraordinary music. Nichols's frustrating life and career is superbly portrayed in A. B. Spellman's *Four Lives in the Bebop Business.* Nichols recorded very sporadically, but his most important music was recorded for Blue Note.

Not every Blue Note album was a classic. For example, Lion seemed to admire a trio called the Three Sounds, which played very predictable piano "soul jazz." And many of the organ albums were less than riveting. But compared to most record companies, their batting average was extraordinary.

However, by the early 1960s, the Blue Note sound became increasingly predictable: trumpet, tenor, and rhythm, with occasional variations. The alternative was the organ albums, which were mostly organ trios played by the prolific Jimmy Smith or by one of the legion of Smith-derived jazz organists.

By this time, critics began to yawn with the appearance of a new Messengers or Hank Mobley Blue Note. After "The Sidewinder" was a hit, Blue Note albums became even more predictable. Every record would feature at least one funk tune, most of them variations on the Morgan hit. In addition, even the personnel of most albums became increasingly predictable. One example: The drummer on most sessions in the 1960s was Billy Higgins, mainly because of his ability to make jazz/funk tunes like "The Sidewinder" really swing. Higgins was and is a great drummer, but using him on so many dates gave the albums a similar texture, and, more importantly, did not challenge the soloist. Blue Note had earned its initial reputation by taking chances, by challenging jazz musicians by putting them in unusual settings. But by the early 1960s the Blue Note sound had become ossified—and that is precisely the music that is being revived today by the neoclassicists. And of course Blue Note was not the only jazz label that released hard bop albums. Prestige, Riverside, Savoy, Argo, as well as a number of other small labels and to a lesser extent the major labels (Columbia, RCA) all released hundreds of hard bop jazz in the latter half of the 1950s and the early 1960s.

I remember that when I first got interested in jazz as a kid in the sixties, most reviews of Blue Note hard bop albums and of those on other labels, many now considered classics, were met with indifference by most critics. This style had played itself out within about five years. Many in the jazz world were looking for innovative music that would once again enliven the scene. Of course, they got it, with maybe a little more innovation than many of them wanted. One of the main reasons that Ornette Coleman and the early free jazz movement was embraced so quickly by many in the jazz world was because hard bop had run its course and there was a real hunger for fresh musical thinking. And of course another key reason was that America itself was beginning to go through major changes, and once again jazz was reflecting the onset of all that change.

THE HARD BOP meat-and-potatoes jazz that was recorded so brilliantly by Blue Note was of course not the only modern jazz being created in the late 1950s. There were several key innovators creating some of the most important jazz that would ever be heard, and some of the best. An adequate perusal of the magnificent music of Charles Mingus or Thelonious Monk or Clifford Brown or George Russell really lies outside the parameters of this book. But their innovations, and their ability to create completely idiosyncratic music that sounded like nobody else's, is in itself an indictment of this present generation of jazz musicians. Many of the neoclassicists constantly drop the names of these musicians. Understanding their music, its harmonies or melodic ideas, is fine. But they don't seem to get the main lesson to be learned from them: that to create jazz that is truly authentic, the music you make must be an expression from and for yourself and the times in which you live; that you must make music with your own *sound*, one different from anybody else's.

As I have stated, there is not enough room in this study to discuss adequately all the important music created by all the important musicians during the 1950s. But there is one musician I particularly want to discuss at length because I believe that his life and career illuminates, at least as much as any other jazzman, what it means to be a jazz musician—and what is so lacking among this current generation. His name is Sonny Rollins.

Rollins is a tenor saxophonist who first reached an apex of fame while still in his early twenties. We have already seen him as a teenager recording with Bud Powell and Fats Navarro in 1949. Even then he had a recognizable sound and style. Rollins grew up in an area of Harlem that, for whatever reason, produced a number of second-generation boppers, including Jackie McLean. The teenagers used to hang out with Bud Powell, who would teach them the latest bop tunes being played on Fifty-second Street. It was an exciting time to be a jazz musician, but also a very dangerous time. Most of these young jazz musicians got drawn into the spiral of heroin addiction, including both Rollins and McLean.

Nevertheless, Rollins worked hard to develop his protean style, playing with most of the important modernists of the period. However, there were two key associations for Rollins in the first half of the 1950s, one with Miles Davis, the other with Thelonious Monk.

Through Miles, Rollins made his first recording under his own name in 1951. Miles himself was working only sporadically, but when he did work he often hired Rollins. One early Miles session with Rollins, released as *Diggin'*, is a classic of 1950s bop in which Jackie McLean makes his debut on record. In 1953, Miles led a notorious session in which both Rollins and Charlie Parker, using his favorite nom de plume (or rather, nom de horn), Charlie Chan, played tenor saxophone. The producer, Ira Gitler, bought a quart of gin to be shared by all the musicians in the session. But Bird took the bottle and drained the whole thing himself and then nodded out. Miles had it out with Parker, one more fracas in their intensely complex relationship, with all its elements of father/son, love/hate, guru/student, and con man/mark (when Parker died two years later in 1955, Miles told Max Roach, "He died before we could get even, Max"). Rollins lionized Parker, looked to him for guidance as both a musician and as a man. Presumably, that is one of the main reasons Rollins got sucked into drug addiction. Parker felt genuine guilt over this effect he had on so many young jazzmen, and he told Rollins what he told so many others: "Do what I say, not as I do."

From playing with Monk, Rollins developed the key to his style. Monk always insisted to those who played with him that they "use the melody" of a tune, not just the chord changes. Since bop, it had become hip simply to ignore a tune's melody and create a solo based completely on the chord changes. But Monk always used parts of the melody itself in his solos, giving performances a kind of structural unity not heard in much modern jazz. Critics like Gunther Schuller would dub this "thematic improvising," and Rollins became a master at it.

In Rollins's own phrase, he recorded "promiscuously" during the first half of the 1950s, including classic sessions with Miles, Monk, the important but underappreciated pianist/composer Elmo Hope, and even with the Modern Jazz Quartet (with whom he recorded again in 1957). Rollins crystalized the basic elements of his style during these years, the powerful tone, sometimes gruff and other times cello-like, the roiling rhythmic conception, the use of vocalized effects, the subtle humor. All of this experience paid off. By the mid-1950s, most modern jazz fans assumed that he was the most important tenorman of his generation.

However, during this period Rollins struggled with his drug addiction and at one point withdrew from the jazz scene in order to kick his habit. He worked as a common laborer in order to stay away from the temptations of the jazz scene and also to build up his body. Rollins would continue to withdraw a number of times from his life as a musician for a variety of reasons; a deeply introspective man, he seemed to wrestle continually with the whole idea of being a jazzman and what that entailed. Miles Davis originally wanted Rollins to be the saxophonist in the quintet he formed in 1955. But since Rollins was on sabbatical, Davis used John Coltrane and, of course, the rest is jazz history. Rollins joined another classic 1950s hard bop group when he did come back to the jazz scene, the Max Roach–Clifford Brown quintet. Tragically, Brown and the group's pianist, Richie Powell (Bud's brother), were killed in a car accident in 1956. Brown had been the most exciting jazz trumpeter since Fats Navarro, who was one of his main influences. Ironically, he lived a clean life, staying away from drugs, which were epidemic in the jazz scene during this era.

In 1956, at the age of twenty-six, Rollins recorded perhaps his greatest album, *Saxophone Colossus*. The entire record is a tour de force, but one tune in particular is considered by several critics to be his masterpiece—"Blue Seven." Perhaps that is because it is such a fine illustration of how a brilliant jazzman can take the simplest of materials and out of them create a transcendent musical statement. The melody is a basic blues with a rather ambivalent harmonic structure. Rollins creates his solo almost completely out of this simple melody itself—rather than just using its chord changes—playing variations on variations but never completely letting go of the melody itself. It is a perfect introduction to Rollins's art, a superb demonstration of the way his musical genius functioned. Gunther Schuller, the composer and writer, wrote a detailed analysis of Rollins's solo that was published in one of the jazz magazines. When Rollins read it, he was astonished at the detail and complexity of Schuller's analysis—he had not consciously been aware of many of the things that Schuller described in his piece. It so confused Rollins that he had to stop playing for a while. This does not mean that Rollins is a kind of native genius, unaware of the sophistication of his music. As Wynton Marsalis has pointed out about Louis Armstrong, if this were true he never would have been able to create music along these lines repeatedly, which Rollins has done. He just thinks of his music in a more intuitive, pragmatic, and visceral fashion than the way it was described in Schuller's piece. Schuller pointed out that it would have taken many hours, if not days, to work out a piece of music as brilliantly conceived as Rollins's "Blue Seven" improvisation. Rollins, of course, improvised it on the spot. The musical invention of jazz musicians comes equally from both the right and the left sides of the brain, which is why an analysis like Schuller's might seem so confusing. For Rollins, playing music is an act that is done with one's entire being, and the choices he makes in creating jazz mean putting everything on the line. And it is affected by the mise-en-scène of the moment in which it is created. More even than Miles Davis, Sonny Rollins is the ultimate jazz existentialist.

As late in his career as the 1960s, after he had made a number of classic albums and won many jazz polls, Rollins would tell an interviewer that he was not sure if he wanted to devote his life to music or not. I think the reason Sonny could express such doubt came from his basic attitude toward the creation of jazz. For Rollins, music is an act of constant becoming. His style has changed so frequently over the years that it seems truer to his spirit to say that it is a style that is constantly in a state of change while remaining unquestionably his own, unlike anybody else's. Rollins understood that commitment to jazz was as much a commitment to a way of living and looking at life as is becoming a priest or a monk.

When I was first getting interested in jazz, I remember asking my older brother about Sonny Rollins, whom I had often seen mentioned in the first few issues of *Down Beat* I had read. "He's not supposed to be too good," my brother told me. And for the first few years I took that as gospel and ignored Rollins. But when I finally did hear him, on the radio, I liked him immediately. Yet I have run into many casual jazz fans who have a negative attitude toward Rollins. I think most of this comes from the fact that, for one of the greatest of all jazz musicians, he has relatively few recordings that genuinely reflect his genius in all its dimensions. Anyone who has seen Rollins on a good night can testify to what an overwhelmingly inventive and exciting musician he can be. Although he has recorded several fine albums, most of them pale next to the best of his live performances. This gap between record and live performance is far greater for him than it is for any other jazz musician I can think of.

For Rollins, jazz, authentic jazz, can only be created in live performance. Only then, in front of an audience, where there are no nets, no retakes, where mistakes cannot be erased or takes spliced together, is a jazz musician in his or her true element. The recording studio does not offer such a milieu. I have long suspected that even when he is recorded live, Rollins does not play as well as when there is nobody recording him (at least to his knowledge—some exciting bootlegs of Rollins performances have emerged). I believe that to Rollins, the phrase *recorded jazz* is an oxymoron: Jazz can only be played once and heard once. That is the jazz experience.

I have twice seen Rollins play solo concerts, without any accompaniment at all. The first time, at the Whitney Museum in New York, he was absolutely brilliant, playing for an entire hour of unceasing invention, keeping his audience hanging on every note. Rollins is one of the wittiest of all jazz musicians. Most jazz musicians I have known have a great sense of humor, but nobody expresses it in his or her music better than Rollins. Much of Rollins's humor can be heard in his use of "quotes" from other tunes, which he drops into the middle of a solo. In the middle of a totally abstract section he will bring us back to earth by quoting from some famous tune—which can range from a Thelonious Monk piece to "Stars and Stripes Forever"—twisting the melody around, turning it on its head, until it is no longer recognizable. Or he quotes one phrase from a tune and then links it to another phrase from another, quite different tune, turning both tunes inside out with a sense of irony and wit that at times reminds one of the work of Vladimir Nabokov. Rollins is a master of musical legerdemain, except one never feels fooled but, rather, elevated. He did this sort of thing throughout his Whitney performance, but always using it to create a musical statement, not just as cleverness for its own sake. Needless to say, the audience was enthralled during his performance, a true tour de force.

Unlike the Whitney concert, the second solo concert, which was performed at the Museum of Modern Art, was recorded and—no surprise—it was not nearly the equal of the Whitney performance. Rollins kept on trying to get into sync, but what came out of his horn was not much more than exercises rather than real music. The joyful gleam in Rollins's eyes during the Whitney concert was not there; rather, he was quite obviously frustrated. He could have his bad nights even when nobody is recording him. But I also believe that on this night the fact that he was being recorded had a great deal to do with Sonny's less than stellar performance. After all, playing solo was the ultimate jazz existentialist experience—there is nobody up there but yourself and certainly no nets at all. For Sonny Rollins recording such a performance somehow violated the basic logic of the jazz aesthetic.

For Rollins, and all great jazz musicians, the music is the man and the man the music. I once attended a concert of his in New York's Town Hall where his appearance marked his return to the scene after another of his sabbaticals from the jazz scene (the rumor was that this time he had gone to India in order to study yoga). After two long, mediocre opening acts, Rollins appeared with the New York Bass Choir—about a dozen bassists as well as piano and drums. As they played various tunes arco, Rollins strolled among them improvising, even at various points walking off through a door backstage, where we could faintly hear him still blowing, and then strolling back onstage, continuing his improvising without letup. Unfortunately, this only lasted about half an hour before the curtains came down in front of a disappointed audience. Immediately there was a clamor for more Rollins, and only after this kept up for several moments did Sonny come back onstage. He explained that the music we had heard was all that had been written and there was simply nothing else to play. The crowd wouldn't hear of it. Sonny put his horn in his mouth and played for a minute or so, after which he asked, "Okay, is that enough" "Nooo," replied the crowd. At this point Sonny began to pace the stage, trying to explain the problem. And this is what I found most fascinating: He would begin a sentence and then finish it by playing on his horn. He did this for several minutes; obviously, his horn was almost an appendage, at least as important for communicating his distress as his voice. This is how central his music is to his life. (Eventually he played an a cappella version of "St. Thomas" and asked if that was finally enough. The crowd gave in at last.)

Rollins, at least as much as most jazz musicians, is aware that improvising on the most exalted level is dependent on factors that affect him in the moment, what might be called jazz's mise-en-scène. A Rollins fan told me the following story, which even if not true nevertheless is indicative of the importance of mise-en-scène in jazz—or at least to the great jazz existentialists like Sonny Rollins. At one time Rollins had a terrible trumpet player in his band, really awful. Someone asked a member of the band close to the saxophonist why Rollins used the lousy trumpeter. "Listening to this guy makes Sonny angry," said the sideman, "and he plays better when he's mad." Things like this are never taught in music school.

In person, Rollins seems to be constantly debating in his mind what it meant to be a jazz musician. Was he a serious musician? Was he just playing the role of a serious musician? Was he simply an entertainer? Rollins has never held together his own group for very long. He has constantly experimented with different sidemen, different instrumentation. As we have already seen, he has even played on several sessions completely solo, without any accompaniment, and has often through sheer bravura pulled it off. But apparently that is not the answer to his search either, because he usually goes back to playing with a group, even if it is just bass and drums.

Rollins has constantly struggled with the question of whether he should please his audience or satisfy his own musical curiosity (this last question is one many jazz musicians have had to deal with, perhaps most famously John Coltrane). He told one writer that, in order to be more of a real "entertainer," he was thinking of changing outfits for each tune so as to be attired in a fashion that reflected the nature of the song. Partly due to his concern for his audience, Rollins has always used a far wider range of pop tunes than most jazz musicians. He once stated that he had a liking for Al Jolson tunes (bringing to mind an album with the title *Rollins Plays Jolson*), and he has recorded several songs associated with Jolson. He has also recorded "There's No Business Like Show Business," "The Most Beautiful Girl in the World," and "I'm an Old Cowhand." Besides offering his audiences variety, using out-of-the-way songs like these is a challenge to Sonny as an improviser, particularly since "using the melody"—thematic development—is such a key aspect of his style. By using unfamiliar tunes, Sonny puts himself—and his sidemen—in the position of having to think in fresh and inventive terms and leaves no room for falling back on just "running the changes" and favorite clichés.

When Rollins was touring the West Coast with Max Roach's group in 1957, he recorded two albums for Contemporary, a California-based label that released mainly West Coast jazz records. Although Rollins was considered the quintessential hard bop tenorman, he had no problem playing with the West Coast jazzmen, again proving how wrongheaded are those who polarize jazz racially or geographically. One of these albums, *Way Out West*, is one of Rollins's greatest accomplishments. Recorded late at night, after a club appearance, the group is a trio. It included the great bassist Ray Brown and the ubiquitous West Coast drummer Shelly Manne. Rollins chose tunes with a Western theme—"I'm an Old Cowhand," "Wagon Wheels"—and in this most basic of settings, loosened by the time of night and the fact that he had already been playing for hours, Rollins plays with such prodigious power and sheer muscularity he seems to seize the music and never let go. Rollins even got to explore, on a limited basis, his idea of dressing in keeping with the nature of his songs. On the cover of *Way Out West*—a classic in itself—he is dressed as a gunslinger, with a saxophone in place of a gun. Rollins was kind of like a gunslinger in that, in the ever-macho jazz world, his reputation was that of the toughest tenorman on the scene.

Make no mistake, Rollins was fully aware of the profound significance of his music and the underlying reasons for his fierce commitment to it. Shortly after *Way Out West*, Rollins recorded a piece named *The Freedom Suite* that covered one side of an LP. Rollins made clear in the notes he prepared for the album (but which did not appear in the original edition of the record) that his concern was with the concept of freedom on a number of levels: musically, in terms of the struggle of black people in America, and beyond that, or along with that, the ultimate meaning of freedom in terms of being human. There is nothing outwardly didactic about Rollins's *Freedom Suite* (as there would be with Max Roach's *Freedom Now Suite* a few years later), but in the work's intensity and its ceaseless momentum forward, Rollins perfectly captured the struggle for freedom on every level, making us aware that they are all intertwined.

Heard now, it is still a wonderful piece of music. But when it appeared it had a special resonance that reflected a time of growing restlessness among African Americans in their continuing struggle for freedom. Not that this struggle is over; it is just different now. This 1958 piece made it clear that nobody was more aware of his place in time than Sonny Rollins.

As a matter of fact, Rollins was, and still is, a lord and master of time, a rhythmic prestidigitator. He does things with rhythm that defy the ear's logic. Even at the fastest tempos, of which Rollins is one of the few masters, he has the ability to seemingly stop the flow of time, or twist it into a Möbius strip. By treating each note as a separate sound, and by being able to give each note a different time value, he creates music that transcends all our expectations and leaves us breathless with his magic, and that shows us that even the chains of the flow of time can be broken if one is truly free.

Shortly after recording his *Freedom Suite*, Rollins would go into another of his sabbaticals. This time—in the late 1950s—it was at least partly because of the growing importance of his friend John Coltrane. Coltrane was delving into musical areas on the tenor saxophone that were unprecedented. And there was much silly talk pitting Rollins against Coltrane in competitive terms, despite the fact that the men were close friends and greatly admired each other.

When Rollins returned, his new group was a quartet that featured Jim Hall, the great West Coast guitarist. Some bigots on both sides of the racial divide were shocked at this selection, but Rollins hired Hall because Hall was one of the subtlest players in jazz, and also because Sonny had never before used a guitar instead of a piano. The group lasted longer than most Rollins combos, But Rollins, like Coltrane, was increasingly fascinated by the music of Ornette Coleman and the possibilities of the new free jazz movement. Rollins had always been, in his own way, a free jazzman, one who set no limits on the perimeters of his musical conception. But now, working with a group consisting mainly of Coleman sidemen (including the trumpeter Don Cherry) his playing zoomed into the outer limits of imagination. This was truly free jazz in every sense of the phrase: you never could guess what would come out of Rollins's horn next. When he recorded an album with his old idol, Coleman Hawkins, one of his primary influences, most assumed that Rollins would play it straight with the veteran. But his playing on this album, *Sonny Meets Hawk*, is some of the most bizarre and weirdly inventive jazz ever heard. Hawkins even follows suit himself, and he too seems at times to be floating toward the stratosphere. Only when a musician is as committed to genuine spontaneity as Rollins is could music like this be possible. Never in a hundred blue moons can anyone imagine Branford Marsalis or Joshua Redman playing music on this level of wild imagination.

Rollins came back to earth, but in the early 1970s he signed with Fantasy Records, and for a while he attempted to adapt his style to fusion, which simply did not work. He produced album after album of music that was not even close to reflecting his genius. However, on a good night he could be as brilliant as ever. Or he could be quite the contrary. I once went to see him play at his opening night at Keystone Korner, a now defunct jazz club in San Francisco. He was magnificent, playing lengthy solos bursting with ideas and humor, and he was obviously enjoying himself, his eyes gleaming with pleasure at his own invention. I told a friend of mine who had no use for Rollins (mainly because he had never heard him in person), and I insisted that he catch Rollins a few nights later. On this night, much to my shock and chagrin, Rollins was awful. More than awful, horrible. He would pick up his horn and try to get into the music but then shake his head and sit down on a stool, letting his accompanying trio play most of the music. Whenever he did attempt to stretch out, it just didn't happen; after a few bars he would run straight into a mental brick wall. He was perfectly sober (Sonny has been for many years a bodybuilder and near fanatical about his health at least partially as a way of making up for his years of addiction in the 1950s); he just could not get inside the music that night. It simply was not happening.

Naturally, my friend never trusted me again when I recommended a musician (he at least got a good laugh—at my expense—out of the experience), and this was quite embarrassing. But it was also revealing. For a dyed-in-the-wool improviser like Rollins, there have to be almost as many bad nights as there are great nights, and probably most nights are something in between. To be truly spontaneous, not to have any idea what you are going to play until the moment you are actually standing on a stage before an audience, is the equivalent of a dangerous trapeze act without the net. To as pure a musical existentialist as Sonny Rollins, anything else is simply not authentic jazz. True, most neo tenormen never have a night as bad as that last night I caught Rollins. But they also never know the glory of that opening night, where Rollins's music was so deliriously exhilarating that even if jazz had been responsible for nothing else but that night of music, it would have justified its existence, at least for me.

Rollins has played a few concerts in which he has had neos as special guests, including Roy Hargrove, Joshua Redman, and James Carter. This is not surprising; these musicians rightfully worship Rollins, and these days playing or recording with the more prominent neos is supposedly the way for veterans to attract an audience. It is similar to the 1970s when Rollins flirted with fusion, as did many important jazzmen, because that was supposedly the way at that time to reach a broader group of listeners, and it was the dominant style of the day. But Sonny now, as he has in every previous era, has transcended any category, and has constantly reminded us of what it means to be a jazz musician.

At the age of sixty-seven, although he does not play nearly as many gigs as he used to, Rollins is still capable of playing magnificently. Living in a bucolic area of upper New York State, he spends much of his time walking through the woods playing his sax, free as a bird. "Music," Rollins once said, "is an open sky." When we listen to Sonny Rollins at his best, the truth of that statement is driven into our minds and hearts—that music, and jazz in particular, is without limits, that it can embrace the entirety of our human experience and enrich our lives with the beauty of the moment, the here and now. His music is really as much retort as anyone needs to the idea that jazz is limited by anything, any tradition or racial and ethnic consideration. It is the music whose true grist is sweet freedom. With its infinite possibilities and magical manipulation of time, Rollins's music is as profoundly spiritual as any music I have ever heard.

Most of the neoclassicist tenormen, of whom there are quite a few, admire Sonny Rollins and have been greatly influenced by him. I am sure they have memorized his classic solos and they can emulate his tone. They can utilize many aspects of his style, but what they can't do is understand or duplicate the inner processes or the particular sensibility that has animated his genius. That is because it developed straight out of his life and the times in which he lived. It seems a simple lesson, but these days, at least among jazzmen, it seems one that is largely being ignored.

AS SHOULD BE clear, Sonny Rollins transcends the category of hard bop, just as Stan Getz or Art Pepper transcend cool jazz. Actually, most of the prominent musicians of this decade, as in previous decades, transcend whatever category we try to fit them into. Unlike today's jazzmen, they played music as a reflection of their lives, not to fit into the closed box of a genre.

By the end of the 1950s, there was change in the air. Hard bop seemed increasingly predictable and ossified, although still capable of producing brilliant albums in this genre. At the end of the 1950s and in the early 1960s, Hank Mobley for one produced a series of classic albums that defined the genre and which were particularly lyrical and emotionally gripping musical statements. In addition, around this time Blakey put together probably the greatest version of the Messengers: the band included tenorman Wayne Shorter, Lee Morgan, and pianist/composer Bobby Timmons. Yet even this great band could not hold back the winds of change.

To the neoclassicists, jazz history ends about here. They admire Ornette Coleman's early work, and they have tried to emulate the Miles Davis quintet of the mid-1960s (much more about that in the next chapter) and the Coltrane Quartet of the early 1960s, but for them jazz history closed down until the advent of Wynton Marsalis. The free jazz movement, according to the neoclassicist view of jazz history, only produced chaos and cacophony.

Or did it? Perhaps we should take a closer look at that contention.

10.

Free at Last

ONE OF THE most stirring moments in American life during this century was in August of 1963, when Martin Luther King, Jr., at the end of his magnificent "I Have a Dream" speech at the Washington civil rights rally, exclaimed the lines from an old black spiritual "Free at last, free at last, thank God Almighty, we are free at last." He was referring specifically, of course, to the struggle of African Americans for their rights as citizens of this country. But the concept of freedom was at the heart of almost all of the social and cultural upheaval of the 1960s. It was in the songs and the rhetoric of the period, and in the pursuit of Ultimate Freedom, lives were uprooted and even new communities created.

When Martin Luther King, Jr., cried out that he was "free at last," he was, sadly, referring to his dream of the future, not the present. But even now, over thirty years later, African Americans are still struggling for true freedom, which cannot be realized as long as racism is so endemic in American society. During his presidency, Ronald Reagan gave a speech extolling the greatness of America in which he made the statement that in this country, unlike other places in the world, everybody had an ancestor who had *chosen* at some point to come to the United States. It was bad enough that he overlooked those who had ancestors brought over here against their will in chains, but he also left out those who were here long before there even was a U.S.A. and who certainly did not choose to come here; rather, America came to them, right on top of their heads.

With such statements coming from the president, do we have to wonder if racism is still rampant in this country?

The nature of freedom has been a key concept to African Americans since they were first chained inside those boats that brought them from Africa to the New World. They have always been painfully aware of the irony that they were first slaves and then "second-class citizens" denied basic rights by dint of their skin color in a country whose founding principle was that of individual freedom. It was in the 1960s that the cruelty of this irony came to a head.

The sixties was the decade in which I grew up, and I was an eyewitness, and often a participant, in much of the tumult of that era. It was also the decade in which I first started to follow jazz, and I can vividly remember the fierce controversy that convulsed the jazz world during this period. At its heart were the limits of freedom—that is, whether there were any. And the social connotations of this controversy were hard to miss.

The meaning of freedom has been at the center of the creation of jazz since its earliest days. New Orleans ensemble jazz was created by black people forced into a ghetto. As we have seen, when Louis Armstrong pioneered the jazz solo, it was clearly a reflection of the new kind of personal freedom many African Americans felt, or at least hoped for, when they had moved north. When one listens to Armstrong's Hot Five and Seven solos, that celebration of freedom is unmistakable. One thing that Armstrong, and those who followed after him, discovered was that playing jazz elevated them to a plateau of freedom that they could not enjoy in American society itself.

Although the term *free jazz* refers to a specific musical movement, it is—once again—impossible to separate the music, from its place in time and the lives of the musicians during that time. Even the intense arguments of critics, fans, and musicians surrounding the free jazz movement all had a social subtext that was undeniable.

The counterculture, the antiwar movement, even to an extent the pop music of the period, were all at least indirectly born as a reaction to the continuing battle of African Americans against an oppressive society. In fighting for freedom, black people were engaged in a struggle that at least seemed to give their lives a profound meaningfulness that many young white middle-class people found lacking in their own lives.

The baby boomers, of whom I am one, were given everything by their parents, most of whom had seen real struggle in the Depression and then the Second World War. We may have been spoiled with material comfort and a virtually guaranteed rosy future, yet many of us felt empty. In their struggle for justice, African Americans led lives of deep moral and spiritual commitment, lives that *mattered.*

In the 1960s, there were growing numbers of blacks who began to wonder if they really wanted to be integrated into an American society that could have tolerated bigotry for so long and which no longer seemed to have much moral or spiritual direction. As James Baldwin put it, did blacks really want to "integrate into a burning house"? Was being a "solid American citizen" truly what Martin Luther King, Jr., meant by "free at last"?

The counterculture of the 1960s stemmed directly out of the black civil rights movement. When blacks began insisting that they be responsible for their own struggle, whites involved in the movement, either as actual participants or as spectators on the sidelines, began to wonder about their own lives. Was middle-class American life what they wanted? Was it truly free? When they began to drop out, it was in the cause of freedom. Letting your hair grow long and growing a beard and mustache and wearing eccentric clothing was a way of instantly putting yourself outside "straight" American society and, to some degree, knowing what it was like to be despised simply because of your appearance. It was an artificial way to create a struggle against the most basic oppression of the street that blacks had been suffering for years; obviously, at any point you could get a haircut and shave, but African Americans could not escape from their skin. Nevertheless, during this period many alienated young white people committed themselves to living outside the American mainstream in an attempt to find genuine freedom.

The psychedelic gurus of the period pushed the idea that you should "free your mind," escape from the strictures of socialization that keep you from being who you truly are and keep you emotionally and spiritually imprisoned. Freedom seemed to become a more popular subject for many of the songs of the era than romantic love: The Who exclaimed, "I'm Free"; Janis Joplin sang, "Freedom is just another word for nothing left to lose"; Hendrix extolled the joy of being "Stone Free"; and one of the most famous anthems of the era was Lynyrd Skynyrd's "Free Bird." John Lennon sang on the last Beatles album, "One thing I can tell you is you got to be free." A song like Bob Dylan's "Maggie's Farm" was implicitly about freedom; when Dylan sings that he's not "gonna work on Maggie's Farm no more," it is clear that by "Maggie's Farm" he means mainstream America; he's dropping out, freeing himself from the restrictions and absurdity of straight American life.

But for jazz, the idea of freedom was explored in a far bolder fashion than that of rock or pop, which still retained traditional musical structures. The free jazz movement was a revolution against every basic element in the creation of music. Rock might have shaken its fist at the tyranny of the "establishment," but free jazz intended to blow it to bits.

According to the neoclassicists, the decade of the 1960s was, to a large degree, a black hole in jazz history. The free jazz movement, which dominated the jazz scene of the sixties, from their view, was one of pretentious, self-indulgent cacophony that turned off many jazz fans and was really just a self-indulgent musical reflection of the black nationalism of this period.

However, there are certain musicians and groups that are essential influences on the neos. For instance, they admire Coltrane's music of the early part of the sixties, and Ornette Coleman's initial "swinging" music, too. Most important to the neos is the Miles Davis quintet of this period, the classic group that included saxophonist Wayne Shorter, pianist Herbie Hancock, bassist Ron Carter, and prodigal drummer whiz Tony Williams. This is the group that Wynton Marsalis at least attempted to emulate with the first groups he led. It is true they were a magnificent group, one of the greatest in jazz history. But, one cannot embrace the music of Coltrane's quartet (that is, his pre-*Ascension* music) or Miles's 1960s quintet without understanding their place in the context of the jazz scene of the sixties, the era of free jazz.

That the most profound music produced by African Americans—jazz—has a history that many have interpreted as one of increasing musical freedom should be no surprise. However, the truth is somewhat more complicated than that. For example, was the advent of bebop a step toward greater freedom? Well, yes, in some ways, but the harmonic complexity of bop, it can be argued, made it harder to improvise freely through the intricate density of chords.

Arguments about whether European harmony is more or less "free" than, say, modes are not as important, I think, as the philosophical, human notion of freedom and its place in the evolution of jazz. Because if one could say there is one subject that lies at the heart of the making of jazz, it is freedom, true human freedom. As I previously stated, the jazz bandstand has often been the one place where African Americans can be genuinely free in this country, can define themselves and express their deepest emotions and ideas completely on their own terms. Of course the same is true for musicians of whatever race. But for obvious reasons, this freedom of expression has special meaningfulness for African Americans.

So naturally the whole idea of freedom is central to the creation of jazz. In the 1960s, there was a testing of the outer limits of that freedom. It was a remarkable time, one from which we can learn quite a bit about both jazz and some of the most profound truths of our lives.

AT THE END of the 1950s, jazzmen were looking for greater freedom to develop melodic ideas rather than explore harmonic complexity, which limited melodic invention. Some musicians were thinking beyond this to the wholesale questioning of the very idea of tonality. We have already seen in the section on cool jazz the attempts by Lennie Tristano, Jimmy Giuffre, and others in singular experiments with free improvisation. The problem with those experiments is that they were nothing more than fascinating minor musical adventures; they did not create music born out of the musicians' hearts and souls, as would certainly be the case with the free jazz of the 1960s.

As the 1950s wore on, an increasing number of jazz musicians, acting almost as prophets of the coming free jazz era, began exploring this direction. The young Cecil Taylor is among the most important of these. Conservatory trained, Taylor experimented with using some of the techniques of modern classical composers with such jazz influences as Dave Brubeck and Horace Silver. By the 1960s, Taylor developed a style that defined the term *energy music*: He didn't "play" the piano, he exploded on it, creating dense atonal outpourings of sound expressed with a febrile intensity.

Charles Mingus had written pieces that were atonal and others that included free-for-alls of caterwauling saxophonists not unlike some of the most intense music of the free jazz period of the 1960s. In 1960 Mingus would form a pianoless quartet featuring Eric Dolphy, one of the first reedmen to be influenced by Ornette Coleman, and the often daring trumpeter Ted Curson. While far more conservative than Coleman's group, the Mingus quartet nevertheless pointed toward a new direction for jazz. Mingus's classic 1963 big band album *The Black Saint and the Sinner Lady* was not free in the formal sense, but in its ferocity, emotional anarchy, and desperately intense lyricism, it was very close to free jazz, at least in spirit.

As usual, Miles Davis was attuned to this growing movement among musicians, and in a 1958 interview with Nat Hentoff he expressed it this way: "I think a movement in jazz is beginning away from the conventional string of chords, and a return to emphasis on melodic rather than harmonic variation. There will be fewer chords but infinite possibilities as to what to do with them. Classical composers—some of them—have been writing this way for years, but jazz musicians seldom have."

The Monk admonition to Sonny Rollins and others to "use the melody" was perhaps the first stirring toward a greater emphasis on melodic rather than harmonic invention. But Miles was undoubtedly speaking of ideas he had gleaned from composer/arranger/jazz theorist George Russell. Since the late 1940s, Russell had been working on his theory called the Lydian Concept of Tonal Organization in which he postulated the substitution of modes in place of chords as the harmonic structure for jazz. Russell was a member of the "jazz Bloomsbury" that would get together in Gil Evans's one-room apartment, where Miles and Russell first came to know each other. It was from Russell that Miles got the idea of the use of modes as a basis for improvisation. Using modes, or a series of scales, gave the musician tremendous liberty to play virtually any melodic idea without breaking the envelope of harmonic structure. Russell himself had made brilliant use of modes since his earliest work one of, the first melding of modern jazz with Latin American rhythms, "Cubana Be, Cubana Bop." Russell explored modal jazz, and other iconoclastic concepts, in his great work of the 1950s and 1960s, including his magnificent 1956 *Jazz Workshop* album, which is one of the most important, and most adventurous, small-group albums of the 1950s. The following year he was commissioned to write a long piece, and he created a masterpiece, "All About Rosie." His big band 1958 tone poem "New York, New York" and his small-group works of the early sixties such as *The Stratus Seekers* and *The Outer View* further expanded on his Lydian modal vision, and later works went even further. Russell's concepts were not only responsible for the modal and free jazz movements of the 1960s, but they also had a great influence on the fusion of the 1970s. Russell has continued to be one of the most continually innovative and exploratory musicians of our time, producing one of the most unique and exhilarating bodies of work in all of jazz.

Charles Mingus, always the musical explorer, also experimented with a simplified harmonic system in the 1950s very close to Russell's modes. So did Dave Brubeck ("Le Souk"). But once again it was Miles who popularized this concept by creating intensely personal music with it.

Miles's first experiments with this new, stripped-down harmonic approach was in a tune originally titled "Milestones" (it was later retitled "Miles" when it was pointed out that Miles had already written and recorded a tune with this title in the 1940s) on the album of the same name. And on the magnificent *Porgy and Bess* album, on which Miles collaborated with the great arranger Gil Evans, there was a version of "Summertime" in which Evans used only one chord on which Miles improvised some simple but strikingly effective variations on Gershwin's classic song.

But it would be Miles's next album that would really establish modal improvising in jazz: the glorious classic *Kind of Blue*. I have written about this album so many times (including in both of my previous books) it is hard to come up with much fresh to say about it. Except that still—still!—it is music that I find overwhelmingly beautiful and moving. I think part of its power comes from the way the players are especially attuned to each other; despite the fact that all of the musicians on this date—Miles, Coltrane, altoist Cannonball Adderley, pianists Bill Evans and Wynton Kelly (who plays only on one tune), bassist Paul Chambers, and drummer Jimmy Cobb—had achieved a personal style, a style as personal as the way they talked or the dreams they had when they slept, they all seemed to be on the same wave-length, discussing, musically, the same matters. I also think it should be obvious that these new, freer structures that Miles used throughout the album (many of them in collaboration with Bill Evans) put these brilliant musicians in the position of having to think and express themselves in new ways, to find new connections between body mind and heart and not to fall back on clichés and the most facile musical ideas.

Although this music does not sound free to most ears, the playing is richly melodic. It reaches us emotionally a lot more easily than, say, Coltrane's harmonically centered "sheets of sound" of the late 1950s, or even some of Charlie Parker's knottier work. Coltrane would take modal jazz even farther in the classic albums he would record in the 1960s, including *Crescent* and *A Love Supreme*. After the latter album he would use modes as a jumping-off place into the deep and often murky waters of free jazz.

Explorations of musical freedom were not being done solely by young black members of what was called the New Thing in the 1960s. Perhaps after Coltrane, the most influential jazzman of the era was pianist Bill Evans. For many years Evans has been accepted as being a great jazzman, the most influential pianist since Bud Powell, whose influence has surpassed being just for pianists. That is until the era of the neoclassicist. Now he is being attacked as lacking true authenticity for not playing within the "true" jazz tradition.

I once overheard Stanley Crouch giving a diatribe against Evans. It was just before a kind of symposium of jazz critics (I was there to observe; I wasn't taking part). Evans, according to Crouch, was a "punk" whose playing could scarcely be considered jazz. He could not swing, according to Crouch, and there was no blues in his playing. When Miles replaced Evans with Wynton Kelly in 1959, he was replacing the "punk" Evans, a jazz pretender, with a truly great jazz pianist. And Tom Piazza, a writer who has admitted his admiration for the ideas of Crouch and Marsalis, wrote this about Evans in his *Guide to Classic Recorded Jazz*: "I must admit that I have trouble sitting still for his work for very long. He doesn't swing enough, he can't play the blues, and I don't feel close to his soul."

Crouch was right about Wynton Kelly—he was a great jazz pianist. But so was Evans, and virtually every musician I know agrees with that, especially pianists, white or black. Even Crouch's hero, Kelly, was influenced by Evans; according to his own testimony, he changed his ballad style after hearing Evans.

Here we have another great example of an important musician whose influence is wide and deep being eliminated from jazz history because of the limitations of the concept of the jazz tradition. It is hard here to ignore that like another musician treated this way by the neos, Bix Beiderbecke (remember Albert Murray's statement that Bix's name has been "intruded" into lists of great jazz trumpeters by white critics?), Evans is white. As a matter of fact, Martin Williams, probably the most respected critic in jazz, has stated that Evans and Beiderbecke are the two most important white players in jazz history.

Evans's impressionistic harmonies, his touch, his melodic inventiveness, the unforgettable melancholy lyricism of his music, put him in the front ranks of players. According to George Russell, who "discovered" Evans, he had an astonishingly impeccable sense of time and he swung hard in his own way, just as Monk does or, for that matter, as Wynton Kelly does. It is interesting to note that both Evans and Coltrane, who of course played together when they were with Miles, had rhythmic sense that seemed to ride over the beat rather than on it. Coltrane, too, was attacked for not swinging, though nobody would dare say such a thing now (well, Philip Larkin probably would if he were still alive).

Besides being a great improviser, Evans led a group that paved the way for much of the free jazz that followed. The trio he formed with bassist Scott LaFaro and drummer Paul Motian developed a concept for this kind of group that was radically different from other piano trios. Rather than the piano being the dominant voice with the rhythm section just being used as accompaniment, in the Evans trio there was a constant dialogue among the three instruments. LaFaro's bass lines were more melodic than rhythmic, and Motian's drumming was often quite abstract, both flattening and expanding the rhythm and allowing for this three-way discussion;

Motian is a master of "sprung rhythm." It took a while to reach the point where these innovations finally came together. But they did when the group recorded for the third time, at an appearance at the Village Vanguard. The dialogue among the three musicians on these recordings is extraordinary, and the successful creation of a small ensemble that constantly improvised as a group was both a key advance for jazz and a glance toward jazz's past, when ensemble improvisation was the heart of the music. It was also the last time they would play together: Eleven days after the Vanguard sessions, LaFaro was killed in a car crash.

The music of this particular Evans group was especially important because, like so much New Thing jazz, it brought true group improvisation back to jazz. This is a key point about the free jazz movement, maybe *the* key point: No longer was jazz just a series of soloists accompanied by a rhythm section. Now, as in jazz's past, ensemble improvisation was once more a central aspect of jazz creation. This can be heard in everything from Ornette's album called *Free Jazz* and Coltrane's *Ascension,* to much of the work of Sun Ra, AACM, and Albert Ayler. This new emphasis on group improvisation is what led the Miles Davis quintet to its great post-bop innovations—and it is exactly what is missing in the neoclassicists who attempt to emulate the Davis quintet. Also, early in the decade, group improvisation was central to the conception of the first Bill Evans trio.

Evans would continue to create beautiful music until his death in 1980, but never would he lead a group as innovative and fascinating as this trio. Echoes of that group would be heard in many jazz groups for years to come, and its influence is still being heard. One perfect example is the Standards Trio that Keith Jarrett has been leading for a few years now (with bassist Gary Peacock and drummer Jack DeJohnette, both of whom have played with Evans).

As for Evans's influence, it is difficult to think of a pianist, other than avant-gardists in the sway of Cecil Taylor, who has not been influenced by Bill Evans. Two of the key pianists of the last thirty years (besides Jarrett), Herbie Hancock and Chick Corea, were very obviously and admittedly influenced by Evans.

Regarding Crouch's statement that Evans could not play the blues, it is true that he did not often play the blues. But there were times when he did, and when he did play the blues, like everything else he had done, he played them in a completely personal and unique fashion. Actually, Evans first gained fame through the blues solo he played on the initial recording of George Russell's marvelous "All About Rosie"; it is considered one of the great solos in jazz history. Anyone who still doubts Evans's ability to play the blues should listen to Oliver Nelson's classic album from the early 1960s, *Blues and the Abstract Truth.* Besides Evans, there are a number of genuine young lions of the period: trumpeter Freddie Hubbard, bassist Paul Chambers, reedman Eric Dolphy, and Nelson himself, who was a wonderful saxophonist as well as a composer/arranger. Every piece on the album is either a blues or has a definite blues "feel," and Evans solos extensively. Solo after solo, Evans plays music soaked in the blues but as personal as anything else he ever played. These are *his* blues; like every other jazzman, he experiences blues in his own way. He makes no effort to sound like anybody else in an attempt at some kind of false authenticity.

Does Evans "sound white"? What if he does? He *is* white, after all, and if his music is authentic it has to be expressive of his own life and truth. The beauty and power and—yes—authenticity of Bill Evans's music is vouched for by the fact that some of the greatest African-American musicians of this century—Miles Davis, George Russell, Art Farmer, Oliver Nelson, Cannonball Adderley, and Charles Mingus, to name a few—all respected him enough to have Evans play in their bands and/or record with him. Miles said about Evans: "I sure learned a lot from Bill Evans. He plays the piano the way it should be played." This is an incredible statement from the usually taciturn Miles.

Listening to *Blues and the Abstract Truth* and hearing the wonderful contrasting individuality and conviviality among the introversion of Evans, the extroversion of Hubbard, Dolphy's harmonically audacious leaps and swoops, and Nelson's down-home funk, we are reminded that one of the most wonderful things about jazz is that, contrary to those who insist on a narrow tradition, there are so many different ways to play it, all of them legitimate and authentic.

AROUND THE SAME time as Miles's first forays into modal jazz, Ornette Coleman, still living in Los Angeles, (where he had moved from his home in Texas) would be recording his first album, *Something Else!!!!* Heard now, it hardly seems like the stuff of revolution. Coleman used a standard bop quintet instrumentation, even using a pianist, the last time he would record with a pianist until very recently (as I write in 1996).

As we have previously pointed out, the record label that first recorded Coleman was Contemporary, which had mostly recorded West Coast jazzmen ranging from Shelly Manne and his Men to Hampton Hawes and Art Pepper. Coleman's next album for Contemporary was called *Tomorrow Is the Question*; most of Coleman's first several albums had similar futuristic titles. One of his first albums for his next label, Atlantic, was called *Change of the Century.* Still another was titled with a faintly belligerent defensiveness: *This Is Our Music.* From the titles of his albums alone it was obvious that Ornette was creating a manifesto about the future direction of jazz.

This second album's instrumentation included Coleman's alto saxophone, Don Cherry's trumpet, bass, and drums—a pianoless quartet and the same instrumentation as Gerry Mulligan's precedent-setting group of the early 1950s. As I said earlier, some critics have written of Coleman that he came to this instrumentation on his own and had little knowledge of the Mulligan group. This is hard to believe, since these recording sessions were held in Los Angeles, where just a few years previously Mulligan's group caused such a sensation. But, ultimately, who did what first really is of little importance. Coleman's music utilized the implicit freedom of the pianoless quartet in ways that were light-years ahead of anything Mulligan, or anybody else, had done before; the music was unprecedented in daring. Coleman often sounded ingenuous when he talked about his music, because in many ways what he was doing was, after all, basically simple and straightforward. He was, in his own words, "playing the music," not the harmonic outline of the music. Ornette's manifesto was based on this simple question: What was the point of taking chorus after chorus dictated by chords when an improviser's natural inclination was to play melody freely, without the nuisance of harmonic perimeters? Playing free—without a traditional harmonic structure—makes sense at least for Ornette Coleman, for whom it was the musical conception that best enabled him to create his often byzantine melodic lines. It also allowed his groups tremendous freedom to improvise collectively, since there was no harmonic weight in this music, unlike bop or hard bop. But was this too much freedom, as some critics and musicians insisted?

At this time of the 1960s, the argument about whether first Coleman, and then the other free jazzmen, were playing new music that had too much freedom at a time when African Americans were fighting for ultimate freedom, instantly polarized jazz. A favorite byline of the sixties was Eldridge Cleaver's famous remark that "if you are not part of the solution, you are part of the problem." One had to decide which side one was on in this debate and become committed, *engagé.* By the sixties, the civil rights movement was being changed by many of the young, militant black leaders. For them, the fight to live lives like those of white folks was senseless. The call for "Black Power" was really a call for blacks to find their own definition of themselves, not one provided by white people. The free jazz movement paralleled this in that most of the musicians wanted to eschew as much of the European element in the music as possible and to reinvent jazz as a purely black, African-derived music.

In the fall of 1964 there was a series of concerts at a New York club organized by Bill Dixon called "the October Revolution." Many of the most important post-Ornette free jazz musicians appeared in what obviously was a call to arms among the young jazzmen drawn to this new movement. Talk of revolutions of all sorts was constantly in the air in the sixties, and in this case the October Revolution had connotations about other, nonmusical revolutions that many of those on the street believed were inevitable. Much of this revolutionary fervor was more fantasy than anything else. But even so, just the thought of revolution, no matter how distant from reality, kept the air alive with excitement during the sixties, and gave individuals the incentive to review the significance of their pursuits and encourage artists to embolden their vision.

So if a white critic maintained that Coleman, or any player in the free jazz movement that followed in his wake, played with too much freedom and should not go beyond the harmonic territory staked out by bop, it sounded far too similar to certain politicians complaining about "uppity" blacks causing all that ruckus in their fight for civil rights and saying that they should be happy with the gains they have made that white folks generously "gave" them.

Much of the significance of free jazz is that it almost completely severed the bonds of European harmony, or at least it tried to. One would have to be myopic to miss the significance of this movement and its relationship to the call for Black Power and black nationalism. The ultimate gauntlet was laid down by saxophonist Albert Ayler when he said, "It's not about notes anymore." Ayler wanted a music that bore absolutely no resemblance to anything stemming out of European tradition.

Ayler's music at its most extreme not only eschewed harmony, it also ignored meter, pitch, and melody. As John Litweiler writes in his book on 1960s jazz, *The Freedom Principle,* "For the first time in jazz, chaos becomes the premise of an ensemble." The only thing European about this music was the fact that he was playing a European musical instrument, the saxophone. But even with this, Ayler's technique on the sax almost turned it into a different instrument—he certainly did things on the horn that its inventor, Adolphe Sax, never dreamed of. Ayler used caterwauling and multiphonics in the creation of solos that were nothing but dense sound, with no reference to melody, harmony, or, as he himself pointed out, even notes. If Miles Davis had taken us to the stratosphere of musical expression with his use of modes, and Ornette landed on the moon with his "harmolodics," then Ayler had shot clear out of our solar system, deep into some other galaxy.

Many critics, including those who were sympathetic to the free jazz movement, assumed that this was music that expressed black rage. Some free jazz players, such as Archie Shepp, agreed. Cecil Taylor asked the question, "What is so wrong with expressing rage in music?" After all, isn't it a powerful human emotion?

Older musicians who had no use for Coleman's music were in a position of sounding like Uncle Toms if they voiced their objection to free jazz. And white jazz critics, for so long self-conscious of their role in an art form dominated by blacks, felt as if they were on a very slippery slope. Things got so polarized that a person's political bent could often be confused by the nature of his or her record collection.

But if Ornette bothered some in the jazz world, they were left dumbfounded by the music of Ayler, the early Pharoah Sanders, Archie Shepp, Sun Ra, and many others. If Ayler was right that jazz was no longer about notes, then what it was about was atonal screeching and caterwauling, intense cacophony the likes of which the human ear has not heard outside of medieval insane asylums. When Coltrane decided to explore this area of music in 1965, it was a dark day for many critics and Trane fans, except for those thrilled by his audacity. After all, at the time he was the most popular musician in modern jazz, thanks to such "hits" as his raga-esque version of "My Favorite Things"; he had a lot to lose. But for Coltrane, jazz was *about* risk. His 1965 far-outside version of the old "Meet the Band" number, "Ascension," brought together many of the young free jazzmen in a work whose screaming intensity has become a kind of jazz benchmark of this era as well as a great way to clear out guests at the end of a party (it is also the name of a book about Coltrane available in both hardcover and paperback).

Coltrane did more than just explore this music itself. He sponsored several of the young free players and was responsible for their being signed by the label—Impulse—for whom he recorded; Impulse was the jazz label of the powerful ABC-Paramount corporation. Before the Impulse signings, most of this music had been released on small labels, especially one called ESP, which was almost to free jazz what Blue Note had been to hard bop (but not nearly as successful). When Coltrane backed these musicians and began playing free himself, free jazz was no longer an avant-garde fringe movement but was now part of the jazz mainstream, an integral part of jazz history despite the negative attitude of many critics and fans toward it, both then and now. And there is no denying that free jazz greatly affected the rest of the jazz world in several obvious and not so obvious ways.

It should be no surprise that there were many voices in the sixties insisting that jazz was truly dead, destroyed by the free jazz movement. Probably there was no one more eloquent about this than the British poet and sometimes jazz critic Philip Larkin. Larkin had a special enmity for Coltrane, saying about him, "Coltrane sounds like nothing so much as a club bore who has been metamorphosed by a fellow-member of magical powers into a pair of bagpipes." Larkin thought that it was bop, which to him suffered from the same kind of modernism as the poetry of Ezra Pound and the painting of Picasso, that had killed jazz; free jazz just snuffed out its final breath. Despite being British, Larkin understood better than many American critics much of the subtext of the free jazz movement, which he interpreted from his racist and reactionary worldview.

Albert Ayler, the early Pharoah Sanders, Archie Shepp, and post–*Love Supreme* Coltrane comprised just one side of the free jazz movement, obviously the most extreme side. That is the music pointed to by the neos as having been disastrous for jazz. And there is some truth in that: It did turn off many jazz fans who heard nothing but pure cacophony in the playing of these musicians. But there was an enormous amount of music from this era—often called "post-bop" or "freebop"—that was brilliantly innovative and certainly could not be construed as being self-indulgent. Some of this music, I am sure, is embraced by the neos. But it cannot be separated from the musical currents of this period, including the more extreme forms.

Blue Note, interestingly, released much of the best 1960s post-bop music. While most Blue Note albums continued to be meat-and-potatoes jazz, organ trios and quartets or hard bop and regular releases of the Three Sounds, Lion and Wolff also produced several of the musicians in the vanguard of the music, and some of the best free jazz in this period. Ornette Coleman and Cecil Taylor both recorded for the label, Taylor producing one of his most important albums, *Unit Structures*. But Blue Note also gave musicians relatively new to the scene a chance to record with all the care and support that was so much a part of the Blue Note operation. Pianist/composer Andrew Hill recorded some of the best music of this era for the label. Hill wrote pieces and improvised with a chromatic density that was different from anything else in jazz. And his music had a powerful rhythmic flow—call it swing if you insist—that gave his music immediate accessibility despite its harmonic twists and turns.

Blue Note also recorded the important tenorman Sam Rivers, who became an especially key figure of the 1970s "loft scene" (see the next chapter). Wolff and Lion also recorded the first albums of vibraphonist Bobby Hutcherson, possibly the most important vibist since Milt Jackson, who straddled hard bop and free jazz, producing albums that had the drive of more traditional jazz combined with an experimental edge and harmonic freedom that gave them relevance. Jackie McLean, a key figure in the hard bop movement, became fascinated with the new music and recorded a series of albums for Blue Note that swung as hard as they were adventurous. The first one was called—no surprise—*Let Freedom Ring*.

Much of this music owed the feeling of rhythmic freedom of free jazz it conveyed as well as its driving hard-bop momentum to the great drummers of the period, particularly Tony Williams, Elvin Jones, and the greatly underappreciated Joe Chambers. They played with what Miles called "that thing," that visceral drive of jazz at its best, combined with a variation of what the poet Gerard Manley Hopkins called "sprung rhythm," rhythm that is disciplined and muscular yet off center, unpredictable, and constantly changing.

The most important of the post-bop groups was the Miles Davis quintet—the one that coalesced at the end of 1964 with Wayne Shorter, Herbie Hancock, Ron Carter, and Tony Williams. Generally, this group was not considered part of the free jazz movement; if anything, Miles was portrayed as something of a reactionary during this period. Cecil Taylor was probably speaking for a lot of young free jazzmen when he said, "Miles plays good for a millionaire." How could someone like Miles Davis be part of a revolution that was social as well as musical? For the most part, his quintet of the 1960s played much of the same book as his previous groups: "My Funny Valentine," "Milestones," "On Green Dolphin Street," "So What," and so on. It seemed as if Miles was trying to hold on to the past while surrounded on all sides by revolution. Yet the group was much more free than it might seem. We have a much better insight into how free that was, thanks to the recent release of an eight-CD set of the group recorded live at Chicago's Plugged Nickel club in 1965. The rhythm section seemed to be a cross between the one in Miles's classic, hard-swinging 1950s quintet (Paul Chambers and Philly Joe Jones) and the innovative, freewheeling one in Bill Evans's classic trio (Scott LaFaro and Paul Motian). Wayne Shorter was not as free a player as Archie Shepp or Albert Ayler, but he *was* free in the mode of Sonny Rollins, particularly the Rollins of the early 1960s. Shorter was for a while mistaken for being another Coltrane imitator, and there was some degree of truth in that; Coltrane was obviously an influence, but in a way Rollins was just as important an influence. Actually, when he played in the Davis group, his style seemed to be a melding of that of his present boss and that of Trane, two styles that on the surface might seem to be inherently irreconcilable. Yet Shorter brought it off, weaving Coltrane's lyricism and sound with Miles's ability to use space and to infer more than he outright states. Shorter's improvisation could turn in seemingly any direction, and it often seemed to have virtually nothing to do with the chord changes (for instance, his lengthy, driving solo on "Round About Midnight," of all things, which turns into an intense burner). Shorter used, though only in certain climactic places, Coltrane's wails and cries. And rhythmically he was his own man; his rhythmic conception was rather like Miles in its combination of elasticity and driving power.

The amazing thing about the group is its ability to improvise as an ensemble. That is, there was no preset arrangement; it was all done adlib. A piece that started off as a ballad could turn into a fast-tempoed wailer. Meters and tempos could change in a piece according to the way the group felt as a whole. Hearing them live, one has the feeling that anything is possible, and frequently that is true. One of the most amazing moments in the Plugged Nickel set is one of the versions of the group's theme. Usually Miles would play the theme, maybe one member of the group would take a short solo, Miles and Shorter may restate the theme, and that would end the set. But this time the group digs into the theme for some reason and turns it into a breathlessly exciting, lengthy duet between Miles and Shorter backed by a cascading rhythm section. It is pure musical magic.

And it certainly seems to be music that should be the definition of "freedom." Yet those who seize on this group as what is "good" about the 1960s and denounce late Coltrane, Ayler, Sun Ra, and the others of that time as what is "bad" don't understand the dynamic nature of the evolution of jazz. All the important music of this era was like a symposium on freedom. Everyone in the jazz world was affected by this ongoing debate, especially young musicians such as those in the Davis quintet. The most extreme radicals of the free jazz movement—Ayler, early Sanders, Sun Ra, Archie Shepp—acted as a prod to others to be more brave, to open things up and to take great chances they might not have previously taken. This was certainly true of the Miles quintet. Drummer Tony Williams openly stated that he would have preferred to be playing free jazz with Cecil Taylor than to play with Miles, an incredible remark, since most musicians would have given an arm or a foot to play with Davis. Wayne Shorter was very close to Coltrane, and Herbie Hancock was fascinated with the free jazz movement. There is one cut on the group's *Sorcerer* album in which they play as close to free as a Miles group ever got. On the tune called "Limbo" there is no set pulse; Tony Williams plays explosively, his rhythms are free but they are also supportive of the soloist, allowing whoever is soloing to go in any direction he pleases, from ballad tempo to that of searing intensity. Recorded in 1967, after the group had been together for close to four years, it demonstrated as good as anything this quintet ever recorded its ability to function as an organic whole and the level of ESP on which these musicians seemed to function.

Miles's 1960s quintet is probably the most influential group on the neoclassicists, or rather it is the group they often cite as being the most influential. Yet none of the groups that have attempted to emulate the great Davis quintet—including that of Wynton Marsalis—has come even close to the inventiveness and resourcefulness of Miles's band. The thing that made that group so exciting—that made its whole so much greater than the sum of its parts—was the feeling of moving the music forward toward fresh discovery. Musicians emulating that group now are doing just the opposite—they are moving backwards in time. The thrill of discovery and risk is no longer inherent in the music, only the outer trappings of the group's basic conception. None of these ensembles have been able to improvise as a group, or to change tempos and meters constantly, or to wander so close to the edge of the harmonic envelope. And the reason this group was so adventurous was because of the time in which it existed. Miles might have been outspoken in his distaste for the more extreme members of the free jazz movement, but there is no doubt that the mood in jazz was one of unbridled exploration of the concept of free jazz, and that he, like every other musician keyed in to the moment, was fascinated by the new constellation of possibilities.

Even musicians like Stan Getz were influenced, at least indirectly, by the free movement. In albums from the period, such as *Sweet Rain* and *Captain Marvel*, the former king of the cool tenor played with a passionate expressiveness and charged intensity that had never previously been heard in his music. He even recorded an album with Bill Evans, which had a rhythm section that included the great drummer of the Coltrane quartet, Elvin Jones. The record is a disappointment, but Jones spurred Getz to play with unprecedented rhythmic expansiveness and drive. Obviously, Getz no longer was satisfied with being "king of the cool" at a time when jazz was beginning to boil from the heat.

THERE ARE A few neos who do acknowledge the free jazz movement of the 1960s. The most prominent is James Carter, the popular saxophonist. However, Carter injects 1960s multiphonics into his solos in a highly contrived fashion, and only plays them long enough to give his solos a certain hip currency and to prove to his audience his emotional commitment. One never gets the sense that his screeches are anything other than pressing a button in order to get a desired reaction from his audience.

As with so much of the neoclassicist music, this is what happens when jazz musicians attempt to play music out of its time. It has absolutely no emotional authenticity. Rather, it is a music of learned effects. Whatever we might think of the 1960s now, it was a time and a place in history, and the music, like that of every other decade, was born out of the social and cultural crosscurrents of that time. Free jazz, even that of the most "outside" players, was an important development in jazz history, like it or not. It had a great effect on nearly every jazzman of the period as well as many who emerged later. And jazz is a big enough mansion to have room for everyone: Ornette Coleman as well as Johnny Hodges, Ben Webster as well as Albert Ayler, Bill Evans as well as Cecil Taylor. Isn't that one reason why we love it?

While admitting that this is true, we must also admit that Wynton Marsalis has a point: Free jazz did turn off many jazz fans, no doubt about it. To a number of those in the jazz world, it was no longer a "people's music," but it was now an art form that seemed to be impenetrable, music to be endured rather than music that truly endured. As Miles Davis put it, maybe jazz had forgotten its folk roots and it was time to find them again. But how could that be done without moving backward, something jazz had never done before? Leave it to a couple of geniuses to find a new way forward.

11.

Dancing in Your Head

If the neoclassicists dismiss the free jazz that dominated the jazz scene of the 1960s, they treat the movement that followed it, the jazz/rock or jazz/funk fusion that first emerged in the late 1960s and which dominated the jazz of the 1970s, with utter contempt. To them, this was the time of the Big Sellout, when jazz musicians turned their backs on the true jazz tradition in a cynical maneuver to reach the vast pop audience.

The young neoclassicists are not the only ones to feel this way. To many, fusion has become almost a dirty word, although the genre is alive and well and is actually still the most popular form of jazz. Look at any chart of the best-selling jazz albums; although a few albums of straight-ahead jazz, including some by the neos, do manage to make the list occasionally, most of the top-selling records are fusion. Kenny G., Spyro Gyra, Bob James, George Howard, Najee, David Sanborn, George Benson, and a number of others play variations of fusion, and all of them are easily the most popular performers in jazz. There is no doubt that this is jazz without its usual edge, bland music without much subtlety or depth or the layers of meaning we have come to expect from jazz, pleasant enough to listen to when at the dentist's office or riding in an elevator. I don't despise Kenny G. or Spyro Gyra as many do in the jazz world. If people enjoy such music, or any type of music, for that matter, that is fine with me. At least Kenny G. or the members of Spyro Gyra or whoever, don't insist that their style is the only way to play authentic jazz within some true tradition.

It is sad that this is what has become of fusion because it colors our vision of the original fusion movement, which, if not another true jazz revolution, was nevertheless a step forward, not just a way for jazz musicians to make a fast buck. It is ironic that fusion, which became the most commercial form of jazz, followed on the heels of free jazz, inarguably the least commercial jazz ever produced. However, as with free jazz, we can see certain elements that would help lead, eventually, to the current cul-de-sac in jazz. But in the beginning, fusion seemed to be a bold innovation and the direction for the future of jazz.

Among the elements that are, in retrospect, disturbing about the birth of fusion is the fact that the two figures most important to the development of fusion were veteran jazz innovators rather than members of a fresh generation of jazzmen. Normally we could expect such a new generation of musicians to be the ones to take the new dire action, with a handful of leaders among them showing the way. But with fusion, the two most important innovators are very familiar by this point: Ornette Coleman and—who else?—Miles Davis.

As we have seen in earlier developments—cool, hard bop, and modal jazz (the roots of the free jazz movement)—and contrary to legend, Miles was not the lone innovator of these forms. Others were as or more important, although Miles did play a key role. But with fusion it is different: if Miles did not really "invent" fusion, nevertheless he was of singular importance. While there had been numerous others who had been experimenting with fusing jazz or R&B with jazz long before he did, his original vision of fusion was a genuine step forward for jazz rather than just a way of winning a pop audience.

Disavowal of fusion is one of the key touchstones of the post-Marsalis generation. When Wynton Marsalis first began gaining fame, he drew almost as much attention for his attacks on Miles Davis, whose music from an earlier period he was quite obviously emulating. Miles was infuriated by these attacks. For one thing, they demonstrated a total lack of understanding of jazz protocol. Apprentice musicians like Marsalis were simply never supposed to attack the masters of the music, particularly those who had so deeply influenced them. I must point out that this occurred after Miles's return to performing after his "retirement" in 1975, when he was playing basic jazz/rock that was far less complex and innovative than his audacious music of the late 1960s and 1970s.

But nobody attacked Miles with more spleen than Stanley Crouch. His rage toward Miles seemed positively apoplectic, as if Miles had personally insulted him. In his essay "On the Corner: The Sellout of Miles Davis," Crouch attacked Miles with the kind of moral outrage more in keeping, say, with denunciations of the more notorious members of Germany's Third Reich or child molesters. Crouch begins his essay with: "The contemporary Miles Davis, when one hears his music or watches him perform, deserves the description that Nietzsche gave of Wagner 'the greatest example of self-violation in the history of art.' " And that is just the first sentence.

After describing and denouncing the performances of Miles Davis at the time the essay was written (the late 1980s, a few years before Miles's death), Crouch summarizes his career, expressing his respect for Miles's pre-fusion music. Strangely, he has high praise for *Filles de Kilimanjaro*, which, if not out-and-out fusion, nevertheless has many of the elements of that style. But it is after this that Crouch writes:

> And then the fall. . . . Beginning with the 1969 *In a Silent Way*, Davis's sound was mostly lost among electronic instruments inside a long maudlin piece of droning wallpaper music. A year later with *Bitches Brew*, Davis was firmly on the path of the sellout. It sold more than any other Davis album and fully launched jazz/rock with its multiple keyboards, electronic guitars, static beats, and clutter.[1]

Among the major problems in Crouch's piece is that he does not differentiate between Miles's fusion of the late 1960s and 1970s and the music of his post-"retirement" period from the early 1980s until his death in 1991. In treating this music as a homogeneous whole, he shows no sensitivity to the value of the earlier music, or at least to how different it clearly is. He does, sadly, score some points about Miles's later music, that of his post-"retirement" period. Often it just seemed as if Miles was cashing in on his legend, playing a kind of faceless, bland jazz/rock and, as Crouch points out, often pandering to his audience. During this period, Miles would pose dramatically onstage, playing the role of "Miles Davis" rather than just being himself, something he had been so resolute about before.

But Crouch is dead wrong about the earlier music; the music of that early fusion period was not the by-product of a pose or a cynical attempt to cash in on rock. It was Miles doing what all jazz innovators have done throughout the music's history: forging a new direction by plugging in to his time in the present and building on the advances of the previous period.

Critics who have been influenced by Crouch have also bought into the idea that Miles had sold out and done grave injury to jazz by exploring fusion. A piece in the *New York Times* written by Peter Watrous, the *Times*'s jazz critic who is notoriously sympathetic to the neoclassicists and their musical philosophy, went even farther than Crouch's essay. Watrous wrote a lengthy piece about what he called "the Miles Davis curse."[2] This "curse" supposedly influenced many important musicians to cease playing "real" jazz and instead take up fusion. Like such moldy figs in the 1940s who insisted that Charlie Parker, Dizzy Gillespie, and the other boppers were no longer jazz players, Watrous states that when Miles and his supposed acolytes started to play fusion, they were no longer really jazzmen. Whom does Watrous list as musicians suffering from the fearsome "Miles curse"? Almost all of Miles's former sidemen from his 1960s quintet, as well as Gil Evans, Ornette Coleman, Sonny Rollins, and George Russell. Watrous points out that because of "the Miles curse," such formerly fine jazz musicians as Freddie Hubbard and Milt Jackson recorded a series of popish albums for the CTI label that were probably the worst albums of their careers.

It is a ridiculous list; sure, maybe Miles *cursed* them (Miles cursed everybody), but the idea that the brilliant musicians on this list had surrendered their musical legitimacy to the dread "Miles Davis curse" is pure nonsense. For example, putting George Russell on the list is especially ludicrous because he was experimenting with much of the substance of fusion—including electronics—long before Miles even made his first attempts. Incidentally, when I asked George Russell about this accusation, he laughed at its absurdity and he pointed out, "Jazz was born as a fusion of music—fusion is the real 'jazz tradition,' fusing together various types of music and creating a new whole."

And Ornette had played with rhythm-and-blues bands early in his career. In fact, in a concert at Manhattan's Town Hall early in the 1960s, he played with a rhythm-and-blues band with an instrumentation not that different from his Prime Time band. And nobody could ever accuse Ornette Coleman, of all people, of bowing down to fashion.

Regarding the "Miles curse" and Davis's colleagues from the 1960s quintet, it is well known that (according to every member of the group, including Miles) the band made its advances collectively. To a large degree, it was through the interest in 1960s rock and funk of the young players in his band that Miles first began seriously listening to this music.

So the idea that they were simply slavishly following his example has no currency. As we have shown many times before, no innovation in jazz has ever come into being because of one man, not even Miles Davis.

More importantly, Watrous, like Crouch, seems unable to distinguish between truly innovative, groundbreaking music like Miles's early fusion or Ornette Coleman's Prime Time and crass attempts to reach a large audience by putting jazz musicians in pop settings. The latter has been going on almost as long as jazz has existed; just recall many of Louis Armstrong's records, in which he sang with a Hawaiian band or in obvious novelty tunes. Another classic example are the Charlie Parker records with strings (which, despite the mediocre string arrangements, are actually quite beautiful, thanks to the lyrical intensity of Bird's playing). And in the last years of his life, Wes Montgomery made a series of best-selling albums that were more pop than jazz. That is the true context for understanding crass attempts to make pop music out of jazz. And before we condemn these musicians too harshly, it should be remembered that making these albums was a way of surviving in the harsh world of jazz economics. Making albums like this is a way for musicians to feed their families and pay the rent, and as long as they still make the great music they are capable of at least most of the time, I think we should hesitate before excoriating them.

But such obviously commercial albums have little to do with *Bitches Brew* or Tony Williams's original *Lifetime,* or Ornette's *Of Human Feelings*, brilliant *jazz* albums in which elements of rock have been utilized to broaden the music's pallet. The early fusion movement had the makings of an important new development of jazz. The thing that diverted it from its great potential was, ironically, its great popularity, as we shall see.

LOOKING BACK, IT should not be a surprise that fusion evolved at the end of the 1960s. That was a time when various kinds of music that seemed to be developing in different trajectories crossed together, fusing at a time when such an occurrence seemed natural and ineluctable rather than forced and contrived. It would have been impossible, really, for fusion to have existed in previous eras in modern jazz because of the harmonic complexity of the latter music. Fusion demanded less cluttered harmonic structures than did bebop or post-bop. Jazz musicians have long made nasty cracks about rock bands who "only play three chords," but since the advent of the modal era launched by George Russell, and explored by Miles and Coltrane, followed by Ornette's harmolodics and free jazz, jazz musicians were improvising with very simple harmonic architecture (recall that Gil Evans used only one chord in some of his arrangements for Miles in the late 1950s) or no harmonic structure at all. Modal music had become very popular in rock; even some of the Beatles' songs were modal, "Tomorrow Never Knows," for instance. That song bears a great resemblance to much of Coltrane's work in his pre-*Ascension* period such as "Afro-Blue" or "Chim Chim Cheree" or his famous version of "My Favorite Things." Coltrane would play on a scale over a bass ostinato pedal point while his pianist, McCoy Tyner, played a continuing vamp. Much early fusion is similar to this kind of modal music—really, the main difference is the use of electronic instruments and jazz/rock/funk rhythms (interestingly, Coltrane was experimenting with electronic music—including overdubbing and an electronic saxophone—shortly before he died).

At the time when fusion first appeared, there were many in the jazz world who thought that jazz was losing ground to rock in terms of the innovative use of musical and recording technology. Some of the more creative rock groups were able to create sonic textures that were unique and unprecedented. Jazzmen seemed to be left behind, no longer the most progressive musicians on the cultural landscape. Of course "classical" musicians had been working with electronic effects for many years. When Jimi Hendrix, for example, created music fusing the "white noise" of electronics to bedrock blues, he was utilizing electronic effects in the service of music that was also deeply felt—Muddy Waters meeting Stockhausen. How could any musician not be curious about such developments? And bands like Cream or the Grateful Dead played lengthy improvisations on electronic instruments, which enabled their players to create a textural depth and with a power heretofore not possible. Sly Stone at this time was making records that were highly innovative in that they fused funk with rock and elements of jazz and seemed to be plugged into the seething currents of the time. Rock and funk seemed to be growing up, and becoming increasingly inventive and musically sophisticated. And on top of that, this new, more musically interesting rock and funk were vastly popular.

The first jazz musicians to dabble in the fusion of jazz and rock were young players who had one leg in the jazz world and the other in the emerging counterculture. Flutist Jeremy Steig led a group called Jeremy and the Satyrs that was possibly among the first fusion bands. Vibraphonist Gary Burton led a group featuring the young guitarist Larry Coryell that was also groundbreaking in its use of rock textures. We must remember that until this point, most in the jazz world had absolutely no use for rock in any form, so although the rock elements heard in these bands may now seem tentative, at the time openly embracing elements of rock was a very bold step.

For these and other musicians who felt the way Miles did toward the end of the 1960s—that jazz had gotten too far from its folk roots—the road seemed obvious: not to turn back from the era of free jazz but to build on certain aspects of that music and give jazz new sonic frontiers by fusing it with certain elements of rock and funk. That is what is clearly going on in the creation of *Bitches Brew*, one of the very few great works from this period. But *Brew* is a badly misunderstood masterwork, as is fusion itself, at least in its earliest years.

THERE IS A story about Miles in my book *Round About Midnight* that illuminates Miles's philosophy concerning creativity and innovation. One afternoon Miles and I had a fierce debate on the subject of whether that day was Tuesday or Wednesday. This was during Miles's "retirement" period, when he would stay up for days at a time. He rarely left his Upper West Side home, which he kept dark day and night, often with only the large-screen projection TV providing any light, making it almost impossible to keep track of time. On this afternoon, Miles asked me what day it was. When I told him it was Wednesday, Miles fiercely growled, "You're a lying motherfucker," a favorite expression of his that he turned into an almost lilting musical phrase. This turned into a little debate, until I finally remembered that I had a copy of the *New York Times* in my briefcase. I took it out and, without much feeling of victory, showed it to Miles. He shook his head, sat down, and then looked at me. "You see all those awards of mine on the wall, Eric?" he asked me. "The reason I won them is because I can't remember anything worth a damn."

As we all know, Miles was a master of cryptic statements, both on and off the bandstand, and this one took me a while to figure out. Of course what he meant was that an artist who can forget past achievements is forced to innovate, to forge ahead relentlessly. And to plug into his own time rather than being stuck in the past, forcing the artist to eschew clichés and to dig deeply in terms of both the art itself and his emotions and ideas. For a jazz musician, who supposedly creates his music on the spot, the "art of forgetting" is essential in order for his music to be truly spontaneous and in the moment, and therefore not sentimentally tethered to the past.

Perhaps the notion that Miles was selling out when he recorded his first fusion albums is based somewhat on Clive Davis's story that appeared in his autobiography. According to the former boss of Columbia Records, he told Miles that his records had not been selling up to par, and that, compared to almost any of Columbia's rock acts, they had been hardly a blip on the screen. After this discussion, Davis (that is, Clive Davis), states that Miles set about to record first *In a Silent Way* and then, and most importantly, *Bitches Brew*, which became the best-selling jazz record up until its time, and which saved Miles's niche at Columbia.

But such an explanation for this key turning point in Miles's career is ludicrously simplistic. For one thing, anyone who knew Miles at all is aware that he was a complex man and that any major decision he made—particularly one that affected his music—was made for a variety of reasons.

And the idea that Miles would produce inferior music simply to pander to the huge pop audience is absurd. As Miles used to say repeatedly, he was too vain to create music that he did not believe was first-rate. The insistence of Miles's detractors like Crouch or Marsalis that *Bitches Brew* is merely jazz-tinged rock has little basis in truth, and such a description bears virtually no resemblance to the actual music. What piece of rock and roll or funk has ever sounded even remotely like *Bitches Brew*? It is without any doubt jazz, and great jazz at that. Obviously there are some rock and funk influences, but to my ears they are not much more pronounced than those heard on parts of *Filles de Kilimanjaro*, for which Crouch expresses such admiration (for good reason—it is a brilliant album).

It is clear from any close examination of the facts that Miles had been working toward first *In a Silent Way* and then *Bitches Brew* for years, experimenting with a number of the elements that he utilized on *Way* and *Brew* both in live performances and in recording sessions. Much of this transitional work was only heard years later, in such anthologies as *Circle in the Round* and *Directions*, and much of the important live transitional work, like that of the supposed "lost" quintet that included Wayne Shorter, Chick Corea, Dave Holland, and Jack DeJohnette, can only be heard on bootlegs.

But a number of those elements can be heard in the recordings of Davis's great quintet of 1964 through 1968. The young musicians in that classic group—pianist Herbie Hancock, bassist Ron Carter, drummer Tony Williams, and saxophonist Wayne Shorter—had their ears to the ground, and were listening not only to free jazz, which dominated that era, but also to much of the pop music. They recognized that pop music was going through a historic change, and they helped make Miles aware of all the new developments, from the Beatles and Motown to Sly and the Family Stone and Jimi Hendrix. This was the music you heard on the street, the music most people were dancing to, the music that dominated the airwaves and was most relevant to people's daily lives. Any musician—regardless of musical genre—insisting on ignoring that change was simply sticking his or her head deep into the ground. The dual influence of modern pop and free jazz could be heard in often subtle ways in the work of the Davis 1960s quintet in the years of its existence, in albums like *Miles in the Sky* and *Filles de Kilimanjaro* (as well as several recording sessions that were not released until years later, on collections such as *Water Babies*). Particularly key is the group's rhythmic conception, which evolved steadily throughout the group's existence and which eventually led to the approach to rhythm heard on the most important early fusion albums.

Joe Zawinul, who collaborated with Miles on much of his early fusion work, including *Bitches Brew*, once told an interviewer that his whole conception of music changed when he heard Miles's quintet's version of Wayne Shorter's "Nefertiti." Anyone who is familiar with that piece, will remember how the horns repeat the pretty, enigmatic theme over and over again while the rhythm section surges, splashes, and burns. Zawinul told the interviewer that he kept waiting for the music to start (since there were no conventional solos). And only when the tune reached its end did he realize the music had been happening all along.

It is not much of a jump from "Nefertiti" to the constantly boiling rhythm section, electric pianos, guitar, and Bennie Maupin's bass clarinet that are the musical landscape of *Bitches Brew*. Actually, the exact same technique used in "Nefertiti" can be heard on the last piece on *Brew*, "Sanctuary."

On such pieces as "Circle in the Round" and "Directions," recorded years before *Brew*, with the quintet plus additional musicians, including Zawinul, and guitarist Joe Beck, we can hear many other elements that went into the making of *Bitches Brew*. So the idea that Miles suddenly decided to change his music in order to reach a wider audience is obviously not correct.

In addition to the evolution of his own group, Miles's innovations of the late 1960s and early 1970s, like all jazz innovations, arose out of, among other things, the musical innovations that dominated the era that just preceded it, particularly that of his former colleague John Coltrane.

In many ways, fusion was a brilliant solution to the perplexing question, What new frontiers were left for jazz after the era of free jazz? It seemed as if jazz had reached a dead end. Free jazz had, in truth, alienated a large part of the jazz audience and young people, including college kids, who were increasingly turning to rock as their music of choice. And maybe it was true that free jazz was simply too demanding of its audiences.

Throughout the 1960s, it is clear that Miles's attitude toward Coltrane was rather ambivalent. In a way, he never fully recovered from Trane leaving his band; even years after Trane's death, Miles would talk about the saxophonist with a sense of reverence and respect that was absent from his discussion of any other jazzman. However, his attitude toward Coltrane's classic group was quite similar to his attitude toward most of the music produced by former sidemen, that they had played far better when they had been with him (and he was correct about many of them). It is also obvious that Miles was more than a bit jealous of Coltrane's fame, and in particular his respect among young African Americans; he clearly felt that Coltrane had co-opted his former role as the dominant figure in jazz and as the jazz musician with the greatest cultural relevance.

But it is also obvious that he took to heart several aspects of Coltrane's music, including his later explorations. *Bitches Brew* bears a marked resemblance to such Coltrane pieces as *Kulu Se Mama, Africa*, his salute to "India"; or even his version of "Nature Boy." In all of these pieces, there is improvising over pedal point and dense polyrhythms (Elvin Jones's drumming). In addition, as with *Brew*, Coltrane often used two bases, one serving as the anchor, the other playing far more freely.

And Miles was also more influenced by innovations of 1960s jazz other than Coltrane's. He might have bad-mouthed free jazz, but he had also been aware of some of the most arresting qualities of that music. Miles's ears were always open, especially to any sort of innovative thinking. Like free jazz, *Bitches Brew* rarely has a definite pitch; its rhythms are complex since as many as three percussionists play simultaneously, and while it is never free rhythm, its density allows the soloist the same kind of freedom. And, perhaps most importantly, there is genuine group improvisation.

Although even at the height of the bop era there was always an element of group improvisation in jazz, basically jazz had become dominated by the soloist with little regard for the polyphony of group improvisation so prevalent in the New Orleans era. The free jazz musicians brought back this element, perhaps most famously in Ornette's classic *Free Jazz* album, and John Coltrane's "Ascension," as well as much of the music of Sun Ra and the AACM and BAG. Everyone in the band was always involved in the music, not just when they stepped forward to take a solo. Miles himself had been including some limited elements of group improvisation in his performances with the quintet; this can be heard as early as the 1965 Plugged Nickel sessions, which have been recently issued in their superb entirety. But *Bitches Brew* explored whole new areas of group improvisation. With its three electric pianos, two bassists, electric guitar, and bass clarinet interweaving with each other and with a soloist, constantly creating changing washes of tonal colors, *Bitches Brew* redefined group improvisation. The group improvisation reaches its height of density at the climax of the first piece on *Brew*, "Pharoah's Dance": While Miles states and restates the primary theme, the rest of the band reaches a cacophonous frenzy that is obviously an echo of *Free Jazz* or *Ascension* at their most intense.

There was another way that the free jazz period led to Miles's fusion era, and that was a rather backhanded, negative way. As I previously mentioned, Miles believed that the avant garde jazz that had dominated the scene in the 1960s had lost sight of, as he put it, the "folk roots of jazz," and that was a main reason that jazz—all of jazz—was losing its audience to rock. It was no longer, in his opinion, a people's music, but a music for elitists, particularly white jazz critics. By bringing elements of funk and rock to jazz, he hoped he would make it relevant to most people's lives again.

Beyond simply trying to create music that he believed was relevant to its time, *Bitches Brew* and indeed all of Miles's late 1960s and 1970s electric oeuvre were in a way a solution for Miles to the previously schizoid nature of his career. In a way, Miles had had two careers (although, unlike Wynton Marsalis, they were both in jazz), one as a leader of small groups, some of the greatest of his time. The other part of his career was the series of orchestral albums he had recorded with Gil Evans (music rarely played outside the recording studio). Each mode lacked an element of key importance to Miles that the other had. The small-group music could be almost completely improvised and had a flexibility and spontaneity lacking in the orchestral works. On the other hand, the orchestral works had dense tonal colors that had been simply impossible for the post-bop small groups that Miles led.

But the new age of electronic instruments changed all that. Frank Zappa once made an interesting point. He said that three rock musicians could produce through sheer volume and electronic effects the musical density and weight of a large orchestra. Miles found that by using electric instruments he could create, at least to an extent, the tonal colors that his small-group music had formerly lacked while maintaining their free-wheeling improvisational spontaneity. So finally he had melded the two sides of his career. Therefore I think it is clear why he never recorded another orchestral work with Evans after he went electric. One footnote: Evans, too, turned to electronic instruments and rock-derived rhythms by the early 1970s, and his own music became looser and relied far more on improvisation.

One more question that was brought up by the detractors of Miles's electric period must be tackled: Is *Bitches Brew*, and all of fusion for that matter, outside the so-called jazz tradition? Music made in the moment cannot be limited by some self-appointed guardians of a very narrow jazz tradition apparently written out on stone tablets somewhere.

But even if you believe in some version of that tradition, what is it about *Bitches Brew*, or any of the best fusion that followed, that pushes it outside that envelope? The use of electric instruments? The idea that only so-called acoustic instruments can be played when performing supposedly authentic jazz is absolutely ridiculous. If anything, jazz musicians have continually been pioneers in making electric instruments viable, giving them real musical life. The electric guitar? Even before Charlie Christian there was Eddie Durham. His recordings with Lester Young's Kansas City Six are indisputable classics. And of course Christian was one of the greatest of all jazz musicians, despite, or probably because of, his electric guitar. Electric keyboards? Does the name Jimmy Smith ring a bell? Would anybody insist that neither he nor his hordes of organ-playing imitators (and the occasional true original, such as Larry Young) are not jazz musicians, squarely in whatever tradition you please to invent? As Bill Kirchner pointed out to me, the electric organ was really the first synthesizer. And as for the electric bass, jazz musicians had been using electric bass for a long while before Miles. One of the first first electric basses was presented to Monk Montgomery, the great guitarist Wes Montgomery's brother, who became one of the earliest masters of the instrument. Dizzy Gillespie (whom Crouch calls, rightly so, "a supreme musical intellectual") used it for many years. Cannonball Adderley also used the electric bass for many years. And although I used to be prejudiced against the electric bass myself, that was before I heard bassists who had mastered the electric instrument like Bob Cranshaw or Steve Swallow play it. Once again, it was the jazz musician who turned this clunky instrument into something that was musically viable. And what about the vibraharp? It is certainly an electric instrument. Should Lionel Hampton, Milt Jackson, and Bobby Hutcherson now be declared "nonjazz musicians"? It should not be a surprise that jazz musicians have been on the frontier of successfully utilizing electric instruments; it is a music, after all, whose basic nature is exploratory and ever expansive. There were many who considered the saxophone a less than legitimate and rather vulgar instrument whose main use was for novelty vaudeville performances. It was jazzmen who showed the depths and subtlety the saxophone was capable of—in the hands of masters.

Then what about rhythm? *Bitches Brew* does not swing, at least not straight-ahead 4/4 swing, right? But as we have already discussed, does all jazz have to be played in 4/4, straight-ahead swing rhythm? That would surely eliminate a great deal of music that has long been considered not only jazz, but some very important jazz. This would include all Afro-Cuban jazz, Brazilian jazz (say, Stan Getz or Dizzy playing a bossa nova), and such indisputable jazz masterpieces as Miles's "All Blues," Coltrane's version of "My Favorite Things," and Sonny Rollins's "Valse Hot." As far as funk rhythms go, certainly Herbie Hancock's "Watermelon Man" or "Cantaloupe Island" or Lee Morgan's "The Sidewinder" are jazz, as well as all those Lou Donaldson "Boogaloo" albums (I am not saying they are necessarily good jazz). The rhythms heard throughout *Bitches Brew* and most of the fusion that followed are often polyrhythms derived from jazz, funk, rock, Afro-Cuban, and Brazilian rhythms. But the bottom line is that they are jazz rhythms in their complexity and flexibility. And the very bottom line is that *Brew* has "that thing," as Miles would put it, that vibrant rhythmic push that he had heard previously in the drumming of Philly Joe Jones, Jimmy Cobb, and Tony Williams.

Certainly *Bitches Brew* is part of any kind of jazz tradition, as is all of Miles's electric work. When Miles released *On the Corner* in 1972, he received almost blanket condemnation from most critics. It was treated as being a crude sellout to funk. Crouch even titled his disdainful essay about Miles "On the Corner." Such music, according to Crouch, was aimed at the "lowest common denominator." But I wonder if critics, including Crouch, were actually more influenced by an interview Miles gave in which he stated that this album was a gift to blacks on the street, as well as the cover artwork, which was an ugly caricature of African Americans "hanging out." The music inside is, once again, something else. It is an innovative, complex, coalescing of jazz ensemble improvisation, rock, funk, Indian raga, Brazilian rhythms, and Stockhausen electronic.

Long before the term *world music* became so popular, Miles was making connections among several musical traditions. It had a tremendous influence on many musicians, particularly the so-called downtown crowd exploring music with this kind of nexus. Whether or not it was entirely successful, anybody listening to *On the Corner* would have to wonder at the idea that it was an example of pandering to one's audience. This dense, dark, multidirectional, multiethnic, enigmatic piece of music, so disturbingly reflective of its time, can hardly be considered a crowd pleaser. Actually, in its spontaneity and genuine innovation, it is far truer to any real jazz tradition than those who play a style that reached its peak even before they were born.

Miles's later 1970s fusion music, as heard in albums such as *Agartha, Panagea,* and *Dark Magus,* became increasingly denser and murkier in spirit. Using multiple electric guitars, sitar, and keyboards, he built cascading walls of sound. Increasingly, Miles used a wah-wah pedal on his horn, which obscured the beauty of his golden sound but better fitted his own playing into the electric jangle of the rest of the band. Naturally, Miles took a great deal of criticism for this. But the wah-wah was really just an electronic mute; in a way, Miles was paying a salute to one of his great idols, Duke Ellington (a piece in his 1974 album *Get Up With It* called "He Loved Him Madly" was a darkly funereal piece dedicated to Duke, who had recently died). Miles's concern for sonic color, which he had demonstrated ever since his first album, *Birth of the Cool,* was to at least to a degree a reflection of the influence of Ellington, who was a master of tonal color and structure. And of course, brassmen in Ellington's band were famous for their use of mutes, especially in the creation of vocalized effects, starting with Bubber Miley and then later such longtime Ellingtonians as Cootie Williams and trombonist Tricky Sam Nanton. Miles, like them, used the wah-wah to create at times subtle and fascinating sonic effects, although at other times he sounded as if he were a stutterer pleading with his audience through his horn, making for a rather unnerving listening experience.

I think one of the main reasons Miles eschewed playing with his natural tone was that its shining beauty was irrelevant to the cauldron of scalding dark emotions and dread that seemed at the heart of his fusion music in the last couple of years before his retirement. No doubt much of this mood had to do with the constant physical pain Miles was suffering, exacerbated by the druggy intensity of his lifestyle at the time. The music seemed to fit perfectly the mood of the country at the time of Watergate; it was the perfect background music for a recital of Yeats's famous poem "The Second Coming," with the lines, "Turning and turning in the widening gyre/ . . . Things fall apart; the centre cannot hold." With its droning guitars and keyboards, Miles's wah-wah pleas, and pounding jazz/funk rhythm, Miles's music of the 1970s seemed to be an overture for apocalypse. Whether Miles's music from this period is successful as art I am still not certain. But it should not be ignored for its dark ambition.

Miles Davis was (after Sonny Rollins) jazz's greatest existentialist, someone who believed that the only music worth hearing was music in which the musician put his entire being on the line. If Miles was the "Prince of Darkness," as some called him, it is because he had looked long and hard into the void, and that was certainly a part of his music. But he was really an Angel of Light, because he constantly showed us that the way to lead a truly creative and fulfilling life was to leave the past behind continually, to live in the moment and to forge fearlessly into the future.

AS WE HAVE seen, Ornette Coleman had little problem with the concept of fusing elements of rhythm and blues with jazz because he had played with R&B bands early in his career and later performed with an R&B band at his famous Town Hall concert. Ornette had never worried about the problems and pressures of iconoclasm in the past; indeed, he seemed to thrive on them. So when he formed his electric Prime Time band, he did it for his own aesthetic reasons, and he was too stubborn and dedicated to his particular vision to pay much attention to those who decried his leaving the jazz "tradition" that supposedly was connected to acoustic instruments and straight-ahead swing. Prime Time, which consisted usually of one or two electric bassists, two drummers, and one or two electric guitarists, produced a thick kaleidoscopic sonic environment over which Coleman would improvise on his saxophone, trumpet, or violin. From the very first Prime Time album, *Dancing in Your Head*, it was clear that Coleman's music had an inner logic and profundity not to be heard in all the Mahavishnu clones. Coleman had been frustrated for years in his attempts to play his major work, *The Skies of America*, which had been written for symphony orchestra, because the work, which included Ornette improvising over the orchestra, was too radical for most orchestras. Like Miles's electric bands, Prime Time solved this kind of problem for Ornette; through the use of electronics he could achieve textures as deep and full as those of a symphony orchestra with just a few musicians who were comfortable with improvisation.

At least as much as Miles, Ornette legitimized the fusion movement. He had always been committed to his vision, stubbornly holding fast even if this put him in continual conflict with record companies and club owners. Throughout the 1970s and into the 1980s, Prime Time continued to make music that, if anything, expanded on its original concepts, and with albums like *Of Human Feelings*, it clearly began to gain emotional depth and to push even farther the parameters of the original conception. Unfortunately, this would not be true for most of the rest of the fusion movement.

AMONG THE MOST important leaders of the early fusion movement were former colleagues in Miles's 1960s quintets. This should be no surprise because it was a group that evolved together. Miles did not lead them, but he did prod them to explore and innovate, and every night they played there were new revelations.

One of the greatest of all fusion groups was the first group that the drummer Tony Williams led after he left Miles. It was called Lifetime, and in instrumentation, interestingly enough, it resembled one of those popular organ trios of the 1950s and 1960s—electric organ, guitar, and drums. But here the organist was Larry Young, the most innovative organist since Jimmy Smith, whose playing veered closer to that of Coltrane or even Cecil Taylor than to the funky style so prevalent among post-Smith organists. And the guitarist was the English John McLaughlin. McLaughlin had gained a brilliant reputation in England and for good reason. His style utilized some of the sonic techniques of rock guitarists combined with the harmonic imagination of someone who, like Young, obviously also had been fascinated with Coltrane, and had also tried to bring elements of Trane's style to his own instrument. He was technically superior to almost any other young guitarist around, and he was a superb improviser, one who took chances and who loved to play his way into the unknown. McLaughlin played on several of Miles's most important fusion albums, including *In a Silent Way* and *Bitches Brew*.

Lifetime's music was similar to Miles's early fusion work in that clearly the music was as influenced by the jazz of the 1960s as much as, if not far more so than, by rock or funk. Like the Davis quintet, the group would improvise as a whole, with changes of tempo, meter, and mood occurring at will; one number could start out in straight-ahead swing, segue into a rock or Latin section, and then into a rubato section or back to straight-ahead—but all these changes were group improvised, not arranged beforehand. It was an incredibly exciting group, one that created the kind of suspense that is generated when a jazz group is exploring new musical territory. Unfortunately, the group did not catch on. They hired Jack Bruce, famous for being the bassist in Cream, the rock trio that Eric Clapton quit because its extended improvisations were "too close to jazz." Bruce loved jazz, but his bass if anything made it much more difficult for the group to improvise as a whole so freely, and shortly after he joined, they broke up.

Herbie Hancock's first group after quitting Miles was a sextet. At first, it was surprisingly straight-ahead, featuring Hancock's arrangements clearly influenced by Miles's old colleague Gil Evans. But as time went by, Hancock grew bolder and, like Williams, his group began taking musical concepts from the 1960s, fusing them with certain aspects of rock and funk and then letting his group find its own way forward. At its peak, the group included the greatly underrated saxophonist Bennie Maupin, the equally underrated trombonist Julian Priester (who for a while played with Sun Ra), the young Miles-esque trumpeter Eddie Henderson, and the drummer Billy Hart. As with the great Davis quintet, Hancock's sextet improvised as an ensemble; oftentimes, one piece would last over an hour, going through several phases from ballad to driving funk or rock or free sections of group improvisation, similar to much of the jazz of the 1960s. Like the Miles quintet that had preceded it, this group's advances were a result of a group effort: Hancock had learned from Miles how to direct a band by appearing not to direct it at all. Or at least he tried to. The Hancock sextet demonstrated by comparison with the Davis quintet how powerful a leader Miles was, despite his appearance of not really leading. Although there were moments of brilliance, the Hancock group often wound up at dead ends, at times playing with no real sense of compass, often giving performances that seemed unhinged and rudderless. Whatever magic Miles possessed, whatever subtle methods he used to direct his musicians (he was notorious for never rehearsing his bands), it worked; he was somehow almost always able to pull taut performances out of his groups, no matter how much latitude he seemingly allowed them. However, Hancock did manage to record a handful of recordings with his sextet (see the annotated discography at the end of the book) and they help illustrate the exciting possibilities of the fusion movement in its early days.

After Hancock disbanded the financially unsuccessful sextet, he formed a group called the Headhunters that had a hit record (the aptly titled "Chameleon"). Hancock retained Maupin, at least in his early Headhunters band, but let go of all the other superb musicians in the sextet. If not nearly as adventurous as the sextet, nevertheless the Headhunters created its own kind of jazz/funk that was quite a bit of fun, if lacking the depth of Hancock's best music. (To give an idea of Hancock's direction with the Headhunters, one funky number is simply called "Sly" as in Sly and the Family Stone.) Of course, there is absolutely nothing wrong with fun. But jazz used to be deep as well as fun, the combination I found irresistible when I first started to love the music.

PERHAPS THE MOST important fusion group other than those of Miles or Ornette was Weather Report. The group was founded by long-time Miles sideman saxophonist/composer Wayne Shorter and Austrian keyboardist/composer Joe Zawinul. Zawinul had helped develop the musical concepts at the heart of Miles's early fusion work, and he played on both *In a Silent Way* and *Bitches Brew*. Zawinul told an interviewer that he and Shorter wanted to create a group in which there were no real soloists and in which at the same time there was constant soloing. What he meant, of course, by these enigmatic remarks was that group improvisation was at the heart of this group. Shorter and Zawinul were going beyond what Miles had done with *Bitches Brew*, where group improvisation was utilized as well as solos; in this group, like that of classic New Orleans jazz, almost all improvising was done as an ensemble.

Much of the music was similar to Miles's: played over a jazz/rock/Brazilian beat (the rhythm section included a Brazilian percussionist) that swung in its own way. And Zawinul's multi-electronic keyboards gave the group a textural depth not previously possible for a group of this size (a quintet). It was a daring conception, seemingly bringing elements of the earliest jazz into play with some of the most recent. This is the way jazz musicians had once used the jazz tradition, not to return to an earlier style, but in order to find new ways to move ahead. However, Weather Report's first self-titled album was a disappointment. It was music that bubbled and simmered and at times achieved textures unlike anything previously heard in jazz, but it seemed too often to be without direction, and it was too meandering to have any direction or muscle. A *Down Beat* reviewer called the record "musical wallpaper," and that was pretty close to the truth. However, in live performances the group grew increasingly strong they did put out a few intriguing albums (such as *Mysterious Traveler*, in 1974).

I believe that in many ways the members of Weather Report, in their best work, were reimagining jazz, overhauling it, and reshaping it into a music that was a continuation of jazz's evolution, not a renunciation of the so-called jazz tradition. If anything, it was a celebration of that true jazz tradition of flux and change. Weather Report used electronic washes to give the music's texture a depth and variety heretofore not possible in a small group. And they were able to meld improvisation with composition in completely new ways. Don't forget how long jazz (small-group jazz, that is) had been stuck with the same old structure: statement of theme, solos, restatement of theme. Only occasionally did musicians come along to try to alter this; the Modern Jazz Quartet, Jimmy Giuffre's small groups, and some of Charles Mingus's work come most immediately to mind.

Actually, Mingus is an excellent example of a jazz musician who was especially frustrated by the fact that the best improvisors, either because of lack of discipline or interest, did not necessarily play his charts correctly. However, those musicians who were skillful at playing charts were, for the most part, mediocre or inept improvisors. It is interesting to speculate that if Mingus had been a young musician in the 1980s or 1990s he might have seen electronics as the answer to his dilemma—using synthesizers to give his compositions the tonal colors he was seeking and using other musicians primarily as soloists. In other words, through electronics he could have had the best of both worlds using only a tight handful of musicians.

As time went on and the personnel of Weather Report changed (except for Zawinul and Shorter), the music became increasingly brittle, with less emphasis on improvisation and far more on compositions, mainly grandiose pieces by Zawinul. In a display of near-Zenlike renunciation of ego, Wayne Shorter seemed to fade into the background, making less and less of a contribution, both as a composer and as an improviser. Often he would play just a few notes here and there, adding just a little color to Zawinul's compositions. This was especially frustrating because Shorter was both one of the great players of his time and one of the most important composers. By the late 1970s, the band's sense of adventure was gone and they had become an "act," well rehearsed and predictable from show to show.

Alas, as went Weather Report, so went the entire fusion movement. Because of the success of some of the early fusion albums, record companies decided that fusion was the next Big Thing. Suddenly, every pianist was playing electric piano, even a player like Bill Evans, who was so famous for his tone. Fusion became increasingly pompous or just plain crass. For instance, John McLaughlin, who had played so brilliantly with Miles Davis and then Tony Williams, formed his own band, the Mahavishnu Orchestra. The music this band played was loud and pretentious. McLaughlin at the time was involved with an Indian guru, and he attempted to play the electric guitar so it would sound like a sitar, giving it a pleading drone that I guess seemed very "spiritual" to young audiences of the time. Unfortunately, everyone else in the band, including an electric violinist and an electric keyboard player, attempted to play with the same whining and pleading tone as McLaughlin. However, since McLaughlin's chops and musical sophistication were far superior to almost any of the rock guitarists of the time and the drummer, Billy Cobham, had amazing technique, the band caught on for a while with rock audiences. But the music was far too overbearing and heavy-handed and repetitious, eventually wearing down the audience with its electric drone and thunder.

Pianist Chick Corea and bassist Dave Holland replaced, respectively, Herbie Hancock and Ron Carter in Miles's quintet. It was that group, which also included Jack DeJohnette in replacement of Tony Williams and the still stalwart Wayne Shorter, that linked Miles's post-bop music to his electric period. Unfortunately, this band lives only on bootlegs—it was never officially recorded. Corea at first hated playing the electric piano that Miles made him play, and would often attack the keyboard like an electrified Cecil Taylor. Interestingly, Miles, who had no use for Taylor's playing, never said a thing to Corea about his very free and aggressive approach to the electric piano. After Corea and Holland left Miles's band, they formed Circle, which included avant garde drummer Barry Altschul and studious second-generation free jazzman Anthony Braxton. It was a fascinating group; Holland, Corea (at least at this point in his career), and Braxton were among the most cerebral of jazzmen. On the surface, the music of Circle seemed far closer to free jazz then to fusion. The music was decidedly polytonal, and the Holland/Altschul rhythm section played a brilliant version of free jazz sprung rhythm. Circle's music it was adventurous and constantly challenging, but compelling and, in its own cerebral way, quite exciting. However, the group did not catch on with the public. So after briefly forming a band called Return to Forever that played Brazilian-flavored fusion, Corea created a band with the same name (which probably had something to do with Scientology, to which Corea had become a devotee) that was similar in sound and style to the Mahavishnu Orchestra. It was loud, metallic music, based around fast chops that wowed its young audience. It became very popular and, like other popular fusion groups, it too was soon playing the large rock venues like San Francisco's Winterland.

Due to the great popularity of these groups, national magazines like *Time* ran pieces very similar to the kind of thing we have seen lately, stating, namely, that "Jazz is back!" Actually, in many ways it was far truer in the 1970s than it is now. Many of these records did sell large numbers, in fact huge numbers for jazz, far exceeding anything by the neoclassicists. Several of these acts could fill large auditoriums all over the country, and the world, too, for that matter (for example, fusion was particularly popular in Japan).

The problem was that as the 1970s wore on, the music really began to, well, in the words of Beavis and Butt-Head, suck. (The cartoon duo probably would have enjoyed the mindless flash of many of the fusion bands.) All the subtlety and nuance of the best jazz was missing in most of the later fusion, producing music that was all chops and volume with little emotional depth. Nevertheless, fusion continued to be wildly popular, actually a bit too popular in terms of its effect on the rest of jazz.

One of the worst consequences of this popularity was that in the 1970s virtually every musician was using funk or rock rhythms; electric keyboards, bass, and guitar; and harmonically stripped-down, or modal, compositions, no matter how ill-fitting these instruments and techniques were to the musician's original conception. For example, Sonny Rollins recorded the worst albums of his life; trying to fit the round peg of his style into the square hole of fusion had the effect of causing this genius improviser to shut down his creative juices and produce the emptiest solos of his career. Reflecting the confused spirit of the times, one tune that Sonny recorded during this period was called "Disco Monk," as bizarre a conjunction of sensibilities as one can imagine.

By the mid-1970s, the original innovations of Miles and his sidemen and a little later Ornette Coleman were lost and forgotten except for the bands of Davis and Coleman themselves (and of course Miles went into supposed retirement in 1975). However, out of Coleman's first experiments with this genre arose two jazz musicians who would explore elements of Coleman's harmolodic fusion in the creation of an original conception, namely drummer Ronald Shannon Jackson and the brilliantly idiosyncratic guitarist James "Blood" Ulmer. In the 1980s, these musicians proved that fusion was still a viable mode for jazz innovation.

Miles's quintet colleagues were also affected by this trend. Hancock's music turned, except for an occasional nostalgic foray into the "free-bop" of the Davis quintet, increasingly closer to straight funk, with fewer strains of jazz (he would have a major hit in this genre, greatly aided by a bizarre video that was a favorite on MTV). Tony Williams formed a series of bands that, once again, used the Mahavishnu Orchestra as a taking-off point; even his drumming, once so original and consistently innovative, now became closer to that of a typical rock drummer.

FUSION WAS NOT the only style that produced innovative music during the 1970s. There were major contingents of jazzmen who were basically second-generation free jazzmen, using the concepts explored by Coleman, Coltrane, and Taylor and taking them in new directions. These movements were far less anarchic than that of the original free jazz musicians, a movement that tried to give coherence and direction to the whole idea of jazz freedom. In New York, avant-gardists began holding concerts in the downtown lofts. Now that Coltrane was dead and fusion was dominating the jazz mainstream, they had a difficult time finding places to play. So many of them created their own spots. Probably the most well known was that of Sam Rivers, whose Rivbea regularly put on concerts of some of the most daring musicians around, including Rivers himself. Unfortunately, for a number of reasons, most of them economic, the scene began to collapse by the 1980s. But the dedication and resourcefulness of jazzmen, so in need of having their music heard, was once again demonstrated during the brief but potent downtown loft scene (a number of albums of music from this scene were recorded, incidentally).

Outside of New York, the most important of these groups of free jazzmen was Chicago's AACM and the St. Louis BAG. Out of these groups emerged some important jazzmen, seriously committed to expanding the ideas of Ornette Coleman, Cecil Taylor, and John Coltrane. Among them were: pianist/composer Muhal Richard Abrams; saxophonists Anthony Braxton, Roscoe Mitchell, Joseph Jarman, and Henry Threadgill; bassist Malachi Favors; and trumpeter Lester Bowie. They also had a sense of theatricality and often combined earlier forms of jazz with the free jazz that was at the heart of their conception. There was something very uplifting about BAG and AACM because they were new communities of musicians who were exploring the farthest reaches of jazz expression, supporting each other as best they could like the New Orleans musicians earlier in the century and the boppers of the 1940s.

I have heard some critics say that it was these musicians rather than the musicians who created fusion at its most creative who were the true innovators of this era of the late 1960s and the 1970s. The reason I find that hard to accept is because so much of their musical conception, including combining free jazz with theatricality and the use of earlier jazz styles, is borrowed wholesale from Sun Ra, who had been doing the same kind of thing for years.

Sun Ra, for those who don't know him, was born with the name Herman "Sonny" Blount. He changed his name to Sun Ra in the 1950s—insisting that he had actually been born on the planet Saturn—and first started leading his big band, which he called his "arkestra," in the 1950s. At first the music was harmonically loopy hard bop, but by the early sixties most of his music was as outside as Jupiter, a planet for whom he wrote one of his catchy tunes. His band included some formidable players, including trombonist Julian Priester, baritone saxophonist Pat Patrick, altoist Marshall Allen, and, in particular, John Gilmore, one of the most original and powerful tenormen of his generation who some claim was an important influence on Coltrane (although he spent most of his time playing drums, for some reason—standing up once in a while to take a startlingly powerful solo). Actually, much of Ra's music also could be construed as early fusion. He was using synthesizers long before anybody else, at times playing two at a time, creating a—well, what else can I call it?—spacy texture. Many of his tunes were as catchy as anything in rock, and were often played with a funk or rocklike beat.

Sun Ra serves as a perfect retort to those neoclassicists who insist that free jazz did nothing but turn off the jazz audience. Ra combined his music with a true multimedia extravaganza, using dancers, singers, changes of costume to fit various numbers, projected images—and he did this long before rock multimedia shows became de rigueur at places like the Fillmore. I brought friends with all kinds of musical taste to see Sun Ra shows, and every single one of them loved them, even when Ra's band played as furiously outside as *Ascension* at peak intensity. But Ra has never gotten his due; critics even give credit for innovations that are clearly his to musicians who came long after, like those of the AACM. I guess it is hard to be serious about a musician who insists on talking about life on Saturn and trips to Mars and such. However, despite his bizarre philosophy and often wacko lyrics (Example: "If you find earth boring, just the same old same thing, come on and sign up with Outer

Spaceways Incorporated" or "I know that I'm a member of an angel race because I was born in outer space"), Ra is a tremendously important and influential jazzman with an enormous body of recorded work (most of which was originally released on his own Saturn label), which needs to be evaluated and given its proper due in jazz history. Even without all the dancing and catchy tunes and multimedia show, Ra's music at its best is wonderful; at times lyrical, other times explosive, he has a band *sound* that is unlike that of anybody else in jazz. He probably would have gained more respect from critics if he had abandoned the theatricality. But he did things his own, weird, eccentric way, and those of us who saw him and his "arkestra" perform will always be grateful. Once again, Ra's music is the result of fusion, with everything from electronic white noise to Mexican mariachi music. Needless to say, it will be a long time until the Lincoln Center jazz program salutes Sun Ra.

AS THE 1970S wore on, particularly after Miles's supposed retirement, fusion wore out its initial welcome. Increasingly, crass greed seemed to drive fusion, rather than the adventurous spirit that originally launched the movement. I cannot blame musicians for wanting to make enough money to support their families and to live in comfort. But there is another kind of sustenance, and that was being forgotten.

Don't misunderstand me—the fusion movement in its first few years produced some wonderful music, as innovative and inventive as that of any other jazz movement. There was just a lot less of it. Yet it is a mistake for jazz musicians simply to ignore the best music from this era, because it suggests fascinating avenues still worth exploring.

George Russell has pointed out that the word *fusion* is a good alternative term for *jazz*, because jazz was born in a fusion of European and African music and has continued to fuse with other forms of music as it has grown and matured. This is one of the reasons why I, and others, consider jazz to be a radical and visionary music. In the jazz aesthetic, all kinds of musical techniques and sensibilities can fuse with the jazz tradition—the true jazz tradition—and its possibilities are endless. The fact that the neoclassicists have such contempt for the fusion movement itself is just further evidence of the reactionary agenda they have brought to the jazz scene. Jazz can fuse with rock and funk, or Afro-Cuban music, or Brazilian samba, or Baroque fugue (as the Modern Jazz Quartet has done) or Norwegian and Swedish folk music (Art Farmer recorded an entire lovely album of Swedish folk tunes) or even the far realms of Stockhausen's glacial sonic textures, for that matter. This is one reason why it is such a remarkable music—it is open to an endless variety of fusion and infinite possibilities, like the country in which it was born. Or at least like that country used to be.

BY THE LATE 1970s most jazz fans were hungry for the lyricism, subtlety, and warmth that was lacking in the later fusion. So when Dexter Gordon, after years living as an expatriate in Europe, returned and stubbornly played straight-ahead, acoustic jazz, he was greeted like a messiah. Gordon, who had been a professional jazzman since the 1940s, played better than he ever had, creating deeply felt music with an autumnal nostalgia that was profoundly moving.

In his casual way, Gordon had shown up fusion as the empty music it had, alas, become. Following Gordon's lead, other musicians packed up the electric pianos and amps, returning "back to bop."

As they say, be careful of what you wish for. As nice as it was to hear straight-ahead music again, returning to older styles was not a solution to the artisitic quagmire that many believed had been created by, on one hand, free jazz, and on the other, fusion. The return of Gordon, followed by the return of Johnny Griffin and other boppers or hard boppers, was fine in itself. But it also created the atmosphere out of which grew the only movement in which a generation of jazz musicians looked backward instead of forward—that of the neoclassicists.

12.

THE VIRTUAL JAZZ AGE

EARLY IN THE 1980s, two of the most influential pianists in the history of jazz died: Bill Evans in 1980 and Thelonious Monk in 1982. Although their styles were light-years apart, each of them had produced a body of work that was highly personal and equal to that of anyone else in jazz history. They were simply irreplaceable. The loss of these musicians and an increasing number of the greatest players and innovators prompted this obvious concern: Where would the new important jazz musicians come from?

And just as important as the growing attrition of jazz giants was the question of where the next generation of jazz musicians would find the apprenticeship so necessary to becoming a jazz musician. That is, where would they learn to understand not just the music and technique, but also the underlying conception pertaining to the relationship between one's life and experience and the creation of this music. Jazz musicians believed that only through experience—by paying your dues—can one be imbued with the nature of the true tradition that is so profoundly essential to playing jazz. The big bands, which had long been an important part of a jazz musician's education (including such latter-day modernists as Miles Davis and John Coltrane), were, for the most part, now part of jazz's past. Even if a young musician only played in a section, sitting beside veteran jazzmen gave him a rich education in what this music was all about. But now even small groups led by the great musicians were becoming increasingly fewer.

If you are familiar with the life of Miles Davis, you may recall that while still in his late teens he originally intended to study music at Juilliard when he came to New York. However, once he hooked up with Charlie Parker, he spent most of his time on Fifty-second Street, listening and sitting in with anybody who would let him—from Bird to Coleman Hawkins. It was there, he insisted, that he got his real education.

Of course, Fifty-second Street, or anything remotely like it, was long in the past for this generation of musicians born in the 1960s. With the loss of big bands and the demise of crucially important jazz giants, there seemed little chance for young jazz players to emerge.

There also seemed to be increasingly fewer reasons that would compel a talented musician to turn to jazz, especially if he was black. In the past, jazz might have been the only kind of music in which a serious black musician might carve out a career. But by the early 1980s, the situation was quite different. Black people could now seriously consider a career playing classical music, especially after the success of André Watts.

And after Jimi Hendrix, black pop musicians could see that pop music had opened up enough that they could explore and innovate while making heaps of cash. One example is Prince, or as he is known now, the Artist Formerly Known as Prince. He is obviously a very talented musician, a true prodigy, who knew what jazz had to offer since his father was a jazz musician. But he turned to pop music without a look back for very obvious reasons: financial, of course, but also because of his fascination with the power of pop images and the interrelationship between pop icons and the society that literally worships them. It should be understandable why these rewards might appeal to a young musician, and if a musician is as inventive within his genre as Prince (or "The Artist") has been, certainly it has been rewarding both for him and his audience. Even Quincy Jones, who for many years was a respected jazz arranger, began making albums that had virtually no elements of jazz at all; rather, he made slick pop/funk albums not dissimilar from those he had produced for Michael Jackson.

On the other hand, pop music has its own demands, and one of them is that its appeal must be that of the lowest common denominator. That is why it is perfect to dance and party to—everybody can hear and "get" it, no matter what their level of musical sophistication. But eventually a true musical genius must feel straitjacketed by the necessary simplicity and obviousness of pop music. Complexity, subtlety, nuance, and depth of feeling are simply beside the point when it comes to creating the music that dominates our popular culture.

I am not deriding pop or rock or funk—they are wonderful for what they are. But some of us need music of greater depth, too. And this is why so many of us listen to classical music and also have looked to jazz. Young musicians observing somebody like Prince, who has won the respect of apparently serious critics while at the same time becoming disgustingly rich, would have to give a lot of thought to playing a music notorious for being a vocation where musicians, even some of the greatest musicians, have struggled just to make ends meet.

So by the early 1980s, one might have predicted that jazz was certainly on its way out. Certainly few would have imagined that in a few years some critics would be calling this present era a new jazz renaissance. As the great jazz musicians got older and died, it looked for a while as though jazz would die simply from attrition. Or if it did survive, it would only do so in its most commercial forms. Take, for example, George Benson, who started off in jazz with critics claiming that he was the most important guitarist since Wes Montgomery. However, after that he had a huge hit with his vocal version of "Masquerade" and then proceeded to make albums that made Montgomery's pop albums sound as complex as Cecil Taylor's, mostly concentrating on his mediocre singing rather than his often brilliant guitar improvising.

By this time there were jazz labels devoted to nothing but what would later be called "lite jazz," pop-oriented music that was pleasant background while you were shopping at Kmart, but had little to do with a kind of music that throughout its history was famous for shaking and riveting its audience. Most young musicians seemed to be turning to this music, which was basically a very mellow third-generation fusion (like that of the Rippingtons or Fourplay—both very popular groups), if they had any interest in jazz at all. (Incidentally, it is interesting to note that Fourplay's pianist—and a best-selling "lite jazz musician" on his own—is Bob James. James began his career in the 1960s as a far-outside avant-gardist whose first album was on the same label that first recorded Albert Ayler and Pharoah Sanders, ESP.) This was the only type of jazz that young musicians seemed interested in pursuing. And pop music had become so respectable, with the work of pop "artists," as everybody was now referred to, being analyzed as if it were the poetry of Eliot or Pound (no surprise, since most rock critics had been English rather than music majors in college). In many circles jazz, once by far the "hippest" music, was now considered almost old-fashioned and square, especially in the late 1970s, at the time when punk and new wave rock were at their peak.

With the fading of fusion, and the absence of any major new development, jazz seemed to be treading water. When Miles Davis ended his years of retirement in 1980 and began playing and recording for the first time in five years, many hoped that he would again point the way for a new direction, as he had done so many times in the past. But Miles's post-retirement bands were straightforward jazz/rock without the dark complexities and stubborn iconoclasm of his music from the early 1970s. One reason for this is that the young musicians in his band (with the exception of drummer Al Foster, who had been Miles's drummer in his last few pre-retirement bands) had not been influenced by the free jazz of the 1960s. That kind of adventurous spirit still existed in jazz if you sought it out. For example, guitarist James "Blood" Ulmer seemed to be the perfect Miles sideman. Ulmer had already played with Ornette Coleman, and he was one of the few musicians on the scene taking chances, playing a music influenced as much by Jimi Hendrix as Ornette. But Miles refused to have Ulmer even appear on the same bill with him when he played the New York Jazz Festival in 1980.

Post-retirement Miles himself was in a relatively conservative mood, although he would never return to a style earlier than fusion. He seemed to have the attitude that his days of battling for innovation were over, and it was time to relax and enjoy the fruits due him. His main interest was in using synthesizers for the creation of musical layers with the same slick sonic surfaces as those of pop. It was around this time that he was becoming interested in painting, so perhaps tonal colors had become his central passion. He no longer felt the urge to continue the existential struggle and deep introspection that so dominated his life as a man and his performance as a musician. Now onstage he was not the taciturn artist absolutely committed to the sometimes agonizing creation of such powerful music. Now he frequently waved to the audience, joked around with his musicians, mugged for his fans, and, amazingly enough, frequently laughed and smiled onstage. It is not that the "old" Miles ignored his audience by being so deadly serious while performing and rarely acknowledging applause. Rather, he felt that through total concentration and involvement he was able to play music on the highest level that he and his band were capable of—and that this was the best way for him to demonstrate his respect for his audience. Now playing tunes by Michael Jackson and Cyndi Lauper and others, Miles's final music was a pleasant jazz/rock that only at rare times had the emotional pungency of the past.

However, I must also point out that a recording of performances from his last few years, released after his death, is surprising in how effective Miles's music from this period eventually became in live performance.

While certainly not on a par with his greatest work of the past (including his best fusion of the late 1960s and the 1970s), nevertheless he was still able to create moments of great beauty with that unforgettable sound of his. But then again, that was Miles, always able to surprise us, even years after his death.

Whatever anyone thought of Miles's music in the 1980s, I think few would disagree with the statement that he was not any longer the great source for direction that he had been so many times in jazz's past. The music he was playing, fusion, no longer seemed innovative and important. Miles would be important to the new generation of jazz musicians but, to his anger and frustration, in a very different way from his role in the past.

AS WITH OTHER movements in the course of jazz history, it was again a confluence of factors that led to the new movement in jazz: the increasing vapidity of fusion; the passing away of many of the most important jazz innovators; the reemergence of some of a number of prominent figures from jazz's past such as Dexter Gordon, Johnny Griffin, and altoist Frank Morgan, playing bop and hard bop not a bit different from what they had been playing a generation earlier; and the apparent musical cynicism of so many younger jazzmen who were playing an obviously commercial form of jazz. It was from this arid atmosphere in the world of jazz that the neoclassicist movement emerged. All that was needed was a young leader.

Of course, such a leader appeared, almost out of nowhere. Well, New Orleans, where Wynton Marsalis was born in 1961, is hardly nowhere, but it had ceased being important to the world of jazz several generations earlier. Another native son, Louis Armstrong, as we have already noted, was the first true jazz revolutionary. So there is a perverse symmetry to the fact that the Crescent City would be the birthplace of the founder of the neoclassicist movement, the first reactionary movement to seize the mainstream of jazz.

Wynton Marsalis was named after the wonderful pianist Wynton Kelly, who had played with Miles Davis in the late 1950s and early 1960s and, equally important, was virtually a house pianist for Blue Note during its classic hard bop period. This was the era in which Wynton's father, the jazz pianist Ellis Marsalis, came to a musical maturity that informed his playing ever since. Living in New Orleans, Marsalis could ignore the currents sweeping through the jazz scene at its heart in New York—modal, free bop free jazz, fusion—none of these affected Marsalis, a superb player who, like many jazz musicians, did not constantly tinker with and change the style and forms of his music like Miles and Coltrane had but who, like the majority of jazz musicians, had worked at making his music deeper and truer to his heart, like his hero Wynton Kelly.

When Wynton Marsalis was born in 1961, hard bop was already just past its peak and a new generation of iconoclasts, led by Coltrane, Eric Dolphy, and, especially, Ornette Coleman and Cecil Taylor, was beginning to have a powerful effect on the jazz scene. According to Marsalis, he did not particularly care for jazz when he was growing up. Rather, he listened to the black pop of the time, and despite the entreaties of his father, did not take jazz seriously. But somewhere along the line he changed, and when he did he devoted himself to playing trumpet. His father served as an excellent teacher as far as the techniques and musical theory of modern jazz. In his niche in New Orleans, Ellis Marsalis was in a time warp not that much different from the revivalist Dixieland groups that entertained the tourists on Bourbon Street. This rather sentimental attachment to older styles was ubiquitous in the New Orleans musical scene. Its place in jazz history was, needless to say, crucial, but almost entirely far in the past. The Preservation Hall Jazz Band was one of the most famous tourist attractions in the city, although many of the original players of the band had passed away. Most of the members of the band were born years after jazz had evolved out of New Orleans and the style that was engendered there. This is the environment in which Wynton Marsalis, and his musician brothers (saxophonist Branford and trombonist Delfeayo) grew up and learned about jazz.

Marsalis's models were Clifford Brown, Freddie Hubbard, and, especially, the boss of the man from whom he got his name, Miles Davis. Wynton turned out to be a genuine prodigy, able to play jazz as well as difficult classical pieces early on. And by the time he had joined Art Blakey's Messengers at the age of nineteen, he had developed a style that, while its influences were obvious, nevertheless was a unique voice. Blakey was one of the few great jazz musicians still regularly touring and constantly working with the young players he so enjoyed playing with. He had been a supporter of the "young guys" ever since the mid-1950s and before the Messengers, when his group was called the "Art Blakey Quintet." The "young guys" in that group included Horace Silver, Lou Donaldson, and Clifford Brown. Playing with Blakey was a great education for a young musician, except for one thing: Blakey's music was stuck in a time warp where the calendar was always set at 1956. Blakey had survived the free bop, free jazz, and fusion eras simply by ignoring them and continuing to play the hard-driving meat-and-potatoes jazz he first started playing in the 1950s. So a young musician could learn many things from playing with Blakey, but he could only stay within the envelope of the Blakey sound. Blakey himself had become the "tradition," and when playing in his band one had to play and compose in that tradition—so playing in the Messengers did little to encourage the kind of iconoclasm that leads to real innovation and to a young musician's ability to connect his music to the reality of his own place in time.

Following Marsalis, there would be an ongoing parade of young musicians with a similar musical philosophy who would do their bit in the Blakey band. It became almost de rigueur for a young bopper to spend at least a little bit of time with the Messengers, which for a while was kind of a neoclassicist boot camp. Blakey even claimed that one of the Messenger bands that included such dyed-in-the-wool neos as trumpeter Terence Blanchard, saxophonist Donald Harrison, and pianist Mulgrew Miller was "one of the best, if not *the* best band" he ever led. Maybe this was just Blakey talking up his band, or maybe he had simply long forgotten about the heights the Messengers had reached in the past, when musicians were in the process of creating the hard bop styles that these youngsters were only emulating. Or possibly it was simply that by the 1980s the hope of finding musicians with the individualism, originality, and musical curiosity of such stylistic innovators—and former Blakey colleagues—as Clifford Brown, Horace Silver, Wayne Shorter, Lee Morgan, Hank Mobley, Jackie McLean, or Kenny Dorham was no longer a realistic hope to such a longtime observer of the jazz scene as Blakey.

One of the reasons Blakey was so impressed with the neoclassicists was their knowledge of jazz history—and Blakey's important place in it—and their understanding of the specific musical technique essential in the creation of modern jazz. But the reason for their mastery of these subjects is also part of the cause for the fact that jazz has become such a conservative art form. Instead of the long period of apprenticeship that shaped all the great jazz musicians, most of this group of jazz musicians have been taught how to play modern jazz in college or music school. From the 1970s on, more and more schools have offered classes in jazz—including jazz history as well as musical theory and technique, many of them taught by prominent jazz musicians.

The teachers for the most part were of the same generation as Ellis Marsalis, so naturally they taught courses in jazz orthodoxy based on the period they knew the best: the post-bop of the late 1950s and early 1960s. These classes turned out very capable jazz musicians, young men and women who probably had a much better knowledge of jazz history than previous generations of jazz musicians. And these classes proved that improvisation *can* be taught. The attitude of Wynton Marsalis and his acolytes no doubt reflected that of their teachers—that is, to clear away the mysticism built around the creation of jazz and in particular improvisation. To them, jazz is just another form of music, like Baroque or Romantic classical music, with a certain tradition, and if one learns the techniques of that tradition, there is no reason why he or she can't be a fine jazz musician.

There should be no surprise, then, that out of these colleges would emerge a generation of jazz musicians trapped in the past, nor that programs such as the one at Lincoln Center would present jazz repertory in a way very similar to that of classical repertory. I hope by now it is obvious that the reason I have misgivings about such repertory programs is not because I believe that jazz is inferior to classical music. Rather, such programs display little understanding of what makes jazz so unique and unlike other forms of music. Is this possible? Yes, Gary Giddins and John Lewis displayed great imagination in their sadly defunct American Jazz Orchestra, developing strategies for giving imaginative musicians the opportunity to confront the past of jazz through the prism of their own sensibility. Yet, as I am sure Giddins and Lewis would agree, even imaginative repertory—as interesting and revealing as it could be—is no substitute for innovators and innovative music.

Jazz without innovation is a dead art form. But how do you go about creating innovators? The challenge of jazz has never been to play it adequately. The real challenge has been creating a mode of expression that reflects the lives that both the musicians and their audience are living in the here and now. Say whatever you want about free jazz or fusion, the musicians playing that music succeeded in doing just that, playing a music relevant to our lives at the time. That is also the only way to create art that contains profound truths that will have meaning to listeners no matter when they actually hear it. Mozart composed music that reflected his time and by so doing produced art that was relevant for all time. The same is, of course, true with jazz.

Those who insist that the emergence of this generation of neoclassical musicians fills the vacuum left by the attrition of so many of the great players have forgotten some of the main reasons we have such great love and respect for these brilliant men and women. The best of the young musicians have all the technique and musical ability of the great jazzmen, but none of the qualities that led to genuinely personal artistic expression and concomitantly true innovation in the past or which made jazz such an important cultural phenomenon of our time. Innovation arises directly out of individualist expression in this way: Jazz musicians come to terms with who they are in the here and now, and by so doing are forced to create a music that reflects the one eternal truth, that of change (more about this in the next chapter).

Probably much of the hoopla surrounding the neoclassicists was a direct by-product of that surrounding the incontestable leader of the movement, Wynton Marsalis. Nobody in the history of jazz got more publicity than Wynton Marsalis after his historic signing with Sony Music (formerly Columbia Records), historic because he was the first musician to sign contracts for both jazz and classical recordings simultaneously. Marsalis would have the full weight of the enormously wealthy and powerful Sony Corporation behind him, marketing him as if he were a new rock star. The publicist famous for getting Bruce Springsteen on the covers of both *Time* and *Newsweek* in the same week was given virtually a blank check to promote Marsalis. After all, here was a jazzman who could be made palatable to the cultural elite—sure, he played that jazz stuff, but he also played classical trumpet! Marsalis fit perfectly into the role of the "serious" musician. He was quite articulate, and his sober, somewhat arrogant manner fit into the cultural elite's expectations concerning the demeanor of an "authentic" musician. This was the continuing subtext of his publicity. At the Grammies, where he won an award both for best jazz album and for a classical album, Marsalis first played a classical piece and then launched into a hard bop tune with his jazz group. The trendies nodded their assent. Here was a nice young black man who must be talented since he played classical music! As was said about Gershwin, Marsalis seemed to "make a lady out of jazz." The truth is, there have been a number of jazz musicians who could play classical music—Benny Goodman and Keith Jarrett come immediately to mind. But the fact that Marsalis is black is of great relevance here.

Do not get me wrong, I am not criticizing Marsalis for playing classical music, which he does very well. Rather, I am trying to help explain the reason for his fast rise to fame. There is no doubt that he is a talented musician. However, there have been myriad musicians at least as talented as Marsalis who have emerged in the jazz world, including any number of key innovators, who have not received a fraction of this amount of attention and fame beyond that of the jazz world itself.

However, I also believe that this dual career is one of the factors that nurtured in Wynton Marsalis his conservative beliefs about the nature of jazz. Although he has constantly talked up the differences between the two musics (and his supposed preference for the challenge of jazz), still he has missed the forest for the trees. He has bought into the idea of a limited jazz tradition in which the concepts of swing and blues are the essential elements. But as we have stated before, these terms are meaningless in themselves and at worst are constricting to a musical form in which freedom of expression is absolutely essential. But when Marsalis learned the technique of, say, Baroque trumpet-playing, he became aware that this technique was part of a tradition, and that when playing this music tradition is everything, and personal vision and innovation have virtually no place. Yes, a classical player has to interpret the work. But it is the composer's intentions that should be the overriding factor in the conception of those who play classical music. However, unlike a classical musician, a jazz musician is essentially *composing the music as he plays.* Even with a composer for big band like Ellington, as we have seen, jazz is always a music created in the moment, and even when it is not improvised on the spot, that feeling of spontaneity is at the heart of the jazz aesthetic.

In an interview in *Down Beat*, Marsalis expressed disgust for those writers who portrayed him as the product of Reagan's America. Talking about his conservative onstage dress and demeanor, Marsalis told a writer, "It wasn't a matter of making a social statement, even though some people were trying to tie us in with Ronald Reagan and all that stuff about conservatism. It was ridiculous." Marsalis goes on to make the connection between jazz and American democracy but ignores the fact of the effect of social forces and cultural currents on what jazz musicians play. In the 1980s this country had a president who ran on a platform of "morning in America," a euphemism for a reaction against the social and cultural change of the 1960s and 1970s and for a return to the vicissitudes of a mythical earlier, simpler period in American life. It is difficult to ignore the fact that at the same time jazz became for the first time a conservative, reactionary art form, focused on a pre-1960s golden era; I think that most would agree there is more here than just coincidence. Not that there is some one-to-one relationship between politics and artistic expression. But when a society tries to retreat into the past, it transcends simple politics and affects everything in its culture. Most jazzmen in the past remained iconoclastic and progressive no matter what political winds were blowing. But the fact that the mainstream of jazz had become profoundly reactionary is a reflection of the fact that this reactionary current went much deeper than simply political fashion.

Marsalis was soon on the cover of *Time*, was a frequent guest on TV, and, by the mid-1980s, was clearly the most famous jazz musician of his generation. He was the first yuppie jazz musician, a description that in the past would have been an oxymoron. Somewhere along the line, he met and befriended Stanley Crouch, who had been going through a major change in his views on jazz. Crouch had been for a while a free jazz drummer. When he stopped playing to concentrate on writing, his interests mainly concerned such avant-gardists as his friend of the time David Murray. But by the 1980s, as he moved politically farther to the right (the first time I met him, he discoursed on his high regard for the president of that time, Ronald Reagan), his views on jazz were changing, too. Through sheer serendipity, this young, conservatively inclined musician, Marsalis, hooked up with a writer and intellectual whose ideas on music were becoming increasingly reactionary, and out of this relationship came the foundations of the neoclassicist movement.

After leaving Blakey, Marsalis toured with what had been called VSOP, a regrouping of Miles Davis's superlative 1960s, quintet—without Miles himself. The first VSOP tour was in the mid-1970s. Everyone in that group had gone on to play electric fusion with the exception of Ron Carter, so the reunion of these musicians where they once again played acoustic post-bop was in a way a preview of the neoclassicism that would emerge later in the next decade. All the members of the group agreed to reform for the New York Jazz Festival, a tour, and a live album. Miles himself hated the idea of looking back. As we have already seen, he would say about this kind of project, "Didn't we do it good the first time?" Miles did not deny that it was a great group—*in its time*. But trying to resurrect a jazz group to him was a negation of the very meaning of the music. "The music is going to be flat," he said, and he refused to have anything to do with this reunion. Freddie Hubbard took Miles's place, which made sense, since he had recorded a number of times with various members of the Miles quintet in the 1960s and had recorded one classic album, Herbie Hancock's *Maiden Voyage*, with the entire group of the time (except Miles, of course, and Wayne Shorter, who had recently replaced Coleman in the Davis quintet.

Miles, as he frequently did, turned out to be absolutely right. I saw VSOP perform in Berkeley, California, a performance late in the tour when one would have thought the band would have cohered and begun to catch fire. The music was fine enough—how could it not be with musicians of this caliber?—but it had little to do with the band of the 1960s. The music was, well, flat. It just did not have the life that great jazz has when it is being created in the moment of its own time. The original band jolted its audience—and itself—with its constant discoveries. Missing from VSOP's performance (both the show I saw and the album) was the original quintet's emotional and musical urgency, as if what they had to say had to be said right now, and the amazing near-psychic moments of connection between the musicians (the first studio album by the original Davis group with Shorter was aptly titled *ESP*). None of that could be heard now, and I do not think that the absence of Miles himself was the main reason. It was no longer music played in the moment. And therefore it was no longer music in what I call the "true" jazz tradition. But it is this kind of empty post-bop that was emulated by the neoclassicists.

So, looking back, it makes sense that Wynton Marsalis toured with a version of VSOP that introduced him to his largest audience yet and announced his ascendancy to a position of importance in the jazz world.

It was Marsalis's growing fame—and Sony's strong support for him—that were among the factors that eventually disturbed Miles Davis so much that he left Sony/Columbia, his longtime label. Miles was convinced that George Butler, the head of jazz production at Sony, viewed him as a relic of the past and was grooming Marsalis to take his place as its in-house trumpet genius. Besides, he wanted to be treated like a major pop act, not as a jazz genius with one of the richest recording legacies in the history of jazz. That jazz legacy was now an albatross around Miles's neck, although the paradox is that it was his legend that drew most of his listeners to his concerts—for which he was being paid by far the highest fees of his life.

Perhaps Miles should have encouraged Wynton Marsalis to accuse him of leaving jazz for the pop marketplace; after all, that is what he seemed to be doing, if you accept statements he made around this time. But Marsalis's criticism smacked of Oedipal rage (to some degree Miles was obviously a father figure to Wynton, both musically and in his outspoken arrogance) and was quite simply a gross breach of jazz protocol. Marsalis was too new on the scene—and too influenced by Miles—to be launching into the great jazzman the way he did. However, for many on the jazz scene it was hard to criticize Marsalis when Miles was releasing albums like his first post-retirement—and disappointingly tepid—album *The*

Man with the Horn or the later pop pastiches that had a bothersome similarity to pop-jazz albums by the likes of Herb Alpert or Grover Washington, Jr.

Marsalis soon gained almost as much fame for his firmly stated views as for his superb trumpet technique. It was really these statements as well as his music itself that were responsible for the burgeoning of the neo-classicist movement that has dominated jazz for a decade or so now. The philosophy of the music, the justification for revivalism, was contained both in Marsalis's statements and book his *Sweet Swing Blues on the Road*, as well as the 1980s jazz writings of Stanley Crouch (of course, as we have previously noted, a primary influence on both of them is Albert Murray). The book itself is interesting enough, giving us a glimpse of the day-to-day experience of a touring jazz musician. Marsalis proves himself to be, in addition to his other talents, an articulate writer and a far more thoughtful man than he often appears to be.

After Marsalis came the deluge. Record companies viewing the success of Marsalis once again jumped on the bandwagon and began signing young players as if they were baseball teams who had spotted potential twenty-game winners. It did not matter that these players were unseasoned, that they lacked a personal sound and conception. If they dressed in the high style of Wynton and could blow bop changes, they were quickly given the status of "young lions."

The trumpeters—Wallace Roney, Roy Hargrove, Terence Blanchard, and others—drew on Miles Davis, Clifford Brown, and Freddie Hubbard to one degree or another. The tenormen—Branford Marsalis, Joshua Redman, Javon Jackson, James Carter—drew on Coltrane, Sonny Rollins, and Wayne Shorter. Pianists included Marcus Roberts, Bennie Green, and Cyrus Chestnut, and they emulated Herbie Hancock, McCoy Tyner, and Cedar Walton. There is nothing wrong with an apprentice musician emulating the style of one of the great players—that is to be expected. But these musicians were all treated by the media and the record companies as if they were mature, important new voices, revitalizing the jazz scene with their youth. In fact, all these players were remarkably conservative, none of them investigating any fresh territory or trying to achieve any genuinely individualist style, but instead trying to stay safely inside the limited strictures of that narrow jazz tradition.

Take guitarist Mark Whitfield, for example. He is a talented guitarist, he has terrific chops, and he obviously knows the jazz guitar tradition, at least through Wes Montgomery. But his style is a mélange of his obvious influences, Kenny Burrell, Grant Green, and Montgomery. And his compositions are not much more than a collection of chord changes. What he needed was to play in a group led by a veteran musician who could help him learn how to find his own unique voice as a jazzman. Instead, he was hastily signed by Polygram to a big-time contract and ballyhooed as if he were a major new voice on the instrument, rather than the talented but not yet mature jazz guitarist he really was. In the long run this does neither him nor jazz itself much good.

The emergence and promotion of these young musicians was supposed to be good for jazz, supposedly giving birth to this new "golden era," which is how a number of writers have described this period in jazz. But in the long run, of course, it was neither good for jazz nor good for these young jazz musicians to be declared masters when they were just at a point of beginning to learn what jazz is all about.

But what really became the philosophical center of the neoclassical movement was the Lincoln Center jazz program. Marsalis was the primary producer of these concerts, and among his chief advisers were—no surprise—Murray and Crouch. It was JALC that really drew the lines in the jazz world: either you supported this program and its view of jazz history or you were agin' 'em.

Lincoln Center is a cultural 800-pound gorilla—no, make that an 800-pound mummy. It was built by the cultural elite, and it was designed to reflect their social and cultural values. So it should come as no surprise that after the *New York Times*'s chief scribe on blues, rock, and modern jazz left his post, a writer deeply sympathetic to the neoclassicist cause, Peter Watrous, would be hired to cover jazz for the paper—nor that "60 Minutes" black correspondent Ed Bradley would be chosen to be on the program's board. Why was Bradley chosen? He may have been a casual jazz fan, but there are literally dozens of people, both black and white, who have a deep knowledge and understanding of jazz and have devoted their lives to the music. Why Bradley? If you recall, "60 Minutes" did a cream-puff interview with Wynton Marsalis in which he was allowed to duck the one question asked him about the criticism concerning the racial orientation of the JALC programs by answering with a non sequitur. That interviewer was Ed Bradley.

The polarization caused by this cultural politics became inflamed after the Jazz at Lincoln Center program caught on and became a popular success. Concerts at the Avery Fisher Philharmonic Hall were often sold out, and many in attendance were young people. Marsalis and his advisers are justly proud that the program is attracting some young African Americans, a group that seemed to have long forsaken jazz for pop music, currently hip hop. However, with success came criticism, some of it scathing. The nastiest jibes were accusations of racism. After years of shows, each spotlighting important jazzmen, the program had yet to do a single show about a white musician. No Bix, or Benny Goodman, or Bill Evans or Gil Evans or Stan Getz (this past fall they finally did do one show about a white musician, the late Gerry Mulligan. Too bad they did not do it while he was alive).

We have already discussed the disturbing racial undercurrents in the current jazz scene, including the programs at JALC. The answer to those critics who expressed concern about the apparent "Crow Jim" bias of JALC was that decisions about which musicians would be the basis for programs were based only on importance to jazz history. But such an answer was obviously disingenuous and caused even greater polarization. A lengthy piece in the *Village Voice* by Richard Woodard provocatively—but accurately—titled "Jazz Wars," documented the polarization in the jazz world caused by JALC and the musical philosophy of its producers. Peter Watrous (of all people) was quoted as saying, "They say they have to put on all the important figures before they get to the lesser-knowns, and there happen to be more important figures who are black. That's complete bullshit. I'd like to know what Dewey Redman or Gonzalo Rubalcaba has contributed to jazz [each of whom was saluted at a JALC concert]."[1] What knowledgeable person would insist that these two musicians are more important than—or for that matter, equally important as—Bix Beiderbecke, Benny Goodman, Lee Konitz, Scott LaFaro, and several other white musicians crucial to the history of jazz? Even if, say, Bill Evans was not to their taste, his importance to the history of jazz is undeniable by any objective measure; it is hard to imagine jazz since the late 1950s without him. Anyone planning programs for the New York Philharmonic may have a personal dislike for, say, Wagner or Mahler. But they are far too important composers by any objective standard to be ignored in any survey and presentation of the greatest classical music. And of course no serious repertory for classical music could leave them out.

As the *Voice* piece documented, disagreement became so venomous that old friendships and alliances were split and new ones formed based on feelings about these matters. Race was, as we have already seen, one of the main issues. I think we can assume this much: if Crouch really believes that Murray's book on jazz is "the most eloquent book ever written about African-American music," and if Murray himself was such an important adviser, how could the program *not* be racist (or racialist)? Murray believes that white people cannot play authentic jazz, period. His book is not a polemic against white jazzmen, but his views on them are almost casually—and very unambiguously—stated in a footnote and picture caption. And those views are certainly part of the subtext of the main body of a book whose purpose is to delineate the one-to-one relationship between the art form jazz—or rather all "authentic" jazz—and the lives of African Americans.

Race was not the only reason for criticism of the JALC program. To offset the criticism that JALC was too mired in the past, it began regularly commissioning works. However, many of the recipients of these commissions were either Marsalis himself or close colleagues of his. Marsalis's own works got, at best, mixed reviews. Marsalis's large-scale works were admirable for their ambition, but for the most part they demonstrated that he had a long way to go before he could become a genuinely convincing composer of such projects. Once again, the cause of this was the unrealistic ballyhoo that had whirled around Marsalis—some of it justified, some of it manufactured—since the earliest part of his career. Instead of doing what, say, Miles Davis had done, that is, learning about jazz composition from a master (Gil Evans), Marsalis apparently had become convinced that he was indeed the savior of the jazz world and was capable of writing long works like Duke Ellington as well as playing the trumpet and leading a group like Miles. He is a greatly gifted musician, but there is much work he still has to do, and he has quite a bit to learn before he can do all the things his ambition makes him want to accomplish.

In various interviews, Marsalis blamed the sniping on critics who were jealous that a black musician was running this program, rather than a white critic (like the American Jazz Orchestra program run by Gary Giddins, although John Lewis was musical director). Once again, he did not really address the charge itself, but went on the attack.

Race, however, was not the only factor that seemed to guide the decisions of the producers of JALC. At one point, they decided to run a program devoted to the music of George Russell, one of the most important composers (as well as musical theorists) in the history of jazz. Russell has been composing important jazz pieces since the late 1940s, when he wrote "Cubana Be, Cubana Bop" for Dizzy Gillespie's band. However, when it was called to JALC's attention that of late he had been using—horror of horrors—electric bass and even at times a synthesizer, he was "de-invited." This kind of parochial attitude gave JALC a hopelessly reactionary aura; George Russell should have been allowed to perform even if he used bagpipes and kazoo. The musical policy of JALC was staid, safe, narrow in view, predictable, and lacking any sense of daring or adventure—in other words, everything that jazz at its best was not.

In the *Voice* article, Stanley Crouch is quoted as making a very strange retort to critics of the program. After his usual ad hominem attacks on a few critics, he stated, "We are selling out concerts. We are presenting the music in a way that it's never been presented before. The rest is bullshit." It is very bizarre to read such words from a man who has nastily attacked so many forms of popular music, insisting that criticisms are irrelevant because the programs have been selling out. Crouch was fired from the *Voice* for striking another critic who happened to champion rap. Any number of rap artists could sell out Lincoln Center three or four times over the most popular jazz programs—does that put rap above criticism? And of course Crouch is right: Jazz has never been presented like this ever before, as a music whose value lies completely in the past, in which innovation and genuinely individual expression are of little value.

My friends—and especially my musician friends—from other parts of the world get annoyed by all the attention, whether positive or negative, given to the Lincoln Center jazz program. New York, they point out, is not the center of the world no matter how many writers and musicians think it is. That may be true, but to me Jazz at Lincoln Center, more than any other factor, has defined the neoclassicist movement. Gary Giddins proved in his repertory programs that there could still be discovery and surprise in repertory; it did not have to be just a kind of musical museum. But JALC and neoclassicism itself, I believe, was a program with a mission, and that was to divest jazz of its status as a progressive and visionary force in American life and to remake it as a staid and conservative art form to fit into a reactionary cultural philosophy. I am not saying that this was a conscious conspiracy. It was simply a reflexive reaction by those who loved jazz yet had a difficult time fitting the nature of this art form into their reactionary political and cultural viewpoint.

SO WHY DID neoclassicist jazz catch on? How did watered-down hard bop find an audience? Wynton Marsalis has often been outspoken in his lack of regard for pop music, especially rock. He has stated, "It seemed like so many people had bowed down to the altar of rock. That was the struggle. . . . And then it was written that I was against rock music and against pop music, which wasn't really true—it was just that I was trying to see it put in the proper perspective." Jazz, he would point out, is far deeper than rock. Basically, I agree with him, although, as I have already stated, I greatly enjoy pop music and I am certain Wynton Marsalis does, too. I think his indignation is understandable in that pop music has virtually vanquished other, more profound types of music, out of our culture. All you have to do is turn on the radio anywhere in this country to see how pop, rock, and funk have come to dominate America's musical landscape almost to the extinction—at least as far as radio goes—of other forms of music.

But it is interesting to note at least one of the reasons—and I think one of the main reasons—for both his success and that of the neoclassicists can be related pretty directly to rock, I believe.

If hard bop is now far more successful than it was in the 1950s, one reason is because a larger audience has come to like and understand music that is largely improvised. Martin Williams once published a book of essays called *Where's the Melody?* It was meant as an introduction to those new to jazz, and the title was one of the main complaints of those exposed to lengthy jazz improvisation for the first time. At least at the time, improvised solos were an acquired taste that most of those weaned on pop music of the 1940s and 1950s found very difficult to appreciate. While it is true that there were improvised solos in the popular big bands of the 1930s and 1940s, such music did not really prepare an audience for a music like bop, which, except for the simplest arrangements, was almost completely improvised.

However, pop music changed drastically in the late 1960s. Rock bands began to feature long, improvised solos, and the young audience came not only to appreciate them, but to love the excitement of spontaneous (or at least what seemed like spontaneous) composition. The tremendously popular blues/rock group Cream played endless solos on each tune; Eric Clapton eventually left the group, although he continued to take stretched-out solos whenever he played. Other groups with vast popularity such as The Doors, Jimi Hendrix Experience, Ten Years After, and even such psychedelic kitsch as Iron Butterfly, as well as countless others, featured lengthy periods of improvisation. Rock groups even borrowed the dread drum solo from jazz, much to the regret of probably millions of rock fans.

Of course the Grateful Dead won its popularity for the jazzlike spontaneity and lengthy improvisation of its performances. Listening to the rhetoric of both this group's musicians and its "Deadhead" fans, one might think that the Grateful Dead invented a music dominated by spontaneity and improvisation in which highly sensitive group interaction is a necessity. It is rather like the case of the man who reinvented the typewriter.

So it should be no surprise that the mass of young adults, or even middle-aged adults, who grew up listening to the rock of the 1960s and 1970s would immediately grasp what left earlier pop-weaned audiences so confused: the art of improvisation. However, the improvisation of rock musicians was of necessity repetitious and obvious, since they had only a limited understanding of the musical principles to allow them to take the music to new places. And, of course, they did not want to confuse their fans, either. So most rock improvisation was made up of clichés and well-worn stock phrases. Rock itself is a very conservative form of music, for the most part, despite its manufactured image of youthful rebellion and iconoclasm. Although groups in the 1960s experimented with the musical language of rock, for the most part the basic musical content of rock, no matter if it is roots, heavy metal, or progressive, or punk or grunge or alternative, is pretty much the same. More important are the lyrics and the way the musicians dress and wear their hair. The point of many rock movements, like punk and grunge, has been to bring the music back to basics, rather than push off to fresh frontiers, as jazz has done throughout most of its existence.

It is rock, then, as well as, of course, fusion that prepared this large new audience for a conservative form of jazz that was comfortable, safe, and unchallenging yet supposedly hip. Neoclassicist hard bop is very similar to rock in that, despite having the outer trappings of free expression, it is actually a very limited and conservative form of music. Having the bonds of a supposed jazz "tradition" keeps neoclassicist jazz musicians from exploring new musical territory, the aspect of jazz that might unsettle some, although it is one of the main elements that has made jazz so unique and so important. This is why so much bland improvised music is popular now: the tinkling bells, liquid melodies, and vapid prettiness of New Age; the dentist's-office jazz of Kenny G. and Grover Washington, Jr.; and the reactionary and utterly predictable watered-down hard bop of the neoclassicists. It is improvisation without risk, without ecstasy, without soul.

Yet if there is one difference among these musics it is this: No one in

New Age music, nor any of the practitioners of lite jazz, insists that their music is the only authentic jazz, the only jazz that was continuing a narrowly defined tradition. Nor do they trot out the genuinely glorious legacy of jazz and the awesome accomplishments of the great jazz musicians as a way of justifying their own music. But I do not hold the young neoclassicist musicians accountable for the creative vacuum at the heart of the current jazz mainstream. They have been taught how to play a music without also being instructed what is the heart of this music, the true source of its power and vitality: commitment to one's individualistic voice in this time now, and, along with that, the great law of growth, innovation, and change. The reason so many great jazz musicians remain so vibrantly creative even in their later years—and as I write, George Russell (74), Sonny Rollins (67), and Benny Carter (90) continue to prove it—is that they understand and even embrace flux and change.

Perhaps the archetypal neoclassicist jazz musician is Joshua Redman. His father, Dewey Redman, is, like his son, a tenor saxophonist, but as with most well-known jazz musicians of this generation, he has an idiosyncratic style. Dewey was idiosyncratic enough to play with that ultimate jazz iconoclast Ornette Coleman, and later with another important individualist, Keith Jarrett. But his son plays a tepid form of modern jazz, kind of a generic tenor sax style (which means part Sonny Rollins, part Coltrane and part Wayne Shorter), into which he occasionally injects elements from rhythm and blues and, far less often, free jazz. Redman's tours are partly sponsored now by a clothing manufacturer; of course Redman wears his sponsor's clothes at all performances. Redman was originally planning to be a lawyer, but he got drawn into music. However, he has gone about his career like an ambitious yuppie, careful to make good deals and planning the strategy of his career with care. Needless to say, he is one of the most popular of the many neo saxophonists. Forget all about what Whitney Balliett called "the sound of surprise"—that's old hat. Redman sounds more like a careerist attempting a new strategy than an exploratory jazz musician whose music is changed through being driven by musical curiosity and the process of looking ever deeper into his soul.

SO HERE WE are in the present. We have seen the currents of jazz since its inception at the turn of the century and through its truly glorious history to this present time now that this century is coming to an end. I think it is too pat to say that the history of jazz is coming to an end along with the century. But for jazz to have a future, we have to learn from this history, not just for the sake of the music but also for the sake of the country that gave it birth.

13.

Lighting Out for the Territory

A BOOK IS, or should be, a journey of discovery for the reader. Sometimes books are journeys of discovery for the writer, too. This has been such a book. If originally my main objective was to point a finger at those whom I believed were destroying jazz and to cry out "*J'accuse!*" the act of writing this book, and particularly my reexamination of jazz history, has made me realize that, as Pogo once said, "We have met the enemy and it is us."

When I have mentioned the title of this book to some people, they have assumed that my agenda was to "trash Wynton Marsalis," as one put it. I did not intend character assassination from the beginning, despite the title of this book. I hope it is clear that I am, like many in the jazz world—including fans, critics, and musicians, both black and white—very disturbed about the direction jazz has taken in recent years. This is a real concern, and trashing Wynton Marsalis is at best only tangential to discussing that concern. Marsalis would not have become so important to jazz if it were not for the fact that he filled a vacuum.

It is important to remember that when Marsalis first became well known, most young musicians seemed to have little regard for the importance of this great American music and seemed more interested in the bottom line rather than in a melodic line. To have a young man, and, let's be honest, a *black* young man, devoted to uncompromised jazz was like the miracle of fresh hope. In comparison to the spectacle of young so-called jazz musicians playing music that was directly aimed at the pop audience, Marsalis's stubborn insistence to play only music in the "true" jazz tradition seemed to be the wish fulfillment of virtually every jazz fan who had dared to dream. But we had forgotten the old maxim about being wary of granted wishes. The genie who granted this wish got it right in that Marsalis was greatly talented, but simultaneously got it completely wrong because, to use the metaphor of the 1996 presidential campaign, Marsalis turned out to be a bridge to the past rather than a bridge to the next century.

In jazz, just being devoted to the "authentic jazz" has never been enough, and as we have seen in virtually every decade, this devotion has frequently stood in the way of the natural innovation and progress in the evolution that is at the heart of this music. Marsalis understood the devotion necessary to play jazz. But he failed to comprehend the absolute necessity for change and growth in jazz, for being constantly in a state of *becoming*, for playing music that was connected to his particular point in time. This is true for every art form, of course, but it is especially true—and more specific—for jazz.

How can a musician be prepared for a music constantly in flux? I don't know, except to be involved in its world and to know and appreciate deeply within his mind and soul its inner dynamic or, as jazzmen put it, to pay his or her dues. I guess the only way to describe it is as a "way of knowing," kind of like the spirtual epiphany experienced by a Zen monk after his mentor slaps his face.

If this seems like mystical nonsense, well maybe it is. But how else do I answer the question that my friend the Canadian jazz critic James Hale asked me? He had been sent two CDs to review, one a new album by the young tenorman Joshua Redman, and the other a reissue of Sonny Rollins's classic *Saxophone Colossus*. Hale asked me, "Since Redman probably has at least as much technique as Rollins, and is probably more sophisticated in terms of formal musical training and undoubtedly has greater knowledge of jazz history and of music itself, why then does the Rollins album have so much more emotional and visceral impact than the Redman CD?"

There is no way of answering such a question from the point of view of strict logic. The best way I can explain it is that *Rollins lives his music and Redman only plays it*. Rollins's music is intrinsically profound. That of the neoclassicists—and of most repertory bands—is simply a recreation of the music that was the world and lives of musicians in the past. The music of the neos comes from the left, cognitive side of their brains. The music of the great jazz musicians comes from both the left and the right sides, as well as their hearts, bodies, and souls. That's the difference.

I think I have made it clear that every direction jazz has taken, including that of the neoclassicist, has been driven as much by the changes in our society and culture and the lives of the musicians playing it as it has been by particular musical concerns.

If it is true that the visionary and creative wellspring of jazz—a music which has survived war, the Depression, rock and roll, and the early deaths of so many of its greatest players—is drying up, blaming a single generation or a few misguided critics is shortsighted. However, I believe it runs much deeper than that. What I think is really happening is not that jazz is dying so much as it is being absorbed and is fusing with other types of music. Jazz as we know it may be dead. But the spirit of the music will be found in the international music scene of tomorrow. Once again, this reflects vast cultural change. The "superhighway of information" is shrinking our planet so quickly that a parochial form of music like "pure jazz" (whatever that really is) is simply no longer relevant. The music will take forms that will be hard to recognize as jazz. But it will have the same spirit of the "sound of surprise" and the celebration of the "here and now." That is too ancient an ecstasy to ever evaporate.

So we are left pondering the issue with which I began this book: Why are there many in the jazz scene who believe this is a golden era and a jazz renaissance, while others feel, as Bill Kirchner quoting Frank Zappa put it, that "Jazz isn't dead, it just smells funny."

To understand what has happened to jazz, we must first comprehend what the nature of jazz actually is. As I have indicated before, jazz is the first art form that *by its very nature* is rooted in an existential worldview; not the existentialism of philosophic debate and ivory tower, but a pragmatic, down-to-earth kind of existentialism with direct relevance to the actual conception and creation of jazz and the sensibility of the musicians who have created it. I realize that the concept of existentialism has been thrown around so much in recent times that perhaps it lost its true meaning long ago and at this point simply sounds empty and pretentious. But the concepts of modern existentialism offer far more than a coincidental explanation for how jazz has been created and developed.

The musicians who developed jazz probably had no knowledge of existentialism in terms of the work of Kierkegaard, or Heidegger, or Sartre (although in my book about Miles Davis, *Round About Midnight*, Miles's intriguing friendship with Sartre, Albert Camus, and Simone de Beauvoir while he was in France in the early 1950s is noted). But they understood on a profound level some of the basic principles of existentialism and created an art form that reflected this.

This should be no surprise, really, for a number of reasons. To black people, freedom and self-definition, principles so close to the heart of existentialism, are obsessions because they have been denied their rights as citizens and been stereotyped as a people for so long. White Americans have tended to forget what lack of freedom is like, even if their parents or grandparents had been immigrants from totalitarian societies. Once a generation became acclimatized to this country—if their skin was white—they took their freedom for granted. This was impossible for black people.

So out of their love for freedom blacks developed an art form where democratic freedom was everything. It was an art form in which the music could evolve and change whenever the musicians went to the bandstand and played. As Sartre has made clear, the heart of existentialism is the statement "Existence precedes essence." That is, before we achieve a specific nature we must make the choices that produce our *essence*. Choice, and the consequences of choice, are at the heart of modern existentialism. In other words, we are free to create the person we want to be and to bring meaning into our lives, and only when we knowingly carry the weight of choice and its consequences can our lives be meaningful.

These themes are central to America's greatest literature, that of Faulkner, Hemingway, and Fitzgerald, and even such writers as Raymond Chandler and Dashiell Hammett. And of course, in that it is a book about a man in search of his true identity, key existentialist themes lie at the heart of Ralph Ellison's *Invisible Man*. This down-to-earth type of existentialism arises out of the American experience. American writers, like jazz musicians, had to forge their own tradition to create a literature that reflected their—and our—lives in this New World.

After all, America was founded for the cause of liberty for the individual in a democratic society (of course, for the Founding Fathers, this applied only to white males). And America, cut off from the European legacy and tradition, had to define itself, create its own essence.

So it should be no surprise, then, that the most American of all music also involved these existentialist themes, not as high-flown theory but as a way of actually creating music. Jazz musicians must create their own musical conception, their own style, their own *sound*. Tradition is not dictated from above, but is in a state of constant creation, flux, and change as jazzmen play and progress. Jazz is constantly in a state of *becoming*, pushed forward by the currents of the river that is our life and culture.

The insistence of the neos that genuine jazz must be based in the blues and swing is a perfect example of what Sartre called "bad faith" because there is no reason to accept this belief as being true. Rather, we are supposed to believe in this "tradition" and in the necessity of swing and blues on faith.

This is the problem with neoclassicism, and it is a profound one. The theory of neoclassicism is based around a supposed jazz tradition, which dictates what jazz musicians should play and how they should play their music. Essence, therefore, precedes existence in the neo conception of jazz. This goes beyond ivory-tower philosophy. In the case of jazz, the consequences of this insistence about the primacy of a supposed tradition are deadly to the music as a living art form. True individuality is curtailed unless it meets the parameters of this tradition. And almost worse, innovation, *true* innovation, becomes impossible because innovation by definition means breaking out of this concept of the tradition and doing something new and unprecedented. This is simply not allowed when you have a straitjacketed tradition that determines whether a musician is playing authentic jazz or not.

Nobody understood the existentialist nature of jazz better than Charlie Parker. When he said, "Music is your experience, your thoughts, your wisdom. If you don't live it, it won't come out of your horn," those could have been the words of Louis Armstrong, Bix Beiderbecke, Lester Young, Dizzy Gillespie, or any other of the great jazz musicians. The freedom that used to be so much a part of the jazz scene is now in great peril. And this has a direct influence on the actual creation of jazz.

If the musical philosophy of the neoclassicists had dominated the jazz of the past like it does the jazz of the present, one must wonder if jazz really would have evolved and developed, and also whether it would have attracted the great men and women who devoted their lives to this music.

George Russell and his music illustrate these ideas perfectly. Here is a composer/arranger who has been creating innovative music since the 1940s. If at that time there was this limiting tradition throughout jazz, he never would have been able to write the first piece that combined modern jazz with Latin-American music, the classic "Cubana Be, Cubana Bop." If Dizzy Gillespie had been shortsighted and committed to the so-called jazz tradition (in which case, of course, he would never have been one of the key innovators of bebop), he would never have commissioned nor had his big band perform this piece, which is based on Latin rhythms rather than straight-ahead jazz swing, supposedly one of the essential elements of "genuine" jazz. Of course, not only did Dizzy perform the piece, but from then on he frequently utilized Latin rhythms.

Almost fifty years later, Russell, after a lifetime of incontestable achievement, was still exploring new sonic highways and was still fiercely innovative. However, at this time, he was "uninvited" to perform Jazz at Lincoln Center (which, coincidentally, is led, of course, by the trumpet player as famous in his time as Dizzy was in the 1940s) because he used one or two electric instruments with his bands. These two anecdotes are perfect illustrations of what jazz used to be and what has happened to it in recent years.

As I said earlier, jazz is an African-American art form, but not for the absurd and obviously untrue notion that only black people can play it. That is simplistic, racist, mystical nonsense, and those who perpetuate such ideas should be filled with shame. As I have stated before, few African-American musicians have ever given lip service to such an idea. And even when they did, like Archie Shepp, they worked with and even hired white jazz musicians.

But this pragmatic existentialism so endemic to jazz, and the resultant progressive, visionary, and constantly innovative nature of this music, are direct results of the African-American experience. Black people have been denied individual identity in this society and have been stereotyped ever since the first slaves came to these shores. Jazz was protest music in that it announced a new sensibility, a meld of both African and European musical techniques and aesthetic conceptions. Nobody is more American than black people in this country. More than anyone else, they understand what this country could be and what it actually is, and they know, to their sorrow, the huge gap in this distinction.

Freedom, the consequences of choice, the discovery and creation of one's true individual identity, these are all key issues to African Americans for the most obvious reasons (as a black female friend has told me, this is also true for women, especially black women). Racism is *bad faith* in that racists believe in certain tenets for evaluating individuals that have no logical validity. They simply accept them as given.

So in many ways African Americans have been weaned almost from birth on this pragmatic existentialism (without it being given such a name, of course); it has been a key to their survival and their ability to prevail despite their continuing mistreatment over the years.

I believe that the young black jazz musician Henry Robinette is right when he points out that "jazz is played by every race, color, and creed. Lack of financial support notwithstanding, it is for this reason, among others, a very successful art form."[1] And this goes beyond the music itself. Jazz is such a visceral art form in that we feel what a musician is feeling or what he or she is expressing while he or she is in the act of creating. Because of its visceral power, jazz can shape our lives profoundly, opening us up to the sensibility of others, making us more compassionate, humanizing us.

Wynton Marsalis and others have often pointed out that the jazz group is reflective of American democracy. But it runs far deeper than that. Since the nature of jazz—the true tradition—is one of flux and change, those who play it must let themselves be changed by the music. And of course, as they change as individuals, so their music must change also. And changes in our culture and society affect musicians and their work, and in turn they are changed by the music. It is a fascinating, continuous circuit, made possible because of the existential nature of jazz.

Now perhaps, looking back from this viewpoint, the history of jazz has an inner logic all its own and is full of new meaning. Jazz was born when black people, playing European instruments created for the playing of Western music, began to play black idiomatic music such as blues and ragtime. It was no accident that there was such a melding of Western and African musical sensibilities; it was a manifesto, a cry to both the heavens and the ears of men in which musicians proclaimed their individuality, their humanity, and their status as Americans.

The rise of neoclassicism was, I think, a case of nature abhorring a vacuum. Free jazz had gone far too outside the envelope, and the later, grossly commercial fusion made too many compromises, and by the 1980s, especially after the loss of a series of key jazzmen, jazz was empty, used up. It should be no surprise, then, that jazz for the first time began looking backward instead of forward. The first revivalists were, as I pointed out, New Orleans revival groups like in the 1940s, the dixieland bands of Turk Murphy and Lu Watters, and in the 1950s, the Dukes of Dixieland. In the 1970s, a new kind of revivalists appeared, who played jazz in the vein of the 1930s and 1940s. The most prominent of these musicians were saxophonist Scott Hamilton and trumpeter Warren Vaché. They were not a "movement"; they just responded to the music of the swing era and tried to capture the mood of Ben Webster, Lester Young, Harry Edison, and Coleman Hawkins. However, they never declared that they were playing the "true jazz" or that anybody playing in a more modern style was desecrating the jazz tradition.

Repertory was not a new thing in jazz, but it gained new luster within this vacuum. And then, of course, the neoclassicism led by Wynton Marsalis and his advisers filled that vacuum with its own kind of revivalism. The neoclassicists revived the music of the hard bop period just as the Dukes of Dixieland and Hamilton and Vaché had revived earlier styles.

I have to confess something here. Like most jazz fans I know, I share a love of the music that the neoclassicists have attempted to revive—the jazz of the 1950s and early 1960s. This should be obvious; my first two books are about, respectively, Miles Davis and John Coltrane. It was a magical period, truly extraordinary, one that included Monk, Mingus, Rollins, Silver, Blakey, Lee Morgan, and so many more. I cannot blame the neos for having such strong feelings for this period; I happen to share them.

So then what is wrong with reviving this music? Why not just ignore the music of the later 1960s and all of the 1970s and turn back the clock to the time when it seemed like virtually every album released by Blue Note or Prestige or Riverside was so wonderful, so warming to the soul? Why not play jazz like it was at this peak?

Because you can't, you just can't. It doesn't work that way, just as we cannot travel backwards in time. We must live in the here and now whether we like it or not. I know I have said this over and over, but it is so central to what I am trying to convey: More than any other art form, jazz is about the immediate. Sentimental attachment to the past has never previously had any part in the jazz aesthetic. Musicians—jazz musicians—should be able to interpret our time in the present into music that illuminates our lives and connects us to the greatest beauty and the deepest truths. This does not mean that their music has to be avant garde, nor does it always have to innovative in a formal way. But it does have to be fresh and true to the musician's sense of his or her life and place in time. For example, Art Farmer never was an important innovator as such; but he was able to create a uniquely personal expression and create a body of work unlike that of any other trumpet player. He may never have changed jazz history in any formal way, but stylistically he is as original a player as jazz has ever produced, and his music has become increasingly deep and strong over the years, with a burnished beauty unlike that of anybody else. And Farmer has never looked back, but has continued to refine and refresh his music.

As I have said before, I think one of the main reasons neoclassicism does not work is that on some level of consciousness the model that is used by those in this movement is that of the European classical tradition. Certainly the whole idea of musical repertory comes from that. And so does the choice of a performer as to the type and period of music he or she wishes to perform. If a classical violinist devotes his or her career only to the Baroque movement and Bach, that is perfectly fine. Or if a pianist specializes in the Romantic period, that is also just as valid. The difference between these musicians and a jazz musicians reviving, say, hard bop is that the classical performer doesn't create the music he or she plays, and *the jazzman does.*

It is not a crime to revive the hard bop of the 1950s, any more than there was anything wrong with reviving New Orleans jazz. But what is wrong is the insistence that this music was simply a continuation of the "true" jazz tradition. By conceptualizing that tradition as the kind of limiting straitjacket against which—as we have seen—jazz musicians have rebelled since the very birth of jazz, the neoclassicists are killing the living spirit that made jazz so unique, so vital in the creation of a truly American culture. And when most of an entire generation of jazz musicians adopts this musical philosophy, jazz seems on the verge of being aesthetically and spiritually smothered.

Modern jazz no longer has the effect of the "shock of the new," which once made it so powerful; I find it amusing what a fad it has become lately. Hard bop—which forty years ago sound so bold and fresh—can be heard currently as background music for commercials selling everything from computer software to luxury automobiles. One commercial actually compares features of a car to the playing of jazz musicians, including Charlie Parker and Wes Montgomery. You know that once Madison Avenue gloms on to some form of art it has almost undoubtedly lost its edge or power to deeply move us and now is just part of the cultural scenery.

So then the question is: Is it possible for there to be jazz that successfully transmutes the essence of this time we are now living in, these last years of this century, into music? Maybe we should just be happy with warmed-over hard bop, after all. Yet this seems utterly absurd to me. I know from my own life how different this world is from that of the 1950s or 1960s. These are such extraordinary times, and artists throughout the world are struggling to come to terms with them in their respective art forms. Except for the mainstream of jazz. Here we are, facing the end of the second millennium, and the mainstream musicians of jazz—the music of living in the moment, of the here and now—is hopelessly mired in the past. Is it possible for someone to create jazz that, built on the innovations of the past, is still relevant to our time now?

The answer is a cautious "Yes." There are a number of musicians who are playing music which is clearly jazz and whose music is vital and relevant to our time. They range from mainsteam musicians who prove that it is possible to play straight-ahead jazz in a way which is fresh, idiosyncratic, and even innovative, to avant gardists who are attempting to redefine the music's vocabulary. There is also a new kind of jazzman, who plays what I would call "post-modern jazz." By that I mean it is more commentary on jazz than self-expression (perhaps their post-modern irony is more emblematic of our age than most of us would be willing to concede). And of course, there are still several remaining jazz giants including such constant innovators as Ornette Coleman and George Russell who still have the power to surprise and amaze us. Russell's latest album, *Its About Time*, more joyously exhilarating than any large-scale works written by musicians half his age.

In his autobiography, published a few years before his death, Miles Davis thought the future of jazz might lie in the international scene. Miles, like many other jazz musicians, was fascinated by other types of ethnic music and at times utilized them in his own music. When asked about the neo-hard-bop movement, Miles would say, "That music was fine in its time but there's so much more to music than that." As the Internet shrinks our world even more, the relevance of a fusion of various types of world music with jazz becomes increasingly important. And indeed some of the most vital jazz these days is being played in places other than the United States. One example is Jan Garbarek. His music is often a fusion of Coltrane, free jazz, fusion, and East Indian and Brazilian rhythms with his native Norwegian folk music, which he uses as American jazz musicians use the folk music of the blues. At its best, such as in his album *Twelve Moons,* this fusion works amazingly well, producing deeply felt music with an eerie lyricism and an interplay of such diverse elements that is profoundly relevant to our time now.

Another example is the Lebanese oud player Rabih-Abou-Khalil. Abou-Khalil has recorded several albums in which he enlists traditional Lebanese and Indian musicians together with American jazzmen, including alto saxophonist Charlie Mariano, Kenny Wheeler, Sonny Fortune, and Glenn Moore producing an unprecedented vibrantly exciting, rhythmically vital, and oddly moving fusion of East and West. Here is another example in which that line from Rudyard Kipling—"East is East and West is West and never the twain shall meet"—is shown to be, at least musically, no longer necessarily true. And these are not the only examples. There are a number of exciting musicians coming out of Brazil, Africa, Japan, and Europe who bring their native musical sensibility melded with that of jazz. To quote George Russell again, "Jazz was born out of a fusion of two diverse musical cultures and there is no reason why that fusion cannot continue." And despite the protestations of the neoclassicists, it is.

The difference—and it is a very large one—between the above musicians and the great jazz musicians of the past is that they are all on the edges of the music, each doing his own thing, not part of an interacting scene like that of the jazz of the past. They are musical guerillas facing off against a neoclassicist mainstream supported by the big record labels. Once in a while, one of the major labels will sign one of these musicians, as when Sony/Columbia signed the inventive reedman/composer Henry Threadgill. But for the most part they exist on the fringes, fighting the good fight as best they can.

I greatly doubt, however, that any of the neoclassicists would share my admiration for many of the above musicians; I doubt whether they would even label it as jazz. After all, Jan Garbarek, for example, does not play with a blues sensibility. He is Norwegian, and his music is imbued with the soulful folk music of his homeland. As for George Russell's most recent works, such as his exciting new album, those fail the neo-test for "authentic" jazz because he uses rock and funk rhythms and utilizes electric bass and guitar. And avant-gardists such as Henry Threadgill and Tim Berne are just too outside for "authentic" jazz, at least according to the neo-line. And so on for virtually all musicians with a far-reaching musical curiousity, such as that in the past of Armstrong, Ellington, Young, Parker, Miles, Coltrane, and so many other heroes.

I think at this point we have to ask the simple question—so what? If George Russell, Ornette Coleman (when he plays with his electric band), Jan Garbarek or Henry Threadgill are not playing jazz, then what kind of music are they playing? Perhaps it should be called MIRM—"Modern Improvised Rhythmic Music." It is jazz's loss—and I believe ultimately jazz's doom—if its perimeters can no longer contain its most adventurous explorers.

The same thing holds true for great players of the past, such as Bix Beiderbecke. If he is not really a jazz musician because his playing lacks blues sensibility, then what kind of music is he playing? All right, if it is not jazz then suppose we call it "brilliantly inventive, personal improvisation played with a style and in a setting that resembles jazz." That is an absurdity. And of course, if by this measure we push Bix into some other category of music, we had better do the same thing with the music of, among others, Art Tatum, Coleman Hawkins, and Earl Hines (since they had little interest in the blues), not to mention Bill Evans, Stan Getz, and even post-1968 Miles Davis and Ornette's music from the early 1970s on, and so on.

When Duke Ellington said, "There's only two kinds of music, good and bad," he was making what may seem to be an obvious point but is actually a very important one. He was refusing to categorize music into little stylistic boxes, each one separate and unable to "contaminate" any other through a process of fusion. When Ellington made his famous comment, he was being self-serving to a degree: He hated having his rich musical imagination constrained in any fashion. So he composed symphonies, lengthy suites, pieces that utilized a large symphony orchestra, a piece with several tuned drums, jazz boleros, and of course "sacred concerts" held in churches. Certainly Duke Ellington was not a neoclassicist.

IF I THINK about what jazz has done for my own life, the one thing I would say is that, besides simply making living more enjoyable, it has given me courage. If the most profound representation of modern European culture is that of waiting hopelessly, and endlessly, for Godot, in this country I know that my life was made meaningful by waiting for Miles Davis's next album. Jazz gave those of us who loved it something to believe in—as a pointer toward community, understanding of self, the nature of compassion, ecstatic awareness and our deepest humanity. Jazz could even, as John Coltrane showed us, help us find the road toward God through looking within.

Jazz is profoundly modernist in that jazz improvisation is the musical equivalent of what is called "stream of consciousness" in literature. That is, a representation of one's inner thoughts and the way the mind perceives reality. Post-Freud and post-Jung, artists began to realize that our inner worlds were perhaps more interesting than outer reality. Joyce's masterpiece *Ulysses* was based to a degree on the stream of consciousness of two men on a day that, on the surface, might seem uneventful. However, viewed through the prism of consciousness, Joyce turned the ordinary events of the day into an epic adventure of the mind. Similarly, Picasso discovered that the way we might perceive an object can be very different from its reality, and he began to paint pictures of people and things filtered through our subjective perception. Faulkner wrote most of his masterpiece *The Sound and the Fury* through the consciousness of a retarded man who is unable to understand the nature and significance of much of the action that surrounds him.

Jazz improvisation is very similar to stream of consciousness. I do not mean that the musician just plays whatever idea flows into his or her head. Rather, jazz improvisation is based on the musician's inner life, and it comes from the deepest part of his or her soul. It has its own logic and structure, not one that is artificially imposed by a composer.

And knowing this, I must think back to the preface of this book, when I discussed how important jazz became to me when I was a lonely and lost boy. I heard in this music the crying out of other souls, and I was deeply moved. It was in the playing of jazz that the black musician could proclaim his individuality in a society that stereotyped him and in which he felt like an "invisible man." And in the playing of the white musicians who became drawn to jazz when they saw it as an art form through which they could express the truth at the core of their souls. Perhaps this is why jazz musicians used to be thought of as being eccentric or even crazy (there is even an old expression, "Crazy as a jazz musician"). Because through jazz they came to accept the far side of their selves and to be unafraid of being exactly who they were and not what society said they should be.

That is the reason jazz is a music of revolution—it is that oldest of revolutions, what R. D. Laing called "the politics of experience": that of the individual against a society that attempts to make it conform to its strictures. This is why repressive societies despise jazz. Both Nazism and communism discouraged the playing of jazz, realizing on a gut level the revolution of the self at the heart of this music.

So for me as an alienated boy, hearing these other inner souls expressing themselves so directly to my own heart meant that suddenly I wasn't lonely anymore. And ever since, jazz has been there for me in even the darkest hours, illuminating my life, pointing a way.

When I said that maybe we are all at fault for jazz's predicament I meant that perhaps we have all lost our way, and lost our nerve. As we have seen, jazz has been reflective of the lives of Americans, in particular the lives of black Americans, throughout the twentieth century. I think that, to a large degree, much of the hope that used to be so prevalent a part of jazz has been suffocated in recent years. After the Vietnam War, and then Watergate, Americans have become deeply cynical people, and black people in particular have begun to have grave doubts that America will ever be a just society free from racism. Without that hope and enthusiasm for the future, belief in the renewal of innovation fades, particularly that of jazz.

America as a country has always thrived on exploring frontiers of every sort, yet even the idea of outer space as the final frontier seems more like something from the optimism of the past. And although it was born through revolution, that revolutionary spirit now seems to have become almost nonexistent in current times. We are no longer in a state of becoming. Our lives have become shaped by the TV remote and the computer monitor. Americans seem to be increasingly concerned only with staying in their nests, surfing the Internet and the hundreds of TV stations that are becoming available. A music like jazz is, in the terms of Marshall McLuhan, too "hot" for a "cool" medium like television (except for the tepid "lite jazz".) And jazz formerly thrived on the American zest for exploring frontiers and continual innovation.

So maybe we have all been murderers of jazz. Maybe we have become so disconnected from each other that jazz, which is dependent on the interplay of audience and musician, can no longer be created in the way it has been in the past. Maybe we have stifled our own passion for living vital lives in the moment. And maybe jazz is dead, or at least on its deathbed.

These are very real possibilities. And I must confess that, like many, I often believe that jazz may be seeing its final days as the century in which it was born comes to an end. But when these concerns get to be too depressing, I go to my stereo and play Coltrane's "Spiritual," or Miles and Gil Evans's *Porgy and Bess* or Ellington's *Far East Suite* or even, for that matter, Jan Garbarek's *Visible World*, and like so many times in the past, jazz makes me a believer all over again.

Discography

This discography is certainly not complete. After all, *Blue* covers the entirety of jazz history and a complete jazz discography covers several hundred pages and would be far beyond the scope of this book. What I have done instead is to choose albums that I think best illustrate the points I make in the relevant chapters. The albums listed are not necessarily personal favorites, but are chosen instead for their significance to the text. There are, obviously, many important albums omitted from this list. Not only are key albums by many of the musicians missing from this list, but a great number of important jazz innovators are not represented at all. But its purpose is only as a limited guide to the development of jazz as that development was discussed in the main text of *Blue*. The albums I have listed should be viewed as starting-off points. I have tried to choose albums that are currently available as CDs. However, in a few instances I have selected albums which are, as I write, not available. But the reissue programs of most record companies are volatile, and albums are constantly going in and out of print. Jazz fans have learned to be ever vigilant about this sort of thing. I hope you will find this list useful:

Original Dixieland Jazz Band—*75th Anniversary Edition* (RCA)
Jelly Roll Morton—*Complete Jelly Roll Morton 1926–1930* (5-CD set—RCA)
King Oliver—*King Oliver and Louis Armstrong* (Milestone)
Sidney Bechet—*The Bluebird Sessions* (Milestone)

Louis Armstrong—*The Hot Fives* (Columbia)
Louis Armstrong—*Louis Armstrong and Earl Hines* (Columbia)
Louis Armstrong—*Town Hall Concert* (RCA)
Bix Beiderbecke—*Singin' the Blues* (Columbia)
Fletcher Henderson—*A Study in Frustration* (Columbia)
(Note: This set is, as I write in early 1997, out of print. Most of Henderson's most important early recordings are now available only as imports. It is hoped that Columbia Legacy will correct this breach soon—this is important music.)
Duke Ellington—*The Complete Brunswick Recordings, Vol. I* (MCA)
Duke Ellington—*Braggin' in Brass* (Columbia)
Duke Ellington—*The Blanton/Webster Band* (RCA/BMG)
Duke Ellington—*The Far East Suite* (RCA/BMG)
Count Basie—*The Complete Decca Recordings* (GRP)
Count Basie—*The Essential Count Basie Vols. 1–3* (Columbia)
(Note: Columbia's reissue of classic Basie sides from the 1930s and 1940s is a mess. Try and grab the British versions if you can. Hopefully, Columbia Legacy will issue a coherent set of this great music soon.)
Benny Goodman—*Carnegie Hall Concert* (Columbia)
Coleman Hawkins—*Body and Soul* (RCA)
Lester Young—*Kansas City Five and Six* (Commodore)
(Note: This great music is out of print along with the entire Commodore label. Although Mosaic—a small company in Connecticut that does superb limited edition jazz reissues—released a complete set of Commodores that is now unavailable. But sooner or later this music should be available again—grab it as soon as it is.)
Lester Young—*Lester Young Trio* (Verve)
Art Tatum—*Twentieth-Century Genius* (Verve)
Roy Eldridge—*After You've Gone* (GRP)
Ben Webster—*Soulville* (Verve)
Charlie Christian—*Solo Flight* (Columbia)
Red Norvo—*Famous Jam Session* (Stash)
Dizzy Gillespie—*Dizzy Gillespie and Charlie Christian* (recorded live at Minton's) (Esoteric)
Dizzy Gillespie—*Shaw Nuff* (Stash)
Charlie Parker—*The Charlie Parker Story* (Savoy)
Charlie Parker—*Complete Dial Recordings* (Stash)
Charlie Parker—*Bird With Strings* (Verve)
Bud Powell—*The Amazing Bud Powell, Vol.1* (Blue Note)

Bud Powell—*The Genius of Bud Powell* (Verve)
Fats Navarro—*Fats Navarro/Tadd Dameron* (2-CD Blue Note)
Thelonious Monk—*Complete Blue Note Recordings* (Blue Note)
Woody Herman—*The Thundering Herds* (2-CD Capitol)
Stan Kenton—*Retrospective* (2-CD Capitol)
Lennie Tristano—*Intuition* (Capitol)
Lee Konitz—*Motion* (Verve)
Warne Marsh—*Ne Plus Ultra* (Hat Hut)
Miles Davis—*Birth of the Cool* (Capitol)
Gerry Mulligan—*Complete Pacific Jazz Quartet with Chet Baker Recordings* (Capitol)
Gerry Mulligan—*Mainstream Jazz* (Polygram)
Chet Baker—*Complete Pacific Jazz Quartet Studio Recordings* (4-CD box set—Mosaic)
Chet Baker—*Chet's Choice* (Criss Cross)
Art Pepper—*Meets the Rhythm Section* (OJC)
Art Pepper—*October Moon* (OJC)
Stan Getz—*At the Shrine* (Verve)
Stan Getz—*Focus* (Verve)
Stan Getz—*Sweet Rain* (Verve)
Jazz Messengers—*Jazz Messengers* (Blue Note)
Miles Davis—*Walkin'* (OJC)
Max Roach and Clifford Brown—*Brown and Roach Inc.* (Polygram)
Max Roach and Clifford Brown—*At Basin Street East* (Polygram)
Thelonious Monk—*Monk's Music* (Riverside)
George Russell—*Jazz Workshop* (RCA)
Charles Mingus—*Pithecanthropus Erectus* (Atlantic)
Charles Mingus—*The Black Saint and the Sinner Lady* (Impulse)
Sonny Rollins—*Saxophone Colossus* (OJC)
Sonny Rollins—*Way Out West* (OJC)
Horace Silver—*Six Pieces of Silver* (Blue Note)
Art Blakey and the Jazz Messengers—*The Big Beat* (Blue Note)
Hank Mobley—*Soul Station* (Blue Note)
Lee Morgan—*The Sidewinder* (Blue Note)
Miles Davis—*Kind of Blue* (Columbia)
Various Artists—*Birth of the Third Stream* (Columbia)
Eric Dolphy—*Out There* (OJC)
Eric Dolphy—*Out to Lunch* (Blue Note)
Ornette Coleman—*Something Else!!* (OJC)
Ornette Coleman—*Change of Century* (Atlantic)

Ornette Coleman—*Free Jazz* (Atlantic)
John Coltrane—*Giant Steps* (Atlantic)
John Coltrane—*My Favorite Things* (Atlantic)
John Coltrane—*A Love Supreme* (Impulse)
John Coltrane—*Ascension* (Impulse)
Miles Davis—*Miles Smiles* (Columbia)
Cecil Taylor—*Hard Driving Jazz* (but now available under John Coltrane's name and retitled *Coltrane Time*) (Blue Note)
Cecil Taylor—*UniStructures* (Blue Note)
Albert Ayler—*Spirits Rejoice* (ESP)
Archie Shepp—*Fire Music* (Impulse)
Sam Rivers—*Fuchsia Swing Song* (Blue Note)
Andrew Hill—*Point of Departure* (Blue Note)
Art Ensemble of Chicago—*Urban Bushmen* (ECM)
Anthony Braxton—*Seven Compositions* (hat Art)
George Russell—*Vertical Structure VI* (Soul Note)
Miles Davis—*Bitches Brew* (Columbia)
Ornette Coleman—*Dancing in Your Head* (A&M)
Weather Report—*Mysterious Traveler* (Columbia)
Mahavishnu Orchestra—*The Inner Mounting Flame* (Columbia)
Keith Jarrett—*The Köln Concert* (ECM)
Keith Jarrett—*Belonging* (ECM)
World Saxophone Quartet—*W.S.Q.* (Black Saint)
James "Blood" Ulmer—*Odyssey* (Columbia)
Wynton Marsalis—*Think of One* (Columbia)
Wynton Marsalis—*Standard Time* (Columbia)
Joshua Redman—*Wish* (Warner Brothers)
Jan Garbarek—*Twelve Moons* (ECM)
Tim Berne—*Diminutive Mysteries* (JMT)
Tom Harrell—*Labyrinth* (RCA)
George Russell—*It's About Time* (Label Bleu)

NOTES

INTRODUCTION

1. Keith Jarrett, "The Virtual Jazz Age," *Musician* (March 1968).

CHAPTER 1: THE CASE FOR MURDER

1. Frank Conroy, *The New York Times Magazine* (June 25, 1995).
2. Tom Piazza, *Guide to Classic Recorded Jazz* (Iowa City, 1995), p. xv.
3. Andre Hodeir, *Jazz: Its Evolution and Essence* (New York, 1961).
4. Keith Jarrett, "Categories Aplenty but Where's the Music?" *The New York Times*, "Arts and Leisure," August 16, 1992.

CHAPTER 2: YOUNG MAN'S BLUES: RACISM AND AGEISM IN JAZZ

1. Wayne Shorter in an interview in the *Toronto Globe and Mail*, December 12, 1995.
2. Albert Murray, *Stomping the Blues* (New York, 1976). Murray's comment appears in a footnote to a photograph caption, pp. 50, 197.
3. Nat Shapiro and Nat Hentoff, eds., *Hear Me Talkin' to Ya* (New York, 1955), pp. 158–159.
4. Wynton Marsalis, *Sweet Swing Blues on the Road* (New York, 1994), p. 142.
5. Ralph Ellison, "Blues People," *Collected Essays of Ralph Ellison* (New York, 1995).
6. Francis Davis, *Bebop and Nothingness* (New York, 1996), p. xi.

CHAPTER 3: THE JAZZ AGE REVOLUTION

1. John Miller Chernoff, *African Rhythm and Sensibility* (Chicago, 1979), p. 59.
2. Kathy Ogren, *The Jazz Revolution* (New York and London, 1989), p. 7.
3. Ibid., p. 3.

CHAPTER 4: GENIUS: THE TRIUMPH AND TRAGEDY OF LOUIS ARMSTRONG

1. Albert Murray, "The Armstrong Continuum," *The Blue Devils of Nada* (New York, 1996), p. 69.

CHAPTER 5: DÉJÀ VU ALL OVER AGAIN

1. Mezz Mezzrow, *Really the Blues* (New York, 1946).
2. Rudi Blesh, *Shining Trumpets* (New York, 1946).
3. Hugues Panassié, *Real Jazz* (New York, 1942).
4. Hugues Panassié, *Guide to Jazz* (New York, 1956).

CHAPTER 6: SWING AND ITS DISCONTENTS

1. Mark Miller, "Getting in the Groove," *Toronto Globe and Mail*, 1996.
2. Stanley Crouch, "Big Jim's Duke," *The All-American Skin Game* (New York, 1995).
3. Nat Shapiro and Nat Hentoff, eds. *Hear Me Talkin' to Ya* (New York), p. 69.
4. Mel Tormé, *It Wasn't All Velvet* (New York, 1989).

CHAPTER 7: JAZZ REDEFINED: THE BOP REVOLUTION

1. Nat Shapiro and Nat Hentoff, eds., *Hear Me Talkin' to Ya* (New York, 1955), p. 405.
2. Ibid.
3. Ibid.

CHAPTER 8: THE 1950S, PART ONE: OUT OF THE COOL

1. Stanley Crouch, "On the Corner: The Sellout of Miles Davis," *The All-American Skin Game* (New York, 1995).
2. Donald L. Maggin, *Stan Getz* (New York, 1996).

CHAPTER 9: THE 1950S, PART TWO: INTO THE HOT

1. Eric Nisenson, *Round About Midnight* (New York, 1993).

CHAPTER 11: DANCING IN YOUR HEAD

1. Stanley Crouch, "On the Corner: The Sellout of Miles Davis," *The All-American Skin Game* (New York, 1995).
2. Peter Watrous, "A Jazz Generation and the Miles Davis Curse," *The New York Times*, Sunday "Arts and Leisure," October 15, 1995.

CHAPTER 12: THE VIRTUAL JAZZ AGE

1. Richard Woodard, "Jazz Wars," *The Village Voice*, August 19, 1994.

CHAPTER 13: LIGHTING OUT FOR THE TERRITORY

1. Comment by Henry Robinette was made on the Internet's "Miles Davis List," and it is reprinted here with his kind permission.

BIBLIOGRAPHY

Count Basie with Albert Murray, *Good Morning Blues*. Random House, 1985.

Jack Chambers, *Milestones*. William Morrow, 1985.

James Collier, *Ellington*. Oxford University Press, 1987.

———, *Louis Armstrong: An American Genius*. Oxford University Press, 1983.

———, *Making of Jazz*. Delta, 1978.

Dizzy Gillespie, *To Be or Not to Bop*. Doubleday, 1979.

Ted Gioia, *West Coast Jazz*. Oxford University Press, 1992.

Ira Gitler, *From Swing to Bop*. Oxford University Press, 1985.

Joe Goldberg, *Jazz Masters of the Fifties*. Macmillan, 1965.

Edward Hasse, *Beyond Category: The Life and Genius of Duke Ellington*. Simon and Schuster, 1993.

R. D. Laing, *The Politics of Experience*. Vintage Books, 1986.

Gene Lees, *Cats of Every Color*. Oxford University Press, 1996.

John Litweiler, *The Freedom Principle*. William Morrow, 1985.

Marc Miller, ed., *Louis Armstrong: A Cultural Legacy*. University of Washington Press, 1994.

Stuart Nicholson, *Jazz: The 1980s Resurgence*. Da Capo Press, 1995.

Eric Nisenson, *Ascension: John Coltrane and His Quest*. St. Martin's Press, 1993.

———, *Round About Midnight*. De Capo Press, 1996.

Lewis Porter, *Lester Young*. Twayne, 1985.

Robert Reisner, ed., *Bird: The Legend of Charlie Parker*. Da Capo Press, 1977.
David H. Rosenthal, *Hard Bop*. Oxford University Press, 1992.
Jean-Paul Sartre, *Existentialism and Human Emotions*. Philosophical Library, 157/85.
Gunther Schuller, *Early Jazz*. Oxford University Press, 1986.
———, *The Swing Era*. Oxford University Press, 1989.
David W. Stowe, *Swing Changes*. Harvard University Press, 1994.
Arthur Taylor, *Notes and Tones*. Perigree Books, 1977.

Index